COLONIAL MEMORY
AND
POSTCOLONIAL EUROPE

New Anthropologies of Europe

Daphne Berdahl, Matti Bunzl, and Michael Herzfeld, editors

Colonial Memory
and
Postcolonial
Europe

Maltese Settlers in Algeria and France

ANDREA L. SMITH

Indiana University Press
Bloomington & Indianapolis

This book is a publication of

Indiana University Press
601 North Morton Street
Bloomington, IN 47404-3797 USA

http://iupress.indiana.edu

Telephone orders   800-842-6796
Fax orders   812-855-7931
Orders by e-mail   iuporder@indiana.edu

Library of Congress Cataloging-in-Publication Data

Smith, Andrea L.
  Colonial memory and postcolonial Europe : Maltese settlers in Algeria
and France / Andrea L. Smith.
    p. cm. — (New anthropologies of Europe)
  Includes bibliographical references and index.
  ISBN 0-253-34762-9 (cloth : alk. paper) — ISBN 0-253-21856-X
(pbk. : alk. paper) 1. French—Algeria. 2. France—Ethnic relations. 3.
Maltese—France—Ethnic identity. I. Title. II. Series.
  DT283.6.F7S65 2006
  944'.90049279065—dc22
2005036037

1 2 3 4 5   11 10 09 08 07 06

Dedicated to my father

CONTENTS

MAPS

ACKNOWLEDGMENTS

The people in this book occupy an ambiguous position between modernity and postmodernity, between colonial Africa and postcolonial Europe. They have migrated from Malta to North Africa to France, and so much of our time together over the past ten years has been spent returning mentally to these former homes and former times. This is a book about how places endure while people scatter, and the dynamic politics of the past: how here conjures up there, and how now reminds us of then.

I gathered many debts as I traveled the globe in search of traces of the pasts we discussed together, in nearly a mirror image of their migratory journey, seeking out consultants and archives across France, Tunisia, Malta, and the U.K. Fieldwork was conducted in France, Malta, Tunisia, and the U.K. from January 1995 through June 1996 and in January 1998, June 2001, and April–May 2004, and funded by grants from the Social Science Research Council, the Wenner-Gren Foundation for Anthropological Research, the American Institute for Maghreb Studies, and the Academic Research Committee of Lafayette College. Writing was supported by the Harry Frank Guggenheim Foundation, the University of Arizona, and the National Endowment for the Humanities. I am grateful to these organizations for their support of this research.

My research in France was greatly enhanced by my many meetings, discussions, and seminars with Michel Wieviorka, Lucette Valensi, and François Pouillon of the *École des hautes études en sciences sociales.* I thank Robert Ilbert, Jean-Marie Gouillon, staff, and students at TELEMME (*Temps, espaces, langages, Europe méridionale, méditerranéenne*), *Maison méditerranéenne des sciences de l'homme,* of the Université de Provence, for inviting me into their stimulating academic community during my stay in Aix-en-Provence. This project never would have gotten underway had it not been for the immediate accueil of Marc Donato. Jean-Jacques Jordi was ever ready to offer advice, guidance, and motivation. Claude Delaye and his colleagues at *Génealogie Algérie Maroc Tunisie* assisted me as I worked for days in their archives, as did the librarians of the *Centre de documentation historique sur l'Algérie.*

In Malta, the staff at the National Archives, Rabat, were remarkably persistent in locating documents for me. I thank Stephen Degiorgio and

Tomas Freller for providing the spirited fellowship which made my research there so engaging. Father Laurence Attard of the Emigrants Commission in Valletta offered important advice. In Tunis, I especially thank Mickey and his comrades, Habib Kazadagli (Université de Tunis, Manouba), and Jeanne Mrad at CEMAT (*Centre d'études maghrébines à Tunis*).

My ideas have been developed through conversations and debates with Jane Hill, the late Robert Netting, Tad Park, Ana Alonso, Hermann Rebel, Kevin Gosner, Jonathan Boyarin, and Susan Carol Rogers, and various "partners in crime": Deborah House, Hsain Ilahiane, Ahmadou N'diade, Helen Robbins, Julianna Acheson, and Todd Fenton. Many people read the whole manuscript or key sections, including Gérard Althabe, Dan Bauer, Jennifer Gilbert, Deborah House, Susan Niles, Helen Robbins, David Rubin, Josh Sanborn, David Shulman, and Thomas Wilson. Lafayette College student Gozde Ulas assisted me with tape transcription, and Jackie Wogotz assisted with bibliographic entries. Nangula Shejavali helped in more ways than I can list. Finally, I thank Douglas Holmes and an anonymous reviewer for Indiana University Press, Shoshanna Green, and my editor, Rebecca Tolen, for their careful commentary and critique.

I am grateful to the Institute of French Studies, New York University, and especially to Susan Carol Rogers, Emmanuelle Saada, Muriel Darmon, and Ed Berenson, for providing a home base of rich discussion and camaraderie during my fellowship there in 1998–1999. Many of my ideas were advanced through discussions with others at New York University, especially Thomas Abercrombie and Thomas Beidelman. I appreciate the warm welcome from John Olsen, Tad Park, Barbara Mills, Aomar Boum, and Mourad Mjahed and other members of the Department of Anthropology, University of Arizona, when I was Visiting Scholar there in 2003–2004. I thank Lafayette College for granting me these research leaves and my colleagues at the Department of Anthropology and Sociology for their steady support of this project.

Of course, my greatest debt is due the many *pieds-noirs* families I met in France. You have astounded me with your remarkable generosity, gracious hospitality, patience, trust, and whole-hearted emotional and practical *soutien* of this research. While I cannot mention everyone individually here, I want to especially recognize the Bonnici family, the Buhagiars, Pierre Dimech, the Julliés, Mme. Verié, the Cauchis, the Cassars, the Azzoppardis, and the Micalefs.

Without the encouragement and role models of Tiger Burch, Oran Young, and Mim Dixon, of the Arctic Social Science Committee, National Academy of Sciences, I never would have set off on this path to begin with. And finally, thanks to my family for their patience over the years while I vanished for months without writing or calling; to Pat, for listening to more of this than anyone should have to bear, and for always encouraging me to keep at it while maintaining levity, warmth, and perspective; and to Abe and Lyndy, for their gleeful distraction when I needed it most.

This book is dedicated to the memory of several mentors who took the time to encourage me along this journey: Pierre Soumille, whose enthusiasm for every new idea was contagious; Gérard Althabe, for believing in this project; Pierre Rochette, for his friendship and commitment to the study; and Robert Netting, for his steadfast support. Finally, to my father, David Smith, whose limitless intellectual curiosity and faith in me are hard to live without.

Earlier versions of parts of chapters 4 and 5 appeared in *American Ethnologist;* portions of chapters 1 and 9 appeared in *Cultural Anthropology;* and a small portion of chapter 4 appeared in *Political and Legal Anthropology Review;* all journals copyrighted by the American Anthropological Association.

COLONIAL MEMORY
AND
POSTCOLONIAL EUROPE

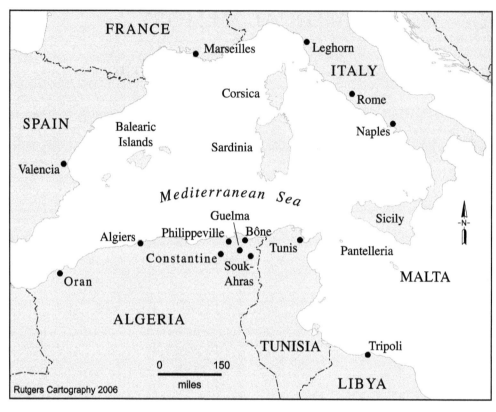

Map 1. Malta, Algeria, and southern France.

ONE

A Song in Malta

"I can remember the First World War," Joseph Zammit[1] announced. We were waiting for lunch in a dusty coffee shop on the Maltese island of Gozo during a tour organized by former colonial settlers of Algeria who were of Maltese ancestry. Joseph continued: "They made a giant effigy of William II, filled it with firecrackers, and blew it up!" Joseph was in his early eighties. A tall man, he seemed even more so due to his careful posture and thick shock of white hair. He dressed formally and traveled through the hot islands that summer in full suit and tie, but his grey eyes twinkled each time he set out to tell yet another surprising tale. There were two others at our table, Michel Pisani and Marie Buttigieg. All of my elderly companions had been born in Algeria but had resettled in France after Algerian independence.

I asked Joseph how it was that he could remember the war—surely he hadn't served? "Well," he exclaimed, apparently pleased to respond, "I was born in 1911—I was seven then. I remember it well because that was when I first met my father." Joseph's father had been fighting in Europe since his son was three years old. "My mother took me down to the port. Men were coming down the plank of the boat, and she pointed one of them out to me and said, 'There he is, that's your father.'" Joseph explained to us that his father had joined the French Army as a member of the *Troisième Zouaves,* one of the *régiments sacrifices* (a regiment with a notoriously high death rate). Michel, one of the leaders of the social club who had organized our trip, joined in the conversation. "Oh, my father was in the *Troisième Zouaves* too," he interjected, his voice animated. He began to outline details of his own family history, but Joseph was not interested. He began to sing, rather loudly, in a language that I assumed was Maltese. The Maltese patrons of the café stopped talking and gave each other meaningful looks that I could not interpret. Marie rolled her eyes and Michel, after listening intently, burst out laughing. As Joseph took a deep breath to start a new verse,

Michel whispered, "It's in *Arabic*!" We listened while Joseph sang verse after verse to the simple march-like tune. It was a touching yet perplexing moment. Joseph later explained to us that the song was a Boy Scout anthem translated into Arabic that he had learned as a child in Algeria for an international Scouts jamboree. This song, and the Arabic language in particular, are important clues in understanding the powerful fascination with Malta that is widespread among these former settlers of Algeria, and characteristic of the ways in which postcoloniality is being experienced in contemporary France.

The excursion to Malta that summer and the club that organized it, the *Amicale France-Malte* (France-Malta Social Club), are not isolated phenomena but part of a wider movement. Following their departure from French Algeria when the colony gained independence in 1962 and their subsequent "return" to France, these former settlers of Algeria (also known as *pieds-noirs*[2]) of Maltese origin formed ethnically based social clubs. They have been traveling individually and in groups to Malta ever since. This pilgrimage has escalated to the point where solo travelers and tour groups representing clubs from different parts of France sometimes meet there by chance. During one such trip, my fellow travelers encountered on three separate occasions people they had known in Algeria. In each case, they had not laid eyes on each other since they had left the colony over thirty years before. It was with astonishment and great emotion that they met again in the elevator of our hotel or just walking along the streets of Valetta, Malta's capital. According to a travel agent I met in southeastern France, so many people were making these pilgrimages to Malta that Air Malta had rerouted its service to include direct flights from Marseilles, a more convenient location than Paris for the *pied-noir* population living in southern France.

This study addresses the spontaneous pilgrimage movement among former settlers, and considers why it is that, several decades after leaving Algeria, settlers of Maltese origin began returning, not to the former colony, but to Malta itself. This movement is all the more intriguing because these travelers have been French citizens for several generations. Current wisdom about French Algeria tells us that when hundreds of thousands of former settlers of many different ethnic backgrounds migrated across the Mediterranean in the wake of Algerian independence, they shared a common culture forged in the *creuset algérien,* the Algerian melting pot. The very existence of these Maltese *pied-noir* social clubs, indicating the continued salience of intrasettler cultural distinctions, challenges this dominant view.

In wider terms, this is a book about diaspora and home-loss, rejection and redemption. Remembered places are often "symbolic anchors of community" for diasporic societies, for whom the homeland idea can serve as a powerful unifying symbol (Gupta and Ferguson 1997a, 39; Cohen 1997; Safran 1991). Among diasporic communities that maintain an ideology of return, the homeland symbol can be intimately connected to the politics of memory and communalization (Bicharat 1997; Slyomovics 1998). However, we know far less about the role homeland plays for displaced people who have no hope of returning, as is the case with *pied-noir* exiles from Algeria. In this study of a particular group of exiled settlers, we will find that here, too, the politics of memory plays a pivotal role. The trips to Malta might be interpreted as yet another instance of a displaced population (in this case, doubly displaced) making sacred journeys to their ancestral homeland in conjunction with an ethnic revitalization movement. The reasons for these trips, the clubs that organize them, and the widespread longing for Malta are more complex, as this study of colonial memory and forgetting, the power of sensory memory, and identity politics in postcolonial France will reveal.

THE SETTLERS "RETURN"

The "Maltese" arrived in France along with other colonial settlers of Algeria in a sudden mass migration during the dawning of Algerian independence. Since most of these settlers had been born in Algeria, and many had families that had been there for generations, this departure truly was a traumatic one. Many migrants could not manage the transition, as evidenced by the high mortality and suicide rates among *pieds-noirs* during their first years in France (Jordi 1993, 186). They arrived in the metropole at a pivotal moment in French history: their resettlement marked the definitive end to France's most important colony, and heralded the demise of empire more generally.

The independence movements that wracked the French empire after World War II would affect social and economic life in the metropole for decades to come, right up to the present day. This is most obvious in the immigration to France of millions of North African former colonial subjects, giving France the distinction today of having the largest Muslim population in Europe (estimated at five million out of a total population of approximately sixty million). During the same postcolonial era, substantial numbers of colonial "repatriates" have arrived as well. These include French administrators, civil service workers, settlers, naturalized former subjects, and Algerians[3] who had served with French military units during the war of independence. During the 1950s and 1960s alone, a total of 2 to 2.5 million such colonials "returned" following decolonization. The first of these migrations followed the loss of Indochina in 1954. Several thousand French arrived from Egypt in the wake of the Suez crisis, and independence led to the repatriation of hundreds more migrants from sub-Saharan Africa and Madagascar. Colonies on either side of Algeria yielded even more: between 1952 and July 1961, 125,000 French were repatriated from Morocco and 132,000 from Tunisia (Dubois 1994, 91). This was an extremely diverse group of peoples: in the case of the North African colonies alone, it included indigenous Jews and Muslims of an array of ethnicities, and settlers originally from across the European continent. Despite this diversity, the migrants were united nevertheless by the official label "repatriate," a term that underscored their unquestioned fealty to the French nation-state.

The longevity and intensity of a given manifestation of colonialism can be correlated with the ensuing decolonization experience. Up until 1962, France's "decolonization migrations" involved colonies that differed greatly from Algeria. While each colonial setting was unique, many French colonies, such as those in sub-Saharan Africa, were initially economic or extractive colonies designed to transfer resources from colony to metropole, and were populated at least at first by more temporary migrants, such as administrators, missionaries, and merchants. Settler colonies differ greatly, and can be characterized by higher concentrations of Europeans originating from a variety of countries. Typically they also had more violent decolonization experiences, stemming in part from the three-way conflict that can arise when settlers constitute a powerful third interest group (Prochaska 1990, 9). While neighboring Morocco and Tunisia attracted settlers, they were protectorates, which some argue involves a less destructive form of French rule than that in French Algeria; they were also colonized for shorter periods of time (Morocco 1912; Tunisia 1881, and Algeria 1830). As a result, the dismantling of French rule was accompanied by comparatively less violence. Former colonial administrators, civil service workers, and settlers left Tunisia and Morocco for France over a period of years, with thousands departing several years after independence.[4]

Algeria's colonial history provides a striking contrast. Algeria was France's premier settler colony, with three coastal *départements* (departments, the largest administrative subdivision) incorporated into the French state as early as 1848. It was also a colony characterized by over a century of violence and oppression. By 1954, more than one million settlers lived there, and, unlike Tunisia or Morocco, emigration with independence occurred precipitously over a period of months.[5] These unique features and the magnitude of the mass migration of Algeria's settlers led to the spread in France of a unique term used to designate them: *pied-noir,* or "black foot," a term I explore further in this book.

The *pieds-noirs* are associated in the French imagination today not only with the embarrassing legacy of the doomed colony, but also with the notorious French-Algerian War (1954–1962). It is difficult to overstate the degree to which that war overwhelmed life not only in Algeria but also in metropolitan France, and to what extent the conflicts raised during this period remain unresolved to this day.[6] Mounting war-related expenses exacerbated an already fragile political climate, leading to the collapse of more than one French government, including the Fourth Republic. At the Republic's fall, military officers in Algeria were organizing a coup, and France itself came close to civil war. Metropolitan French were further implicated through their military service: approximately 2.3 million French soldiers served in the war effort, of whom over twenty-four thousand perished (Ageron 1991, 160). Estimates of Algerian fatalities are still actively debated and range from two hundred thousand to over 1 million.[7] The war garnered considerable international attention, not only because it was a dramatic and ultimately successful war of liberation that heralded the demise of the French empire, but also because of the horrifying revelation that the French Army had turned to the systematic use of torture as one of its principal weapons. This last fact, although known for some time, was suppressed for years and has erupted on the public stage only recently as war veterans, torture victims, and the French public now debate the problems of public accountability, punishment, and restitution for the perpetrators and victims of these war crimes.[8]

The horrible "secrets" associated with this war, and the *pied-noir* connection to it, may go a long way toward explaining why so many *pieds-noirs* felt that they could never return to their beloved Algeria, even to visit, and why many metropolitan French, upon learning about my research subject, would visibly shudder. Arriving in the aftermath of this nation-wrenching conflict, the former settlers became targets of rage and frustration. They were often blamed for the war, for the political turmoil it engendered, for colonialism in general, and, in the case of those who lost loved ones in the war, even for their personal losses. Not surprisingly, their assimilation into French society has been difficult and remains in many ways incomplete. Now, several decades after this tumultuous period, *pieds-noirs* are still viewed by much of wider French society with distaste. They are associated in academic and popular presses with right-wing movements in France, specifically as supporters of nationalist politician Jean-Marie Le Pen. The debates regarding the systematic use of torture during and even before the French-Algerian War have only reignited negative associations with the former settlers. Perhaps for these reasons, remarkably little in-depth research has been conducted among *pieds-noirs.* They remain a population marginalized both socially in France and in the academic literature, tangible reminders of an embarrassing colonial past that scholars, politicians, and the general public alike would rather forget altogether.

FIELDWORK AND THE
FRENCH-ALGERIAN WAR

When first formulating this project, I felt that it would be feasible only as long as I avoided the French-Algerian War.[9] I feared unleashing what I imagined would be hours of narratives about the war from my informants. I did not want to hear these stories—partly because I felt they would be endless or would reach no resolution, but also because I imagined they would represent an attempt to vindicate the "wrong" side. I knew that this war was infamous for the French army's use of torture and I did not want to engage my informants on this subject. There were limits to ethnographic objectivity, I felt, and I did not want to put myself in the position of knowing what the people I met had done during the war years. When I first spoke with the leaders of the *Amicale France-Malte* to present to them my research plan, I stressed that I was interested in people's memories from before the war, what they had heard from their parents and grandparents about life in Algeria in the first decades of the twentieth century, and what they had experienced from the 1930s on. Their response to the project was overwhelmingly positive, and in our initial discussions we ignored the war years completely.

But in southeastern France, with high percentages of *pieds-noirs* and immigrant Algerians, the war was a constant presence. I learned this during my second week, while sitting in Aix-en-Provence one afternoon at an outdoor ice-cream shop along the Cours Mirabeau, a handsome avenue lined with sycamores and sidewalk cafés. An elderly woman at the next table was talking with her two young grandsons while they ate their ice creams. A song by the Cranberries was playing on the outdoor stereo. I had seen the music video accompanying the song, which consists of a collage of images in black and white from various armed conflicts, including footage of Northern Ireland and of the wartime devastation, as well as the peacekeeping of United Nations troops, in the former Yugoslavia.

"Who is this singer?" the grandmother asked the children; "is it an Israeli, that woman, 'Noah'?" "Nah," one boy said, "it's a Scottish woman."[10] "It's against the war!" the younger boy chimed in. "Hmm?" the grandmother asked, not really listening. "Yeah," exclaimed the younger boy, "It's against the *Guerre d'Algérie!*" "You think so?" the grandmother asked, paying more attention now. "Yes, yes, I saw it on TV, it has the *casques bleues*" (literally, blue helmets, a French expression for UN peacekeeping forces). "Ah! But there weren't any *casques bleues* in Algeria!" the woman said, somewhat relieved. The children started laughing. "Oh, no, I think it's about Bosnia," the older one said. "Well, yes, *that* could be, there *are casques bleues* in Bosnia," the elderly woman replied. "Yes," said the older boy, "it's against the war in Bosnia." "Yes, yes," the younger one added, eager to participate, "it's against war . . . against war in France." The grandmother concurred, "Yes, yes, I am against war too . . ." and they began talking of other things.

A few weeks later, an exhibit of local artists filled the Cours Mirabeau. While I wandered up the street, looking at the strange sculptures and garish oil paintings, I ran across a man selling his artwork as well as a book he had recently published about the *harkis,* the Algerians who had volunteered to fight during the war on the side of the French.[11] I spoke at length with the author, a retired French soldier who told me he was ashamed of the treatment the *harkis* had received in France after their years of faithful service. He felt that this was one of the most unpardonable aspects of the war, and therefore was compelled to write his own book about their plight.

Later that year, in the dead of winter, there was an extended demonstration by the grown children of *harkis* in Aix. Twenty or more young men in their twenties camped out in the main square in front of the town hall. People crossing through town had to circumvent their row of sleeping bags. They put up signs outlining their complaints and announcing their hunger strike. They were protesting their high rate of unemployment, lack of funding, and general abandonment by France. They stayed there on the pavement, in their sleeping bags, for weeks, and I feared that they might die of exposure.

While it wasn't always obvious or overt, the war also was a constant presence in the imaginations of my elderly interlocutors. In fact, I believe unspoken tensions regarding the war led many to reinterpret for themselves the focus of my research at the start of my fieldwork, and even my identity as a researcher. When I was introduced to members of François and Michel's Franco-Maltese club on their annual Ascension Day outing in May, we collectively negotiated my role in their community. We traveled by boat down the Rhône, from Arles to the end of the river delta. Dinner was served on board, and association members sat grouped together with their friends at a series of eight large tables looking out onto the river. After a few general announcements about the association's membership, financial status, and future projects, the president and other club officers shepherded me around the room and introduced me to those seated at each table.

Club president François Xuereb is a very articulate and animated elderly man, then in his late seventies. He was originally from Tunisia, and thus had lived through a markedly less violent decolonization experience than the other club members, who were largely from Algeria. For this reason, he sometimes was viewed by Algeria-born *pieds-noirs,* even by members of his own association, as an outsider. He started by introducing me without great delicacy, announcing simply, "I would like you to meet Andrea Smith, a young American student who will be in Aix this year. She is interested in studying the memories of the French of Algeria, the *pieds-noirs* . . ." He and Michel Pisani shepherded me from table to table. Each time he began to address the subject of my research, the expressions on the people's faces shifted from smiling openness to frozen wariness, as if they were thinking, "Who is this foreigner and what does she really want from us?" Xuereb seemed less than sensitive to the degree to which the colonial past is laden with unmasterable memories and forbidden topics for settlers from Algeria. But he too must have soon sensed the tension, for he began to stress that I was especially interested in the pasts of the Maltese in Algeria, the immigrants of Maltese origin, and trans-Mediterranean migrations in general. With this revised presentation, each time he highlighted the Maltese focus of my research, the relief on the listeners' faces was visible. A group at one table even applauded at this point in his presentation, not so much at the joy of having a foreigner arrive in their midst to question them, but more, it seemed, with relief that I wasn't primarily interested in the painful saga of the French-Algerian War. The Maltese migration represented a narrower and, in their minds, much "safer" topic.

Through this collaborative effort between the elderly club members, its main spokesman (of ambiguous insider/outsider status), and myself, a revised definition of my project was developed. Instead of seeing it as a study of the collective memories of life in Algeria of a subset of *pieds-noirs,* a topic that could be construed as one including the long war years, they imagined a "safer" study, one concerning a more distant past, that of their Maltese ancestors. Throughout the fieldwork, even though people shared with me their memories of daily life in the colony, they continued to introduce me to other *pieds-noirs* as someone interested in the history of the Maltese emigration to Algeria and imagined me to be more historian than anthropologist.

A few months into my fieldwork, I began to study the war in earnest. Learning about the war, of course, was essential to my study, for it enabled me to better understand the kinds of traumas the interlocutors might have lived through, and better interpret taped conversations. Silences related to the war years not only shaped the structure of conversations but also fostered a particular kind of nostalgia that would nourish a later connection to Malta.

IDENTITY POLITICS IN CONTEMPORARY FRANCE

The ethnic origins of the settlers are an important source of their alienation in France. At least half of the French settlers of Algeria were originally from Spain, Italy, Malta, and other European countries, and became

French citizens only upon settling in the colony. Thus, many of the thousands of "French" men and women who were "repatriated" moved to a country that had never been theirs, and which most had never seen before. By exploring the ways in which the Maltese social clubs respond to this very dilemma, this study provides a new and timely vantage point on identity politics in contemporary France.

France is often viewed as a nation that is unusually unified culturally, a characteristic commonly attributed to the homogenizing institutions of the French state. Although France, like the United States, is a country of immigrants, it is usually not viewed as such. France's immigration heritage has been silenced in the collective memory, resulting in a "fable of primordial continuous Frenchness disrupted only occasionally by external invasions" (Tilly 1996, vii). Unlike in the United States, where the expression of ethnic diversity has been tolerated or even celebrated at various historical moments, in many French circles since the Revolution there has been a persistent belief that the very survival of the Republic depends on its being composed not of separate religious, ethnic, or class-based subgroups, but of individual citizens equal under the law. In this ideology of republican universalism, membership in the nation is a choice, and national solidarity is founded on the sharing by citizens of a common culture and language (Balibar and Wallerstein 1991, Jaffe 1999). This belief that the country functions as a political community because its members are all part of a common national cultural community persists today (Beriss 1990, 2004). Whatever one's background, "one is expected to be assimilated, to be simply 'French'" (Gross, McMurray, and Swedenburg 1996, 128; see also Blum 2002).

Scholars have debated the degree to which cultural homogeneity has in fact been achieved, and the role played by the state in this process. In his classic work *Peasants into Frenchmen,* Eugen Weber suggested that late-nineteenth-century modernizing efforts, often initiated by the state, were responsible for creating a national consciousness and forging a collectivity from the rich plurality of ethnicities, linguistic groups, and regional identities that separated the state's inhabitants before the 1870s. However, social scientists since Weber have challenged the idea that the nation would "eventually erase all cultural difference" (Reed-Danahay 1996, 207). They reveal instead the continued persistence of regional diversity and argue for a far more nuanced view that shows how local traditions have persisted alongside rapid change (Gerson 2003; Reed-Danahay 1996). Distinct languages and cultural forms persist not despite modernization but perhaps even because of it (Jaffe 1999; McDonald 1989). Susan Carol Rogers found so-called "traditional" customs such as the *ostal* enforced in the rural Aveyron, thanks in part to the improved conditions for local agriculture

that accompanied modernization, and writes that centralization and regionalism are not in opposition, but "dialectically related" (Rogers 1991,
198). In *Education and Identity in Rural France* (1996), Deborah Reed-
Danahay challenges the hegemonic notion that French schools are the assimilating force *par excellence* and unproblematically transmit French culture. She analyzes the everyday forms of resistance of rural French families,
which involve a deft negotiation between local and national identities, between family and the state. As Reed-Danahay writes, the question to ask is
not whether French society is diverse or not, but "how it is that people
learn to manage diverse identities" (1996, 207).

This question brings us to the heart of intense debates about the nature, benefits, and hazards of cultural difference, which have engaged intellectuals, politicians, and the general public in contemporary France. In the
late 1960s, these debates turned from the preservation of distinct regional
cultures to consider those of France's growing immigrant population. Increased racist attacks starting in the late 1970s and the rise of ultra-right
political parties such as the National Front have prompted responses by
immigrant organizations and anti-racist groups such as *SOS Racisme,* who
make a corresponding demand for *le droit à la différence,* or the rights of
ethnic minorities to retain their distinct cultural traditions. Since the
1980s, concerns have mounted around the problems of unemployment,
deindustrialization, and failing educational and health systems, and many
have raised questions about the role played in such trends by immigrants.
As Balibar writes, people in France are reaching a new "threshold of intol-
erance," and it is now commonplace to hear people of all class statuses pro-
claiming that France has an "immigrant problem" (1991, 219–20). Today
some people view every social problem as if it were caused or at least aggra-
vated by immigrants.

Many politicians and scholars have attributed contemporary conflicts
over Frenchness and difference to the fact that the largest subgroup in
France's recent immigration wave, that of North African Muslims, differs
from that of previous waves in their practices, cultural outlook, and, notably, religion. This "neorepublican discourse" calls for cultural assimilation, blaming the cultures of the immigrants for their failure to integrate
(see Hargreaves and McKinney 1997). The current "headscarf affair" is but
one of the many manifestations of this concern in France. However, as
Noiriel and others have pointed out, even this discourse has strong parallels
with ideologies prevailing during two previous eras of xenophobia: the
1880s, which culminated in the Dreyfus affair, and the 1930s, which led
into the Vichy regime, during which it was the cultures of Belgian, Italian,
and Polish workers and of Jews in general that were the focus of attention.[12]

Surprisingly absent from these discussions of immigration and difference in France are the settlers, millions of "French" who migrated "home"
at the end of the wars of independence. The settlers offer an important opportunity to explore the significance of such factors as class and occupational sector, nationality, placement on some imagined scale of cultural
"similarity," race, and, finally, the colonial legacy in discussions of cultural
difference and France's "immigration problem." The fact that the settlers
have not featured in any serious fashion in contemporary debates reveals
much about the salient features of the category *immigré* (immigrant) in
France and postcolonial understandings of culture and race.

SETTLER ETHNOGRAPHY

Before I left for France, I was apprehensive about working with former settlers and wondered about the limits of my empathic capacities. I quickly
found the community refreshingly open, honest, and direct. When first encountering François Xuereb and Michel Pisani, I was interrogated by the
elderly men at length. "Which university are you from? Oh, never heard of
it!" François, the elder of the two, began. Then, down to business: "Who is
your favorite American politician? What do you think about George Bush?"
The men watched me carefully for my reaction. I had to decide right away
to what extent I could or would hide my political views. "Well, I'm a De-
mocrat," I admitted, wondering if I had just eliminated any chance of carrying out a project with their organization. "Aha!" François exclaimed with
a twinkle in his eye. "Me, I am *very* much on the right—I'm 100, no, 200
percent for Chirac! And Ronald Reagan is my personal hero," he went on,
apparently delighted to find someone with whom he could disagree. François Xuereb and Michel Pisani turned out to be quite enthusiastic about
my research ideas, and I proceeded to spend the next two years with them
and their friends.

The *Amicale France-Malte* is based at a thriving community center for
French from overseas, the *Maison des rapatriés* (Repatriates' House, or simply Maison), in the department of the Bouches du Rhône in southeastern
France, which has a high settler concentration.[13] The Maison groups over
twenty such repatriate organizations in a "collective," and I spent much
time there over my months in France, and again with every return visit. My
presence at Maison activities was at first viewed with some suspicion, however. Early on in my research, François, Michel, and I crossed paths with a
woman in her mid-fifties with bright copper-colored hair, dressed profes-
sionally in a crisp floral shift. They introduced her as the director of the
Maison, and explained that I was the American interested in Maltese history. "Yes, I know who she is," she replied coolly, and shook my hand. She

then talked briefly about my interests in North Africa, and told me to be careful: the Maison represented the French, the whites of North Africa, and should not be confused with other North African interests. "Some people think the Maison is for the Arabs too—No!" she exclaimed. "We are completely different from them, the two groups are completely distinct." Michel and François seemed uncomfortable with her outburst and tried to hurry me down the hall. We passed a skinny older man, apparently the building's guard and custodian. He treated the two men with considerable respect, but, on the way out, he said to me as an aside, making sure that they heard, "Watch out what they tell you about the Maltese! They are nothing but bandits and pirates." Michel and François laughed heartily at this comment.

Several weeks later I arranged for a formal meeting with the director, who still seemed to view my interest in Algeria with some concern. She asked point-blank why I was interested in the Maltese experience there. I thought for a minute, and explained that there was no easy answer, but that I had noted some interesting parallels between the migrant experience in Algeria and that of immigrants to the U.S. Apparently this explanation was acceptable, for over the course of the subsequent months, she and her husband greeted me warmly at Maison events. During large gatherings in particular, such as lectures by renowned *pied-noir* authors, she or her husband sometimes introduced me publicly, perhaps to allay the concerns of those who had never met me before. Sometimes I was put on the spot: "What does our American guest think about this history?" I was asked in front of eighty elderly repatriates gathered for a lecture. On other occasions, the director's husband would simply weave into his commentary a statement that alluded to my presence, explaining that this history was so powerful and yet so little known that an American researcher had arrived in their midst to study it. I sensed that these comments or questions were prompted by others' curiosity regarding the presence of a woman whose youth marked her as an obvious outsider, and to placate those who might find such a presence threatening.

Initially, I did not know if the former settlers would willingly participate in this study or want to discuss their memories of the colonial past. Upon arriving in southern France in 1995, I soon found that the past was ever-present for this diaspora community, and memories regularly erupted like Joseph's song, as if out of nowhere. The project was surprisingly enjoyable after all. The people I spent my time with were irreverent, intelligent, and sometimes quite funny. They were old enough not to worry too much about how they were perceived and, perhaps because they had been living as near pariahs for the past three decades, they were not too worried about what I thought of them either. Most were retired and many felt dissociated from France. I soon found that the colonial past itself was of great interest to these elderly refugees from a prior world order, yet a topic that they were rarely able to discuss except with each other. They were thus eager for an audience, someone to whom to direct their life story and to try to convince that it had meaningful shape, purpose, and morality.

The Maltese-origin settlers seemed particularly delighted by my presence—perhaps because they thought it would attract more people to their events. My project may have also given them a renewed pride in their background and heritage, for I had come all the way from the United States to study neither the *pieds-noirs* in general, nor the Spanish or Italian legacy in the colony, but the Maltese in particular. In order to discern how the Maltese club related to the wider *pied-noir* community, I also attended meetings of the regional *pied-noir* associations such as the Friends of Souk-Ahras, a club uniting former settlers of all ethnic origins from that eastern Algerian town. My status as a much younger person from a U.S. university, and thus an obvious outsider, greatly facilitated this research, as I was assumed to be a blank slate, someone with few fixed prior biases. Several of the most active participants were widows or widowers, and some were estranged from their children. I had the impression that they found their twilight years to be quite lonely at times. Toward the end of my project, I was in demand, and sometimes I felt more social worker than anthropologist. Informants contacted me regularly to find out when I would have time to meet with them again. Perhaps thinking that I might be slowing down our meeting frequency because I found their discussions about the past repetitive, people began combing their apartments for books, articles, and any other kind of memorabilia that might provide a pretext for inviting me to return. Their generosity and interest in this research were boundless.

DIASPORA ETHNOGRAPHY

Although I was based in one town in southeastern France, Aix-en-Provence, this is not an ethnography of settler life in that town, but rather an ethnography of an entire diaspora. The people I interviewed lived scattered across a wide region of southeastern France (some as far away as Paris and Dijon), and do not constitute a community fixed in one locale, the traditional focus of ethnographic fieldwork. They found each other after their exile to France through their membership in various settler social clubs that connect people along different dimensions of their colonial lives, such as places of residency, schools, unions, workplaces, and so forth. Sometimes quite large, even multiday, events unite settlers from whole cities or regions of Algeria or Tunisia. Some clubs organize annual trips—to Barcelona and southern Spain by coach, for example. Club members bring nonmember friends or

Figure 1. Settlers socializing. Photograph by the author.

family members, thus allowing for the forging of additional postcolonial connections. All of these activities attract people from a wide region of France, and it is not unusual for them to drive several hours to meet each other. This is thus an ethnography of social practices engaged in in rented halls, during day- and week-long trips, and in other temporary spaces, in the interstices of the settled villages and city neighborhoods that have been traditional loci of study (see fig. 1).

Like the settlers, I traveled extensively over the course of my twenty months in France. Before I purchased a colleague's ancient car, I used France's extensive public transportation network. My fieldwork relied on this excellent system, as well as on the postal service, and it was not unusual for interviewees to send me a copy of the local bus schedule in the post with the correct bus starred, so that I would arrive for our planned meeting with plenty of time to talk before the all-important midday meal. A typical interview day for me would involve walking early into the center of town to purchase flowers or cake from one of the fine patisseries along the elegant Cours Mirabeau, and then a quick hike down to the *gare routière* to catch a bus to the village center of Manosque, Bouc-bel-Air, Salon de Provence, or the Aixois countryside, where I was invariably greeted by one of the elderly settlers waiting for me in a car. I would return the same way sometime after seven P.M., or even well after, since people often insisted I share their light supper.

Being based in Aix-en-Provence was nevertheless an important part of this fieldwork experience. I became closer to families living locally, and my interactions with other Aixois provided me with a strong sense of the ways that the settler and Maghrebin presence has shaped life in this once sleepy bourgeois town, which was quickly becoming a burgeoning population center with growing connections to Marseilles, some thirty miles away. But I never felt that I was fully integrated in Aix: most of the settlers I spent time with there were clear outsiders and isolated even from their closest neighbors. They were connected to other repatriates, but not to Aixois, and I don't think that I was ever given the telephone number or address of a nonsettler, a "true" French man or woman, to contact.

Even some local historians who became mentors were insider/outsiders, having spent most of their lives overseas and arriving in southern France only after the rapid shrinking of the French empire. Such was the case of Pierre, a historian of Tunisia and beyond who greatly assisted me with this research. When he and his family left Central Africa, where he had been teaching history, they moved to a villa in the then outskirts of Aix, where they raised their children. After his children left, and following the premature death of his beloved wife, Pierre found himself alone in his large home, and generously invited scholars traveling from overseas to board there, in a separate wing of the house, during their research stints at the *Archives d'outre-mer*, the French national archives on overseas possessions and the main collection of documents on colonial Algeria. Along with his former students and colleagues from overseas, I too stayed there during month-long research trips in 1998 and 2001. I couldn't help but notice that while he was a remarkably energetic, open, and generous man involved in a range of projects with scholars at the Archives and across the globe, the only neighbors I saw him interact with closely lived a block away, and they were *pieds-noirs* from Algeria also involved in historical research.

My non-pied-noir friends were also alienated from mainstream Aix society. Most Aixois in their thirties and forties had families and were undoubtedly preoccupied with work and children. I spent time instead with an almost exclusively single crowd. Mireille, a forty-something woman with straight dyed-blond hair, stylish glasses, tight black pants, and a bomber jacket, worked for the city tourist office. She was hoping to fall in love and settle down herself, and keenly felt the absence of her married friends, who she believed were obsessed with their children. I met her through a friend of a friend, who needed someone to fill out a local cooking class with Yvette, a stunningly beautiful, earthy, fifty-something Aixoise artist-weaver who ran the class out of her early-nineteenth-century farmhouse, which was now engulfed by the city's rampant growth. Jean, a balding thirty-something Corsican man, once a musician, who worked at a local hotel, was good friends with my landlord, a spunky, hardworking, self-reliant *restauranteuse* in her late fifties and divorced, as were most single people her age. Pierre, a young computer programmer at a steel mill outside of Marseilles, was also an outsider, as he had moved to the area from the Pyrenees; I met him and his friends through Béatrice, the late-thirties daughter of one of my primary interviewees, who was quite actively involved in labor union organizing. I sometimes felt us all to be misfits, newcomers or outsiders to local social life, although it was never clear who the "insiders" were, given the region's dramatic growth over the past three decades.

My impressions of local Aixois life, while probably reflective of the outsider positioning of my principal informants, may also be shaped by the kind of alienation Douglas Holmes writes about in his work *Integral Europe,* alienation Holmes attributes to multiple rapid socioeconomic changes associated with "fast-capitalism" and the developing European Union. He calls our awareness to the skillful ways a particular form of left/right, proto-fascist political movement, "integralism," has been able to exploit the apprehension associated with these changes. The ways this alienation may fuel settler associative activities as well is addressed further in this work.

This study is based on data from several sources, including participant observation, informal interviews, transcripts of taped conversations, and archival research. After our initial meetings, association leaders included me in all club activities as an adopted member. I met with club members and leaders at their offices in the Maison, or, increasingly, at their homes. I attended many pan-*pied-noir* functions at the Maison, including lectures, meetings, cocktail parties, and city-sponsored lectures on North Africa and related themes. I spent time in the *Centre de documentation historique de l'Algérie,* a settler-run resource center which at the time was housed in the municipal library complex. I met with bookstore owners and historians at the University of Provence, and immersed myself in local news and daily life. Because I was living in a region with a high concentration of settlers, even trips to the laundromat or cafés yielded a wealth of volunteered commentary on France's *pied-noir* or Maghrebin "problems." I taped a large number of the interviews. Because I was interested in the informants' memories not primarily for their factual value but as a way to understand how the past has been remembered and how it emerges in daily conversation, I directed taped conversations as little as possible, carefully avoiding introducing new terms or periodicity into the ways people discussed past events and eras, methods suggested by Joutard (1983). This tape-centered technique, while time-consuming, was rewarding, as it allowed me to gain a detailed understanding of how and at what point the past entered the present, the different qualities of gaps in the conversation, and the role played by interruptions and changing group composition. Long passages here are excerpts from these tapes. I complemented this work with archival research, immersing myself in the lost world of French Algeria, to develop a distinct, archive-based understanding of the Maltese experience there with which to compare the oral testimonies. Because the *Archives d'outre-mer* also house the colony's genealogical records, which are of great interest to *pieds-noirs,* even trips to the archives could be viewed as a form of participant observation, and I often met potential elderly interviewees while helping them thread the microfilm machines or decipher the computerized document request system.

Over the course of my time in France, I traveled across southern France, through city centers to the outskirts where the post-1960s concrete-block high-rise apartment complexes were and where many settlers had lived since they were first built, and to the more suburban villas. I met and spoke at length with hundreds of people, over half of whom were Maltese, but also others of French, Spanish, Italian, and German backgrounds. The average age was seventy-two. Most were from Algeria, but I also met their friends who were repatriated from Tunisia, and one couple from Morocco.[14]

THE ALGERIAN MELTING POT
AND THE MALTESE ENIGMA

The Maltese organization I was working with was not unique. Since the late 1960s, at least a half dozen other Franco-Maltese associations have been established throughout France. Through interviews with six founders of such organizations, I found that their slates of activities closely resemble the calendars of the nonethnic, regionally based settler organizations, such as the Friends of Souk-Ahras. On the other hand, the Maltese associations differ from other *pied-noir* organizations in that they have been consciously created around the members' common ethnic heritage.

According to French historians of colonial Algeria and many contemporary French anthropologists, these social clubs should not exist. While French Algeria was a colony of remarkable ethnic diversity, most historical and contemporary sources claim that, by World War I, all of the non-French settlers of various origins had thoroughly assimilated to French cultural norms in the *creuset algérien,* the Algerian melting pot, developing into a new French settler society.[15] This dominant "melting pot" view asserts that once the foreign settlers became French citizens by legal decree in the late nineteenth century, the great assimilating tools of the French state, which included the educational system, compulsory military service for men, and an array of political and legal institutions, as well as social practices such as intermarriage, acted together to dissolve any remaining cultural barriers. When close to a million of these former settlers arrived in France, they were treated as one bloc by the state, legally equivalent to each other and to other French nationals as French "repatriates." Clearly, their official national identities were French: they spoke French, felt French, and acted French.

The elderly settlers of Maltese origin who belong to the *Amicale France-Malte* seem to be prime examples of this dominant narrative. They have lived in France since the end of the French-Algerian War, having arrived there as French citizens. Most are members of the second to fifth generation of their families born in Algeria, and many club members have ancestors who were in Algeria as early as the 1840s. There is no question in their minds about their French nationality: they speak French, sometimes only that language, and certainly not Maltese. They attended French schools, and most of the men served several long years in the French army during World War II. To them, their "Frenchness" is unquestioned and unquestionable. It is only their participation in the Maltese *pied-noir* social clubs that calls into question the official ideology of complete cultural assimilation. Yet given the strong assimilationist ethic that still pervades French society, even the creation of a social club based around a group's ethnic origins, let alone the inclusion of Malta in the club name, can be viewed as a radical act, an assertion of a distinct identity. The existence of so many of these clubs suggests that assimilation in colonial Algeria was in fact far less complete than advertised.

One of the first puzzles to consider is why this phenomenon appears only among the Maltese. Why do we find no Hispano-French *pied-noir* associations, and none uniting the large members of *pieds-noirs* originally from Italy? Despite an official narrative that suggests that all of the settlers "melted together" by the early twentieth century in the Algerian melting pot, the presence of the clubs indicates the continued persistence of a distinctly Maltese identity and memory. I will detail the ways in which settler assimilation in Algeria was far less perfectly achieved than most official accounts attest. Colonist difference, rooted in class and ethnic distinctions, lasted until the end of the colony. Answers to the mystery of the Maltese social club phenomenon lie in the hierarchical nature of French-Algerian colonial society in general, in Maltese colonial liminality in particular, and in the forms of social memory they generated.

THE POLITICS OF FRENCHNESS
IN A COLONIAL SOCIETY

The Maltese began migrating to Algeria, along with immigrants from across Europe, almost immediately after the first French military victories in Algiers in 1830, motivated by dire conditions at home and a promise of a better future overseas. During the next half century, the spontaneous migration of hundreds of thousands led to the formation of a complex multiethnic and multilingual settler population spread across an ever-expanding swath of North Africa. The majority of these early colonists were not French: most came from southern Europe, particularly from peripheral regions along the Mediterranean, or from such Mediterranean islands as Sardinia, Sicily, Malta, the Balearic Islands, and Pantelleria (see map 1).

Over the next 130 years, through relentless resistance and counter-offensives, all-out war, and continued migration, a settler colony was forged, one with a particularly strong connection to the French state. Throughout much of its history, parts of French Algeria were legally part of the French national territory. Three of its departments were created in 1848,[16] and the colony was increasingly subject to metropolitan legal and administrative structures in a process that accelerated dramatically with the establishment of the Third Republic. Whole regions of Algeria, like the hinterlands of France, were subsequently exposed to many of the same assimilating institutions that Eugen Weber highlighted in his work on the creation of modern France. In fact, Weber himself noted overtly the connections between this process and colonization.

French Algeria can thus be viewed as a test case for the debates that have raged since Weber regarding the significance of the state in shaping social identities, for it saw the imposition of similar, if not identical, legislation and normative practices in a wholly removed place. This is a study then of the politics of Frenchness in a colonial society, with many parallels with the state's approach to regional difference in Corsica and Brittany, for instance. Yet Algeria was first and foremost a colonial society that had a long prior history and rich cultural heritage of its own, and our exploration of the politics of Frenchness there must always start with that basic fact.[17]

Ottoman Algeria

From the end of the sixteenth century until 1830, the "Regency of Algiers" was a remote and semi-independent province of the Ottoman Empire. This vast territory was ruled indirectly by a decentralized bureaucratic military involving some fifteen thousand Turkish troops who monitored a population of approximately 3 million (Julien 1964, 7, 15). The region was divided into four provinces, including three *beyliks,* ruled by leaders, or *beys,* who reported to the *dey* (governor) in Algiers.[18] The area was further divided into other political units, relatively autonomous yet interconnected through crosscutting networks of trade, religious organizations, and pilgrimage. Only 5 to 10 percent of the ethnically diverse population, including Turkish officers and bureaucrats, lived in urban areas, largely situated near the coast; semiautonomous tribes (*kabila,* Arabic[19]) lived in the periphery (Bennoune 1988, Clancy-Smith 1994).

Ethnicity and religion were interrelated and important dimensions of social life. The society as a whole included multiple ethnic groups understood to be hierarchically organized (Valensi 1977, 7). At the apex of this hierarchy were a small number of Turkish functionaries, followed by so-called *Couloughlis,* offspring of Turks and North Africans. In addition, there were Andalusians or "Moors,"[20] Muslims exiled from Spain; Arabs, descendants of the conquerors of the seventh to eleventh centuries; Berbers, the indigenous population, living primarily in Kabylia, the Aurès mountains, and the Sahara; and M'zabites, originally from Iraq, who founded towns in the northern Sahara in 1000 C.E.[21] At the bottom of the hierarchy were Jews, descendants of multiple migrations to the region starting perhaps as early as the ninth century B.C.E., a community enriched by later migrations of Jews from Spain and *Juifs francs* from Leghorn; and, finally, sub-Saharan Africans, often enslaved (Bourdieu 1962; Chouraqui 1968, 8; Julien 1964, 11).[22] Despite their many linguistic and religious distinctions, by most accounts the residents of the Regency were connected by a common cultural base and by trading networks.

Cities were heterogeneous and inhabited by the Turkish ruling elite, who lived in palaces and massive barracks, as well as by artisans, merchants, and apprentices. The Turkish rulers relied on the taxation of peasants living in the country's vast rural expanses, on piracy, and on their monopolies on products such as oil, grain, and salt, which only they could sell overseas (Gallisot 1975). Yet the vast majority of the Regency's residents lived in rural regions, where land was key to the local subsistence economy. Most people were engaged in a mixed agropastoral economy that involved agriculture, animal husbandry, and the cultivation of fruit trees in various combinations according to the exigencies of local geography. In the fertile Tell, intensive agriculture was practiced, and residents traded their surplus grain and fruits for the animal products of the pastoralists and the luxury goods of urban craftspeople (Bennoune 1988, 23). In Kabylia, the Berbers produced olive oil, figs, wool, and livestock, which they traded for wheat. In the dryer regions to the south, less agriculture was practiced except in the oases, and pastoralism was more developed. This "Algeria" was not unknown to the French.[23] The region had been connected to European centers for decades through a robust international commerce.[24]

French conquest involved a destruction of the entire social order, leading to pauperism and eventually the proletarianization of the majority of the population. It occurred in stages. During the first fifty years, there was a gradual development of colonial capitalism, slowed by both intense resistance throughout the country and the incoherence of French policies. This period was followed by the development of mature capitalism, with an economy geared to the extraction of mineral and vegetal raw materials to be exported to French industry. The latter years of the colony (1931–1954) were ones of stagnant agricultural production due to the unwillingness of the French to industrialize the colony (Bennoune 1988).

Creating a Settler Society

Algeria's cultural, linguistic, and religious diversity increased with the arrival of French troops and the thousands of European immigrants in their wake. These immigrants were incorporated differently into the colony's economy and social and political life, leading to the formation of a hierarchy of colonist ethnicities. French settlers were the elite: French-origin families held the most important administrative positions, and owned the more profitable factories and businesses and the largest farms and estates. Spanish and Italian migrants were next, and members of these groups often worked as laborers or foremen on French-owned farms and factories. The Maltese, and eventually the naturalized Algerian Jews, were situated at the bottom of this hierarchy. Class and ethnicity/nationality were mutually reinforcing distinctions; to paraphrase Fanon, in French Algeria "you were rich because you were French, you were French because you were rich" (1961, 32). Of all the immigrants arriving on Algeria's shores, the French and other northern Europeans found the Maltese the most difficult to define, and often described them as a liminal population, a hybrid boundary-defying people uniting West and East. There are many grounds for this assessment of the Maltese, and the first to consider is the islands' very location.

Maltese Liminality

Malta's position in the Mediterranean Sea, between the European and African continents, not far from Tunisia, is implicated in Maltese colonial liminality. Malta is a small, rocky archipelago of three islands, Malta, Gozo, and tiny Comino, located in the center of the Mediterranean, sixty miles to the south of Sicily and 180 miles north of the North African coast (see map 1), at the margins of Europe and Africa. Geographers categorized the archipelago as part of Africa until 1801, when it was redefined as belonging to Europe (Donato 1985, 18). However, this repositioning was challenged nearly a century later. Gabriel Charmes, who stopped in Malta on his way to Tunisia, noted several times in his 1888 publication that he found it difficult to say whether Malta should belong to Europe or Africa. In the end, he equivocated, stating that the island "is part of both continents. Its sterile earth, burnt by the sun . . . seems more African than European." The arch-ipelago had been conquered in turn by Phoenicians, Greeks, Carthaginians, Romans, and later Berber-Arabs of the Aghlabid dynasty based in Tunisia.[25] Muslims ruled for over two hundred years (870–1090). The ruling group that most influenced contemporary Maltese understandings of the bound-aries between self and other, however, was the Sovereign Military Order of the Hospital of Saint John, the "Knights of Malta," an anachronistic mili-tary order of noblemen from the European continent that was created in 1113 (during the Crusades) by Pope Pascal II, and that governed Malta for nearly three hundred years.

Under the Knights' rule, Malta, in the imaginations of Europeans and Maltese alike, was the last bastion of Christendom facing an encroaching Islam. The Maltese people themselves were devout Catholics throughout this time, and the *raison d'être* of the Knights was to "wage perpetual war against the omnipresent Muslim Turk" (Cassar 2001, 260). This vision of Malta's role in world history can be seen in the annual celebration in Malta, observed to this day, of the Knights' defeat of the Ottoman leader's army in 1565. As Maltese historian Henry Frendo writes, "The Turkish siege of 1565 symbolizes their legend: the Knights and the Maltese, then under Grand Master La Vallette, repelled Suleiman the Magnificent's invading force, an event which came to be seen not only as a defeat of the Muslims by the Catholics, but also as a European victory over the Ottoman Empire" (1988, 186–87). However, throughout this time, the origins of the Maltese people were in question, due in large part to their language, mutually intel-ligible with North African Arabic.

The Maltese who migrated to Algeria in the early nineteenth century occupied a unique, and uniquely stressful, status position in the colony. They were among the poorest of the Europeans to migrate across the Medi-terranean, some arriving with no possessions whatsoever, not even shoes (hence their occasional appellation *va pieds-nus* [goes barefoot]). They were also a colonized people; the British had claimed Malta at the beginning of the nineteenth century and would continue to do so until 1964. Ironically, even their strong adherence to their Catholic faith marked them as less "Eu-ropean" for many of the French elite. Perhaps most questionable was their language, which linguists now describe as a Semitic language closely related to ninth-century Maghrebine Arabic, and which had come to Malta with North African conquerors of that era along with Islam (Brincat 1991). Surely if they speak a form of Arabic, they must be Arabs, one imagines other settlers saying. Their linguistic practices did confer one dubious ad-vantage, for the Maltese migrants could communicate relatively easily with the Algerian populations, but this ability only reinforced uncertainties about their origins and loyalties.

Making the Settlers French

In the first years of French Algeria, tourists and French writers reported on the bewildering array of dress, customs, and languages (Morell 1854; Bard 1854), while later politicians highlighted the high concentrations of non-French settlers in certain regions, citing for instance the fact that Spanish was the language spoken in whole regions of the colony. Such a state of affairs could not last long in a colony. Because they were based on extreme power differentials and the rule of the many by the few, colonial societies always faced resistance and risked disintegration. Divisions between colonists within such a society could prove fatal to the entire enterprise, and, consequently, the ruling faction often presented a unified image of itself to hide the potentially fatal fault-lines from those it dominated (Stoler 1989; Stoler and Cooper 1997). Liminal or hard-to-categorize social groups are often viewed as especially polluting or dangerous (Douglas 1966; Leach 1964), and we find this to be the case in French Algeria, where the Maltese were viewed as a particular threat to the stability of dominant rule. French officials and fellow European settlers accused them of manifesting un-European, "Oriental" business practices and cultural traits, and these attitudes hardened into fixed anti-Maltese stereotypes and prejudices as early as the 1840s. There is strong evidence that these attitudes endured; I heard quite similar views expressed by non-Maltese *pieds-noirs.*

In response to widespread fears of losing the colony, either literally or symbolically to foreign cultural norms, the French state developed incentives to encourage more French citizens to migrate; however, these official colonization schemes were notoriously unsuccessful. When it was clear that the state management of demography was a project of limited success, state officials turned to the naturalization of the non-French, and their transformation into French men and women, as the only remaining alternative. But even this tack was largely unsuccessful; foreigners apparently wished to retain their nationalities. Finally, seemingly in desperation, the state removed the element of choice and established a naturalization law in 1889 that forcibly naturalized most of the non-French European population *en masse.*[26]

The mass naturalization of foreign settlers did not lead to the rapid cultural and social assimilation that the dominant narrative would have us believe. In his landmark work, *Making Algeria French* (1990), historian David Prochaska has demonstrated the persistence of marked social and economic distinctions between French and non-French colonists well into the twentieth century, even between "original" and naturalized French. The lower-class whites are described by Prochaska as a "colony within a colony," and people referred to this persistent "subaltern colonist" population as *petits blancs* into the twentieth century. While the naturalization laws did not instantly transform all settlers into Frenchmen, after 1911 census data no longer distinguish French colonists by their ethnic origins, and little archival evidence is yet available,[27] making research into this problem difficult. For that reason, to understand the degree to which foreign settlers became French, we will turn to the testimonies of those who lived through this time, the elderly Maltese-origin *pieds-noirs.*

LIEUX DE MÉMOIRE AND
THE POLITICS OF MEMORY

Any discussion of social memory in France must take into account the work of French sociologist and Durkheim disciple Maurice Halbwachs (*Les cadres sociaux de la mémoire* [The Social Frameworks of Memory], 1925), as well as Pierre Nora's multivolume magnum opus, *Les lieux de mémoire* (1984, 1986, 1992). Halbwachs insisted on a social source of memory. He proposed the existence of "frameworks of memory," social frameworks within which individual memories and thoughts are meaningful. While he admitted that individuals have unique memories due to different life circumstances, he believed that even these individual memories are basically social, for they leave a lasting impression to the extent that they are linked or interrelated to the thoughts "that come to us from the social milieu." He considered collective memories of the family, religious organizations, and social classes, which function as models that serve pedagogical aims, teaching the group's qualities, flaws, and values. Social groups are bound together and understand themselves through their collective memories.

Pierre Nora has taken many of these ideas to a remarkable conclusion. Not only has his multiyear, multivolume enterprise on French "sites" or "realms" of memory influenced how scholars now perceive and discuss collective memory (Wood 1999, 17), but his volumes achieved such widespread popular appeal in France that they themselves now play a role in shaping the very activities that he set out to analyze and critique in the first place.[28] It is Nora's contention that modern societies have a new relationship to the past: memory is no longer experienced directly, but is now mediated via history. Later in this volume I consider the shifts Nora argues have occurred in the salience of French republican memory and the decline of the French nation-state as a unifying framework of collective identity. Here I address Nora's contention that "modern" societies no longer experience memory directly.

In Nora's view, memory is integrated, unselfconscious, spontaneous, "the remnants of experience still lived in the warmth of tradition, in the silence of custom, in the repetition of the ancestral" (1989, 9), ideas quite consonant with those of Halbwachs.[29] The quintessential repository of collective memory, according to Nora, is "peasant culture," fast disappearing. History is part of the problem, for its true mission is to "suppress and destroy" memory (1989, 9). His *Lieux de mémoire* project represents a response to this loss of living memory. A *lieu de mémoire,* in his view, is "any significant entity, whether material or non-material in nature, which by dint of human will or the work of time has become a symbolic element of the memorial heritage of any community" (Nora 1996, xvii). The French relate to their national past through these *lieux.* In an introductory essay he argues quite passionately for the need to get to work: There are *lieux de mémoire* "because there are no longer *milieux de mémoire,* real environments of memory" (1989, 7).

The analytical distinctions Nora draws between "memory" and "history," while heuristically useful and the motivation for quite compelling research, are not as useful a starting place for an ethnography of memory. In his seminal work, *Time and the Other* (1983), Fabian argues that the anthropological claim to power is most clearly visible in its uses of time when constituting its object, and he focuses in particular on the distancing of those observed from the time of the observer, what he refers to as a "denial of coevalness" (1983, 1, 25). A similar distancing is apparent in Nora's model, in which radically different historical consciousnesses are proposed for peoples with memories and those with histories, with "modern" societies disconnected from memory and "traditional" societies still living in the embrace of the ancestral. The applicability of such distinctions worldwide is open to debate; I am not convinced that even in France we find ourselves in a world devoid of memory, in which the generations no longer speak to each other, in which family, religious, or class traditions are no longer transmitted directly, between people. As Goebel asks, "Have *milieux de mémoire* really vanished? Have institutions like the family indeed ceased to function as vectors of transmission?" (2001, 854). In this work, I show that that they have not, using as a starting point an ethnographic study of the ways living memories persist despite great disruption across the colonial divide that highlights their place and function for Maltese settlers.

"Social memory" refers here to collective representations of the past shared by a group of people. These include written and oral narratives and representations that exist in nonlinguistic form. Since any society consists of multiple, heterogeneous subgroups, we can expect that distinct vantage points on the past will emerge, interrelate, and come into conflict from multiple intersecting and dialogically related "communities of memory." Power matters. The Maltese were situated at the bottom of an emerging hierarchy of settler ethnicities; it follows that their vantage point on the colonial past should reflect this social position, and should differ from that of settlers of other social strata, especially the French elite. At the same time, their views will have been forged in a colonial context, one ruled by the French, but one in which they shared many of the benefits. They will have been exposed to, if not strongly influenced by, dominant ideologies and practices fostered by the elite. Like other subordinate peoples elsewhere, the Maltese will have distinct memories of their particular experiences, but may have also internalized some of the ways they were viewed by the French, resulting in a kind of "double consciousness": they will be able to perceive the world in their own terms, while internalizing how the elite viewed them, adjusting their behavior accordingly.

Concepts from writings of the Popular Memory Group (1982) are especially useful for exploring the social memory of subaltern colonists forged in such a power-riven setting. They highlight the presence in all societies of a public "theatre" of history, which will be occupied by actors who enjoy varying degrees of power, with some organizations or individuals more closely aligned with central state institutions and others endowed with increasing degrees of autonomy, such as private museums, educators, historians, and the media. The resulting "field of public representations of history" is "crossed by competing constructions of the past, often at war with each other," and through these struggles, a dominant memory is shaped (1982, 207). The conflict that occurs in this public field is representative of the larger struggle between competing social groups, and power plays a significant role in dictating which versions become most successful, which memories are silenced, and how the many versions will interrelate (Alonso 1988).

But a knowledge of the past is also produced elsewhere, "in the course of everyday life," or in what the Popular Memory Group refers to as a "popular" memory—in talk, and narratives and other forms that do not necessarily enter into the public field. A study of this "popular" memory cannot be concentrated here alone, however, but must be relational in its focus, and consider both the ways various memories in the public field interrelate and the interaction between these public representations and more private popular memory. Popular or subaltern memories are forged in response to or in interaction with dominant historical discourses: "it is often these that supply the very terms by which a private history is thought through" (Popular Memory Group 1982, 211).

While a detailed accounting of the battles that have occurred in the "public theatre" regarding representations of French Algeria is beyond the purview of this study, we will consider salient characteristics of the resulting dominant memory. This representation of colonial Algeria silenced many facets of the colonial past, not insignificantly the more difficult experiences of the non-French settlers. In fact, if their experiences were addressed at all, they were incorporated into a rosy account of an assimilation process already presumed to be complete. Dominant memory is vulnerable to attack, however, for subaltern groups in society may retain their own accounts of the same past, as we will see is the case in the social memories of the "subaltern settlers," the Maltese. A discourse-centered approach is particularly well suited to an analysis of the social memories of people in such an ambivalent social position.

Social memory studies, like the historical representations described by Alonso (1988, 34), often hide the hermeneutics of their production. The problem of locating a "social" memory and explaining the mechanisms by which collective understandings of the past are developed, reproduced, and transformed within a particular community has led scholars from a wide array of disciplines to various strategies and distinct dimensions of social life, including written histories and other forms of official discourse, formal speech, and nonlinguistic forms such as embodied memories found in ritual.[30] There is, of course, another clear source of data for understanding social memory creation, reproduction, and analysis. As Irwin-Zarecka writes, if social memory is a socially articulated and maintained "reality of the past," it makes sense to "look at the most basic, accessible means for memory articulation and maintenance—talk" (1994, 54–55). Using everyday speech as my main source of data on Maltese conceptions of the past allows me to detail patterns in settler ways of speaking and reveal the imbrication of memories from different sources that are apparent in interview transcripts. To elucidate these patterns, I employ Bakhtin's notion of heteroglossia (1981, 1986), the interface of competing perspectives or voices, each presenting a distinct point of view on the world. Different voices indicate the maintenance by the Maltese settlers of many ways of perceiving and talking about the colonial past. Some of these voices strongly parallel representations found in official sources, such as school textbooks, and the dominant memory more generally. Others seem to stem from less public individual, family, or group memories of life experiences in the colony. The resulting multivocality is especially apparent in the settler discourse on assimilation, ethnicity, and Frenchness in the colony. When extensive tape transcripts are explored in this fashion, we can detect zones of amnesia and the effects of audience, topic of conversation, and even present-day concerns on the selection of voices, and so better understand the emotional or ideological resources that nourish them.

THE COLONIAL IN EUROPE

Through my encounters with *pieds-noirs,* I learned that colonialism is not just "elsewhere," and neither are the "colonists." The former settlers reminded me of this fact regularly by bringing up the parallels between our histories. They often referred to Algeria as the "Wild West," and to the history of Algeria as their "Western." "The only difference," one woman explained to me over dinner, "is that we didn't exterminate our 'Indians.' Maybe that was our fatal flaw." Such parallels between the histories of colonial Algeria and the settling of the United States were highlighted throughout my fieldwork. Many of the people I interviewed had ancestors who arrived in Algeria around the time that mine had arrived in the United States. This was brought home one day when an elderly woman was showing me photographs from her cherished family album. Upon glancing through it, I froze: here was an image of a rural farming family at the turn of the century. The elderly man was white-haired, bearded, and wearing overalls; the woman had hair pulled back in a bun, several long cotton skirts, and a severe expression. They were standing in front of a wooden wagon with two small children. This photograph was strikingly similar to an early photograph of my Ohio/Kentucky farming ancestors. My strong feeling of recognition, and then immediate shock at the actual foreignness of the scene, brought into sharp focus the fact that I could not distance myself—morally or otherwise—from the *pieds-noirs,* imagining that *they* were guilty colonists while my past was pure. In studies of colonialism, however, such distancing has been rather commonplace, perhaps especially so on the part of anthropological researchers.

Until recently, the anthropology of colonialism and that of Europe have been worlds apart. This may not be surprising. Even during the height of European imperialism, a project that many have argued was what made pre–World War II anthropology feasible to begin with in that it allowed for an intimacy between anthropologists and their object of study (Asad 1973, 17; see also Gough 1968), anthropologists either failed to perceive the wider colonial context within which their research was situated, or argued that the study of the colonial system was beyond their expertise (Balandier 1951). Anthropologists had a "strange reluctance" to consider the power structures within which the discipline existed (Asad 1973, 15). Although anthropological theory and practice has since shifted toward a more critical examination of the relationship between power and knowledge in specific colonial situations and of colonialism's impact on anthropological knowledge creation,[31] continuities remain with colonial-era research. In a critique of contemporary anthropological theory, Edward Said observed that few scholars reference U.S. imperial intervention as a factor affecting theoretical discussions (1989). The bracketing off of anthropologists as morally neutral, an important strategy during the discipline's colonial era, continues, and scholarship on colonial questions usually is concentrated on formerly colonized regions and on the past, thus distancing researchers from their research subjects (Fabian 1983) and from any clear association with contemporary imperial practices. This distancing is nowhere more apparent than in the dearth of research on European colonists themselves in the colonies, and in the anthropology of Europe.

Anthropologists have been studying the impacts of colonization on peoples worldwide since the creation of the discipline, even if this was not outlined explicitly. Yet for a discipline that advocates understanding cultural phenomena from the insider's perspective, it is remarkable how little work has been carried out to date with dominant colonial actors—administrators, settlers, or former settlers. As Thomas Beidelman writes, "It is as though anthropological curiosity stopped at the color bar" (1981, 2). The unwillingness to consider European colonists in the anthropological gaze may be construed as implying that Europeans are somehow natural "dominators," or that the process of becoming a colonizer is a straightforward one. These are, at the very least, problematic notions indeed. I begin with the opposite conviction: learning to be a colonist is a problem in and of itself requiring further study. We have more to learn about the Europeans who emigrated to the colonies and how it was that they established new, decidedly colonial, societies. The case of the Maltese, who made the journey from colonized to colonizer, allows us to elucidate this process. In conducting this research, I have taken into account the statements of Césaire (1955), Fanon (1961), and Memmi (1967), who argued that the dynamics of colonial life were damaging to colonists as well as to the colonized portion of the population. In his *Discours sur le colonialisme* (1955), Césaire warned that the brutalization inherent in colonialism would have lasting negative consequences not only for the victims of colonial policies and those perpetrating them, but ultimately for metropolitan Europe as well.

Given the early bias in anthropology toward the study of non-European peoples and the difficulties early anthropologists faced in addressing the colonialism that was all around them, it is perhaps no wonder that anthropologists working in Europe have been similarly afflicted. Europeanist anthropology blossomed with village studies focusing on local agricultural economies, kinship and household structure, and the effects of modernization on Europe's more rural or peripheral regions. These works have been followed by challenges to the modernization paradigm, important studies of gender, industrialization, and class, and analyses of the ways in which anthropologists have been implicated in creating identities and regions understood as peripheral. More recently, revolutionary changes in postwar Europe have received noteworthy attention, including immigration and its effects on migrant and host societies, ethnicity, ethnic conflict and urban life, postsocialist transitions, and the establishment of the European Union. Anthropologists looking at Europe were not perceiving the effects of imperialism.

This has been a remarkable oversight, one that the former settlers of Algeria recognize only too well. As we drove across the city of Marseilles, one elderly man liked to rant when we passed the grand old buildings of the nineteenth century: "Here you can find the colonialists! Look at this extravagance! This city was built on colonialism, built on the backs of our hard work, and that of our parents and grandparents. The French like to blame colonialism on us as if we were the only ones who benefited, but you can see here that this country was founded on wealth from overseas!" Aside from tracing the economic foundation of many European states in colonial-era wealth, scholars are only now recognizing that imperialism also fostered the development of ideologies about self and other, technologies of rule, and forms of governmentality that migrated between metropole and colony (Said 1978, 1993; Stoler and Cooper 1997; Rabinow 1989; Thomas 1994). Contemporary European literary critics and historians are returning to the archives and using these sources to narrate an alternative national and literary history, one more explicitly tied to the imperial past (Burton 2003; Kumar 2003; Kennedy 1996; Said 1978, 1993; Wilson 2003). In her study of French interwar cinematic and literary works by authors not known as "colonial" writers, Elizabeth Ezra finds abundant evidence of a "colonial unconscious" that pervaded metropolitan cultural life (2000). And clearly colonialism's many influences on European cultural forms have not ended with decolonization. As Etienne Balibar writes, "contemporary France was formed in and through colonization" (1984, 1741). The end of Empire required momentous shifts in the economies of former colonial powers. Equally significant have been the impacts of decolonization on national identities, as many countries—France, Britain, and the Netherlands in particular—suddenly had to formulate radically new national "narrations" (Bhabha 1990), new templates, morals, and heroes around which to build a reconstructed national past and collective identity. Immigration from former colonies has altered European societies in more tangible ways. Xenophobia and the integration of foreigners are aspects of the "new" Europe, and the arrival of more visibly different ex-colonized peoples is often considered a starting point for racial strife or proto-fascist nationalist movements across the continent (Brubaker 1989; Castles, Booth, and Wallace 1984; Cole 1997; Noiriel 1996; Schnapper 1992; Weil 1991; Wihtol de Wenden 1987; Wieviorka 1992). Yet scholarly amnesia regarding the settlers followed them as they resettled in Europe.[32] Social scientists are only now beginning to consider the many ways that the migration to Europe of 5 to 8 million colonial "repatriates" has had lasting effects (see Smith 2003). We have yet to discern how Europe has changed with the arrival of these newcomers, how they may have brought with them colonial cultural practices and ideologies, or how they might shape European polities and cultures in the new century.

NOSTALGÉRIE, NATIONAL MEMORY, AND THE MALTA ENIGMA

Through my conversations and taped interviews with elderly former settlers over the years, I found an oppositional social memory among those of Maltese origin. This is not a construction of the past based on a common memory of the ancestral homeland, as I had expected, but one rooted in a collective memory of their subaltern colonist status and the ambivalence of assimilation. Most Maltese-origin settlers are bound by *nostalgérie,* the *pied-noir* term for a longing for Algeria, which I found was shared by *pieds-noirs* of all backgrounds. The extent to which *pieds-noirs* long for Algeria was brought home most forcefully during an annual two-day reunion of former settlers from the eastern Algerian town of Souk-Ahras. The reunion had been planned for months, and the attendees were clearly delighted to meet up again, this time in a rather sterile rented space at a holiday camp on a beach in southwestern France during a cold winter weekend. It was a few hours into the first day. People gathering that Saturday afternoon during *tchatche* ("chatting," *pataouète*[33]), or happy hour, were loudly greeting long-time friends who had traveled from across France. The noise level in the rented hall was incredible as people milled around, shouting, hugging, kissing newcomers, and dragging metal chairs against the concrete floor to make room for new arrivals at their tables. A crowd stood waiting at the bar to order *pastis* or *oranginas* and to secure some appetizers to bring back to their friends. I was told that two hundred people were expected.

At first I wandered somewhat aimlessly, looking at the blown-up copies of old postcards of Algeria that were for sale as well as the large display of photographs of the people reunited that day, showing them at age five or ten in posed group shots of grade school classes and school football teams. The people who had invited me were deep in discussion with old friends, some of whom they had not seen since 1962, and I did not want to interrupt these emotional reunions. One of the meeting organizers, a young woman in her late thirties, saw me and invited me to sit with her and her cousin. These two were by far the youngest people present. Marie told me she attended these meetings because they provided an opportunity to spend time with her aunt, uncle, and mother. She liked seeing them so happy, she explained. We talked. She was a linguist and had conducted research for her doctorate among African Americans in Los Angeles. She told me that there were many similarities between the former settlers in France and African Americans in the United States and outlined her view of their similar lack of integration. I probably wouldn't be able to understand how it feels to be African American in the States, she explained, because I was white. Since I was from the dominant culture, I would never be able to imagine how it feels to be at once a member of society and yet so separate.

I asked if this is how *pieds-noirs* feel: separate, not a part of France. She paused for a minute, and then pointed over the crowd to a man with grey hair, his arm around another of a similar age, sitting and laughing. "You see that man over there, my uncle? He is always talking about North Africa. Everything is always reminding him of his home, of his home town, of Algeria. He'll see a plant, and it will remind him of a similar species that grows back there. A tree reminds him of the one in front of his old house there. A shift in the light, the clouds . . . There are always echoes back . . ." She searched for words, for another way to explain this to me. "You see, these people here," gesturing this time to the entire room, "they are not really here. They are not here. Sure, they are here physically, certainly, but not mentally. Mentally, we are all at this moment in North Africa."

Colonialism was in many respects a foundational project charting the course of several European countries, such as France, the Netherlands, Britain, and Portugal. This may be nowhere more apparent today than in the changing face of social life since decolonization. The Maltese social clubs are a subset of the hundreds of clubs *pieds-noirs* have formed in an effort to make a home for themselves in postcolonial Europe. Many important questions remain: why are the *pieds-noirs* of Maltese origin so especially afflicted? Why Malta, why now? Are the Maltese social clubs and the stories their members tell about the past signs of a long-suppressed "hidden transcript," finally allowed to emerge in the safety of contemporary France? Why would so many individuals who share such a background choose to travel to Malta, and what does this place represent to them?

TWO

Maltese Settler Clubs in France

MEMORIES AND MALTA

The very existence of the *Amicale France-Malte* and other Franco-Maltese settler clubs suggests the perpetuation of a distinct Maltese identity sustained by distant memories of Malta in the colony and now in contemporary France. This is not unheard of: a shared knowledge of a lost homeland and a people's departure from it can serve to unite people for generations, if not millennia. The bonding of former settlers today around their Maltese heritage, in this view, would indicate that some shared knowledge of that heritage persisted in the colonial period and has been reawakening in France. And yet club leaders François Xuereb and Michel Pisani both challenged such an interpretation on the day we met. When I outlined to them my proposed study of the social memory of Maltese-origin settlers in early spring 1995, they were dubious, but advised me as to how I should proceed with my research: "Find people who are at least fifty years old, because the younger generation won't remember anything. And even then, the memories will be vague." We were sitting in the Maltese club headquarters in the *Maison des rapatriés,* the local "repatriates" center. François and Michel were sitting at their desk, pulling materials from a file cabinet for me.

The past two days had been hectic. The preceding morning the elderly men had picked me up in the crowded center of Aix-en-Provence and had driven me to their office. For this first encounter, they were dressed in suits and ties, and their manner was similarly respectful and formal. François, who had volunteered for the French First Army in 1943, at age seventeen, spent much of the preliminary phase of our visit discussing his war service and upcoming visit to Washington, D.C., where he would participate in the events commemorating the end of World War II. He is an energetic man, in his late seventies when I first met him, and endowed with a quick wit and captivating speaking voice. Michel Pisani, his co-organizer, is a somewhat shorter, muscular, balding man with wire-rimmed glasses and the slightly tanned skin of somebody who has spent much of his life in the sun. François's junior by more than a decade, he often deferred to him, only to regret it on more than one occasion. During this meeting, François explained in detail the origin of his last name, Xuereb: Phoenician, he said, like that of many of the original Maltese families, and he showed me a book illustrating his *blazon de famille,* his family's coat of arms. The two elderly men then responded to what they saw as my interest in Malta by outlining in unison much of the archipelago's history: its early conquest by the Phoenicians, St. Paul's shipwreck there and his conversion of the populace to Christianity, the long rule by the Knights of Malta, and the brief foray by Napoleon at the turn of the nineteenth century, followed by British rule until 1964. They detailed the political affiliation of the current president of Malta, recounted the long-term alternation between nationalist and socialist control of the government, and discussed whether or not Malta should join the European Union. Their helpfulness was almost overwhelming, and our discussion of topics well beyond my research focus consumed much of our brief meeting time. At its end, we decided to meet again the following day. François Xuereb said that he was unclear what my interests were, and perhaps I could make a formal presentation to them at that time.

The next day, I reiterated my interests in a collective memory of the Maltese experience in North Africa. I thought that, being directors of a social club for people of this background, they might have something to say on the subject. François took the floor, attempting to answer all of my questions right then and there. "Yes, well, yes, I can help you. I will tell you how this emigration occurred. There were two kinds of emigration—either by choice, or of the very poor. There were the Maltese who were in North Africa long before the French, such as my family, and then there were French of various regions, the Italians, and the Spanish. You should speak with our friend who is in charge of the association of the *rapatriés d'Oranie* [repatriates from the Algerian department of Oran]. He can tell you all about the Spanish emigration—does that interest you, or just the Maltese?" I asked them if they thought I should consider studying all of the various European migrations to Algeria, or if there was something unique about the Maltese experience in the colony.

They considered this question very carefully. A special feature of the Maltese, they concurred, was that they blended into French culture very quickly, more quickly than other immigrant groups, in fact. The Maltese were assimilationists *"extraordinaires,"* they told me. But, regarding a memory of Malta, they were skeptical: "People today will have no memories of Malta, none [*aucune mémoires de Malte, aucune*]. Nothing will remain . . . well, there will be echoes back, especially regarding traditional cuisine, but otherwise, nothing will remain." This statement puzzled me. The club leaders were telling me that knowledge of Malta had all but vanished, yet as I looked around their office, I saw that it was proudly decorated with images of the islands that they had cut out of magazines and taped to the freshly painted white concrete-block walls. Moreover, our conversations had revealed that they themselves were fixated on the place. They each told me when and how they had first "discovered" Malta, how many times they had traveled there since, and when they planned to return. Malta was clearly a symbol of some significance—the archipelago served as the sole visual focus of the room and the main subject of discussion in those two meetings. And yet, paradoxically, they argued that Malta would not feature in the collective memories of organization members.

THE *AMICALE*

After these initial encounters, I moved to southern France and spent nearly the next two years with François, Michel, and the members of their Franco-Maltese *amicale*. François Xuereb had founded it some six years before, following a visit to Malta with another repatriate organization. "I did it to give myself something to do, and to help those with a Maltese background," he told me one afternoon while we sat in his living room in a Marseilles suburb. Club members are people of Maltese origins, on one or both sides of the family. "These are people seeking their roots," François explained. "They join out of nostalgia, they want to find out where their family came from, where their ancestors used to live." He told me he has helped out many people—both members and others—by accompanying them on group trips to Malta, or by bringing back copies of documents or their family coats of arms. The members are mostly elderly, in various life circumstances—widowed, married, or single, but usually retired—and live in towns and neighborhoods scattered across the urbanized Aix-Marseilles area. They meet several times a year for dinners, parties, and outings; the highlight is undoubtedly the week-long trips to Malta they try to take annually. In the mid-1990s, François counted approximately 130 to 150 families among the club members.

At first we met at their association headquarters or at functions open to all local *pied-noir* club members, such as lectures or happy hours, during which they would introduce me to those present. Soon we became close friends. Their interest in helping me was great: Michel invited me regularly to his small apartment, especially when he and his wife had guests visiting who he felt could help me with my research. He was having quite an active first year in retirement, and regularly walked several kilometers into town to map out his various business dealings. His wife, Rose, is taller than he, and regularly admitted that she was overweight and needed to go on a diet. With permed short brown hair and brown eyes, she looked like many other Maltese-origin women I met. I almost always saw her at her home, where she dressed casually in floral cotton housedresses. She was often at work when I visited, preparing meals or doing laundry and ironing. Yet age was catching up with her and she was starting to really feel like the grandparent she now was.

We would sit into the evening on their low floral divans that surrounded a coffee table, drinking tea and eating Rose's latest marmalade-glazed tea cake, or a treat I had brought them from a bakery in town. Their daughter lived two floors down in the six-story building, and their seven-year-old granddaughter often was with us, coloring or playing with her toys. Her parents worked in Marseilles. When Michel became very involved in my research, Rose seemed happy to have someone visit who could help distract him. I sometimes wondered if he didn't miss his work, of which he spoke so fondly. In Algeria, he had been a salesman who traveled the rural regions to the south selling beverage products, while in France, no doubt due to his long stay in Algeria (he and his family remained there until the 1970s) and fluency in Arabic, he was assigned to manage a crew of *harkis* working in the national forests. He seemed well suited for that kind of work, which involved continual movement out in the countryside, and appeared to me somewhat pent up in his apartment in the rather closed community of Aix. He and his wife were actively involved in a regional association as well, the Friends of Souk-Ahras, and when relations between François and him soured, he made sure I continued with my research by inviting me to attend that association's functions as well, leading me through the milling throngs of hundreds at festive dinner parties to single out those of Maltese origin for me to meet.

I also traveled twenty minutes by car or bus to visit François Xuereb, who lives in a comfortable yet simply furnished villa along a national highway between Aix-en-Provence and Marseilles. He seems taller than his true height, and has the presence of a powerful, physically fit man. After emigrating from Tunis in the late 1950s, he first lived in the village center, where he established a restaurant-cum-hotel that he built by hand. Perhaps because he spent his life in the restaurant and bar business, he seemed comfortable hosting dinner parties, which in my experience was rare for elderly single men in France (he is divorced). He often invited me to dine with him when his relatives were visiting from out of town, and hosted a grand paella dinner for my parents when they visited. Others who knew him well sometimes found him authoritarian or otherwise difficult, or alluded to his having participated in unsavory activities associated with his business. I, however, found him direct, generous, and blessed with a remarkably quick mind and ready sense of humor. It was François who first insisted that we shift from the formal register in French to the more intimate *tutoyer,* and who would ask point-blank questions about my single status with a twinkle in his eye.

LA VIE ASSOCIATIVE
IN FRANCE

The Amicale France-Malte is an *association,* a type of organization that is a distinctive feature of French civil society. The right of citizens to organize without prior state approval was debated over the course of French history, but finally was granted with the law of July 1, 1901. *Associations* are a specific type of institution created by two or more people who share common interests, and they have prospered: millions have been formed since 1901. Today there are over eight hundred thousand *associations* in France, representing a whole array of social activities. A study in 1990s found that sports-related clubs were the most common (19 percent) followed close behind by cultural and tourism clubs (17 percent), and then by health and social services groups, often run by quasi-governmental organizations (12 percent). Clubs with a primarily social mission are often called *amicales.* It is estimated that one out of three French men and women belong to an *association,* with membership slightly more common among men (Defrasne 1995, 70). They are attractive for the kinds of human contacts they provide, and are viewed as an important means of fostering social networks and democratic life (Debbasch and Bourdon 1995).

It is difficult to overestimate the role of *associations* in France. In many respects, then, Franco-Maltese clubs are exemplary of a distinctly French approach to socialization and identity politics. *Associations* have long fostered processes of regional identification. *Aveyronnais amicales* in Paris have for generations served to unite former residents of the Aveyron region, for instance, financing projects back home, organizing parties, and even serving as a marriage market (Rogers 1991, 55–56). As one elderly man explained, "In Aix, there are the people from Burgundy, you have an *association* of Alsatians, et cetera. People try to find each other through their common origins." Immigrants too, especially after World War I, have formed *associations* that serve as local sports, cultural, or mutual aid societies. These clubs are sometimes integrated into national-level organizations strong enough to put pressure on the state, even leading to friction between France and the immigrants' countries of origin. Some of these networks have been quite extensive: in the 1930s, five hundred voluntary organizations of Poles were integrated into a national superstructure comprising some hundred thousand members (Noiriel 1996, 139).

Figure 2. Association Day, Aix-en-Provence. Photograph by the author.

Associations often receive small subventions from the state or local municipalities. The Franco-Maltese club is one of the thousand or so such clubs funded by the city of Aix-en-Provence. According to a city official, organizations that provide social services or which have a goal of wider cultural enrichment receive the most municipal funding. When I attended the annual Day of Associations in Aix one year, I found the central Cours Mirabeau crowded with tables, displays, and people of all ages milling about (see fig. 2). The diversity of *associations* present was astounding; there seemed to be organizations for every common interest, including any sporting activity imaginable, even archery and indoor scuba diving. There even is a regional association to promote *la vie associative* (the *Association régionale de promotion de la vie associative de Provence-Alpes-Côte-d'Azur,* or APROVA). Nevertheless, within such a proliferation of clubs the only overtly ethnic clubs I saw that day were the Aixois branch of the Association of Moroccan Workers (*Association des travailleurs marocains*) and the Antilles Association of the Aix Region (*Association antillaise en pays d'Aix*).

The existence in southeastern France of one *association* for repatriates of Maltese origins might not merit attention; the fact that this club is just one of many, on the other hand, suggests something other than the interests of a few people at work. Once settled in France, I began to learn about many more such organizations, and eventually met with most of their former or current leaders. The first of the Franco-Maltese clubs was created in Paris in

Figure 3. Club members in Malta. Photograph by the author.

the late 1960s, and thrived throughout the 1970s and 1980s due in part to the enduring friendship and tremendous energy of the *association* leaders. The *association*'s membership has dropped off somewhat, but it continues to meet and is now led by two women. Because it was difficult for people to travel to Paris for regular meetings, interested parties established local branches. An active club met regularly in Lyon until recently, and another was established in the Marseilles region in 1972. When this Marseilles club became defunct in the mid-1980s, Mr. Xuereb decided to fill the void with his own organization. While I was in France, yet another major association for repatriates of Maltese origin was thriving in Toulouse. This organization was the most popular of all the Maltese *pied-noir* clubs in France at the time. Their meetings are so large that they require a veritable army of organizers. Finally, yet another such club was formed in 2001 in Nice.

These clubs' yearly calendars of events are quite similar. The *Amicale France-Malte* meets four to five times a year, attracting twenty-five to sixty attendees each time. The first event of the year is held during the French festival of the *Galette des rois* in early February. This is an afternoon event to drink coffee and eat cakes in which small prizes are hidden. At the same time the *Assemblée générale*, an annual business meeting mandated by French law, is held, during which the club members elect the five required leaders for that year. They also meet regularly on Ascension Day in May for day-long outings. During my first year, this involved a bus trip to Arles and a day-long boat trip along the Rhône. The next year, we went to archaeological sites and a museum in Avignon, and on to the Camargue for a midday meal in Ste. Marie de la Mer followed by a walking tour of a local botanical garden. In the late summer or early fall, the association organizes its biggest event of the year, the Malta trips (see fig. 3). These events are not expensive and require advance subscription.

Generally speaking, these are clubs for the elderly, and are not unlike other *associations* in France or organizations elsewhere uniting seniors in the context of an atomized, postindustrial society, with the goal of enhancing their social contacts and enriching their lives. Yet otherwise this collection of individuals appeared to me to have suffered special burdens. After the first day-long trip with the *Amicale,* I wrote in my fieldnotes that the organization's very existence appeared due less to some common ethnic heritage and more to France's failure to offer its members any hope for the future. One woman, Janine, worried about her son, who was twenty-seven. He had already worked for three years at a bank but without a permanent position, instead holding a succession of three-month contracts. He was awaiting the results of an exam he had taken that could yield a permanent position. Yet there were thousands of applicants, she told me, and some days he was quite discouraged. Another member talked with pride about his children, including his son, a successful entrepreneur working overseas. I asked if he had any other children, and he paused before finally explaining that yes, he had another son, who had been in a motorcycle accident and was now a quadriplegic—he lived in a group home, as he needed twenty-four-hour care. He quickly changed the subject. The youngest person there, Catherine Mifsud, was in her late forties and had been unemployed for two years. She had recently applied for a new position but, due to the postal strike in Marseilles the previous month, her application wasn't received in time. Since she speaks many languages, I asked her about her work opportunities in this field. "I wish," she responded, and then told me her story. She was in a childless marriage, and was coming out of a depression. Over the course of the next year, her depression seemed to return. Another woman seated near me at dinner was lively and cracked jokes the whole time, but as I walked along the edge of the boat to enjoy the view of Avignon and its famous bridge, I learned that she too had endured difficult times recently. While on a vacation in Russia, her husband had had an aneurism, and she had had to "bring him back in a coffin." The next year, her twenty-four-year-old son had slipped while walking in the woods, hit his head, and died.

Many of the stories I heard reflected a general anxiety about the future, particularly regarding the limited employment opportunities for youth. I was first in France during a difficult time: multiple strikes paralyzed Paris and then much of France in the winter of 1995–1996, followed by a series of bombings in the Paris subways and attempted bombings on the TGV high-speed train lines. A radio program I heard confirmed my perception of a generalized unease regarding the future. A French writer who had attended his children's graduations in both France and the United States was struck by the optimism permeating U.S. graduation ceremonies, where children are told, "The world is waiting for you, now it is your turn, the big adventure begins today." This struck him as odd. In France, he explained, the message his daughter heard was "School is over, the best years of your life are finished. You will always remember these years as the happiest of your life." Graduation in France was more a looking backward, because, he felt, the future was so uncertain.

The preoccupation of the elderly association members with the careers of their children and grandchildren was pervasive. It is something they may have shared with others in wider French society who were also facing a changing economy associated with deindustrialization and U.S. hegemony, as well as the increasingly important European Union. These forces of change are succinctly captured in Douglas Holmes's work *Integral Europe,* as I discuss further on. But this was not just any group of French elderly. After the day's journey, when it came time to say our goodbyes as we descended from the bus and began to make our way to cars or public transportation, men embraced each other warmly and then shouted their parting goodbyes in Arabic.

The Franco-Maltese associations also are similar to immigrant *amicales* in that they have been formed by newcomers seeking a means to assuage the alienation that they feel in their new home. Unlike other "immigrant" associations in France, however, the members share two additional attributes: they are all French nationals, and, most importantly, they are all former settlers, their families having spent several generations in French colonies in North Africa on their way from Malta. It is also quite interesting, moreover, that this North African heritage is not underscored in any of their literature, nor is it signaled in any way by the various club names, which invariably stress Franco-Maltese cultural ties. At least overtly, these clubs represent a celebration of a Maltese, not North African, heritage. Throughout meetings, meals, interviews, and gossip sessions with club members, I looked for signs of a Maltese, and not simply French, repatriate, or *pied-noir,* identity. I sought out key symbols of "Maltese-ness" that might unite club members, friends, and family members and transcend their contrasting colonial backgrounds, their different generations, and the great assimilating pressures of colonial Algeria. To begin to understand what these symbols might be, we need to return there and consider the islands' rich, sometimes bizarre, and always fascinating cultural heritage.

MALTA, THE KNIGHTS,
AND THE MALTESE

The Maltese archipelago has a remarkably rich history considering its diminutive size and lack of significant resources. Due to its strategic location in the Mediterranean (see map 2), it has played a major role in international affairs for the past few millennia. Settlement was early: megalithic temple ruins are found on both Malta and Gozo, dating to 3–4,000 B.C.E. The Phoenicians arrived in the tenth century B.C.E., and were followed by Greeks in 736 B.C.E., Carthaginians, and Romans. In the ninth century C.E., the islands were conquered by Berber-Arabs of the Aghlabid dynasty, based in Tunisia, and Muslims remained in power at least until the late-eleventh-century Norman occupation.

Of all of Malta's invading rulers, perhaps the best known was the Sovereign Military Order of the Hospital of Saint John, the "Knights of Malta." This order was established in Jerusalem in the twelfth century, following the first Crusade, ostensibly to serve European pilgrims arriving in the newly conquered Levant. Following the Crusaders' defeat in 1291, it moved to Rhodes, from which it was again routed, this time by Ottoman leader Suleiman I. It moved to Malta in 1530. At this time, the approximately seventeen thousand Maltese inhabitants were supporting themselves with subsistence agriculture and by working as sailors for European enterprises trading in the Mediterranean (Blondy 1994, 75; Mallia-Milanes 1992b, 8). A small local nobility had their homes in the inland city of Mdina. Suleiman followed the Knights to Malta, and attacked the islands in a long siege in 1565, now called the Battle of Lepanto, during which the Order and Maltese forces managed to repel the invaders. This battle is still viewed by the Maltese as a key symbolic event and serves as the basis for Malta's claiming a pivotal role in efforts to maintain a Christian Europe.

Over the next three centuries, Malta was governed by the Knights, a heterogeneous collection of European aristocrats, who replaced the local self-government *(Universitàs)*. Strict regulations limited access to the Order to members of European nobility, and even the Maltese nobility was kept from all but the lowliest positions. From this point on, "the inhabitants had no say at all in the government of their country" (Ciappara 2001, 34). A rigid social hierarchy developed, with a foreign minority population of northern European nobles led by the Grand Master dictating local affairs. The Maltese did benefit from increased prosperity and a higher standard of living under the Order's rule, however. During the sixteenth and seventeenth centuries, piracy, a common practice along both shores of the Mediterranean, was a principal source of income for the islands. By the end of the sixteenth century, the Order of St. John was not only capturing non-

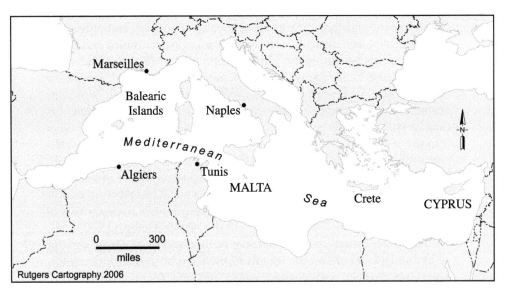

Map 2. Malta in the Mediterranean.

European pirate ships and enslaving their crews, the only piratical activity permitted to them by their statutes, but had also begun to pillage nonpiratical ships of non-Christian states as well.[1] After 1605, piracy became a full-fledged commercial endeavor carried out under the Maltese flag. Associations of financiers bought the necessary boats, equipment, and provisions, armed the men, and divided the earnings, with a predetermined percentage of the proceeds benefiting the Order (Blondy 1994, 77). The Order also tried to foster economic growth in other, more legitimate, ways. It built the largest hospital in Europe in Valletta, offering free care to all. When the hospital was expanded to include quarantine facilities for ships, Malta became a crucial Mediterranean port of call, especially during epidemics (Blondy 1994, 80). By the eighteenth century, it was an important warehouse for merchandise shipped between the Levant, North Africa, Sicily, Leghorn, and France, and an increasingly important center of exchange and trade. This international trade benefited a small but growing middle class of local and foreign businessmen, shopkeepers, and traders, many of whom spent much of the year away from the islands (Ciappara 2001, 51).

The Order owned sizeable estates in Europe and spent a large amount of its annual revenues on the islands in the form of public works, subsidized food, charities, and pensions, and in the Order's maintenance, expenditures which benefited the Maltese both directly and indirectly (Price 1954, 2). Maltese were employed by the Order's navy, on its galley ships, in its dockyards, as guards at its slave prisons, and as gardeners, bakers, and cooks (Ciappara 2001). The relative prosperity was such that the populace was able to rely on imported items for two-thirds of its food supply, and the islands' population grew from twenty thousand in 1530 to a hundred thousand in 1798 (Brincat 1991, 98). As the Order developed the fortifications of the harbor at Valletta, the population of this area swelled, with migrants from Sicily and other parts of Europe arriving to work in construction and on ships. Malta became remarkably cosmopolitan, with not only immigrants from Mediterranean Europe, but also thousands of slaves from the whole Ottoman Empire, who interacted regularly with urban Maltese (Ciappara 2001).

This relatively comfortable situation changed abruptly at the end of the eighteenth century, after the French Revolution. By 1792, the Order's sizeable estates in France, Germany, Naples, Portugal, Sicily, and Spain were either confiscated or heavily taxed. In 1797, the Order's income had fallen to a third of its 1788 level, and in June 1798, Napoleon invaded the Maltese archipelago and expelled the Order from the islands altogether. With the Order gone, the Maltese economy foundered, and the populace struggled through the next four decades of political upheaval and economic decline.

THE MALTESE LANGUAGE:
PHOENICIAN OR ARABIC?

The knowledge that one of the many invading powers that colonized the islands was Muslim troubled later Maltese historians, who, in their effort to demonstrate the innate "Europeanness" of the Maltese people, developed many false traditions, sometimes even based on forged documents. It was important in this geopolitical context to demonstrate that Malta had always belonged to Christian Europe and thus stood in opposition to the Ottoman Empire, Islam, and Africa (Luttrell 1977). The debate over the continuity of Christianity on the islands during the years of Arab occupation (870–1090 C.E.) has been particularly fierce (Luttrell 1994; Mitchell 2002, 29–30). It was and still is widely believed in Malta not only that its Christianity was continuous, but also that it had quite early roots, stemming from St. Paul's early conversions after his purported shipwreck there in 60 C.E. As Jon Mitchell points out, the St. Paul story is central to contemporary Maltese identity, and recent scholarship suggesting that St. Paul may have been shipwrecked elsewhere has been vigorously refuted in the Maltese press (2002, 22–32). Through this story, the Maltese not only lay claim to being European, but also position themselves as among the first Christians, having converted to Christianity even before the conversion of Rome.[2] Yet potentially undermining this belief in Christian continuity is the problem of the Semitic (Arabic) roots of the Maltese language.

The Phoenician colonization of Malta provided sixteenth-century Maltese historians such as Agius de Soldanis with a convenient way to deflect attention from Malta's Arabic and Muslim past, in part because so little is known about the Phoenicians, even today. While this very brief and early colonization dates to the eighth century B.C.E. and has left few visible remains, it was documented in Greek and Roman literary sources,[3] and through this synechdochical relationship, it has served to link the Maltese and their language, not to Arabic and the Orient, but to the Greeks, to the roots of European antiquity, and thus to Europe itself. A thesis of a Phoenician origin for the Maltese language was first promoted in the sixteenth century (Luttrell 1977, 127), and by the nineteenth century it had become so widespread that Maltese linguists and archaeologists alike reveled in a "Phoenician mania" (Sznycer 1973, 148). During this time, all pre-Roman artifacts were attributed to the Phoenicians, despite the fact that very few true Phoenician artifacts were excavated before 1963.

The debate over the origins of the Maltese language is part of a larger debate about the islanders' relationship to Europe. The Phoenician origin language ideology can be understood as resulting from processes of "fractal recursivity" and of "erasure," semiotic processes identified by Judith Irvine and Susan Gal that allow people to construct ideological representations of linguistic differences. Fractal recursivity "involves the projection of an opposition, salient at some level of relationship, onto some other level" (2000, 38). Here, the opposition between Christianity and Islam and between Europe and the Ottoman Empire and Africa, powerful conceptual models in the Mediterranean for centuries (Herzfeld 1987), is projected onto the relationship between the Maltese and Arabic languages: Maltese/Phoenician is to Arabic as Christianity/Europe is to Islam. Considerable erasure is needed to produce this effect, however. In this process, language ideology, in simplifying the sociolinguistic field, "renders some persons or activities (or sociolinguistic phenomena) invisible. Facts that are inconsistent with the ideological scheme either go unnoticed or get explained away" (Irvine and Gal 2000, 38). What had to be "explained away" in this case is the preponderance of evidence of an Arabic basis to the Maltese language.

It is only recently that Maltese scholars have been able to explore this question dispassionately, and their findings have been nothing short of revolutionary. Not only do archaeologists and early historians now believe that Christianity all but disappeared from Malta at least during the two centuries of Muslim rule (Luttrell 1977), but there is some evidence that the Muslim invasion coincided with some kind of population replacement, and certainly a thorough and rapid language shift (Wettinger 1972, 1986). Little is known about the language spoken on the archipelago prior to Arab conquest, for virtually no evidence of the previous language can be detected in place names recorded in fourteenth-to sixteenth-century documents. Instead, the overwhelming majority of early Maltese place names have Semitic or Berber origins (Wettinger 1972, 1986). Wettinger believes that Berber-Arabs probably brought with them an Arabic close to that spoken in Tunisia at the time. Arabization was extensive, accounting for the "thoroughly Arabic character of the local place-names" (1986, 95). He has traced Maltese place names not only to Arab personal names and surnames but also to Berber tribal names and surnames of North African Jews (1972). Because place names provide practically no evidence of the earlier language, he believes that it is quite possible that during the Muslim conquest, the local people were expelled and entirely replaced with Arabic speakers (1986, 90–91).[4]

Linguistic analysis of the Maltese language provides further support for the repopulation hypothesis. Linguists now describe Maltese as the result of the convergence of two unrelated language families, with a North African Semitic (Maghrebine Arabic) base, a southern European Romance superstructure, and English loan words. According to contemporary scholars, the history of this language begins with the Arab invasion and the complete replacement of the previously spoken language, whatever it may have been, with North African Arabic (Brincat 1991, 93–94). A slow and cumulative Latinization began in the Norman period and accelerated during the era of the Crusades. During the tenure of the Order of St. John, starting in 1530, the large presence of Arabic-speaking slaves on the islands may have had a conservative influence on the language, although the number of foreigners speaking Romance languages increased dramatically during this period as well. Foreign contributions to the evolving Maltese language were from Sicilian until the seventeenth century, followed by Tuscan Italian, and finally modern Italian and English since the nineteenth century (Vanhove 1994, 168; Cassar 2001).

Despite overwhelming evidence to the contrary, the Phoenician language ideology persisted in Malta well into the twentieth century and was promoted by various scholars and politicians, such as the British Lord Strickland.[5] At the time, the thesis that the language had Arabic roots was strongly opposed by "all sectors of Maltese society" (Cassar 2001, 270). Even through World War II, it was viewed as retrogressive to promote the idea of Arabic origins for the Maltese language, for "Arabic was the language of Islam" (Pullicino 1979, 19). With similar anti-Muslim logic, some people in the early twentieth century postulated that the Maltese "race" had Hebrew origins, because the "Hebrews" were viewed as "the people of Christ," while the "Arabs" were the "people of Mahomet" (Pullicino 1979, 19).

The Arabic basis of the Maltese language is an important clue to much of what follows. It helps explain why so many Maltese migrated to North African shores in the nineteenth century and felt so comfortable there that they put down roots. It also explains why, when these regions were definitively under French rule, the Maltese were relegated to a status approaching that of the indigenous populace, an awkward liminal status that in turn underlies the very formation of the Franco-Maltese clubs. But before we get to this stage, we need to consider one last colonizer of the Maltese islands, the British, whose rule lasted until 1964.

BRITISH RULE AND NINETEENTH-CENTURY EMIGRATION

Following Napoleon's week in Malta in June 1798, the French evicted the Knights, imposed new taxes, tried to form a republican government, looted the Order's palaces, and imposed the French language. On September 3, 1798, when Napoleon's troops began selling off the treasures of the islands' many churches, the Maltese revolted. After a two-year siege, the

French finally surrendered, and the British took their place. The British continued to occupy Malta during their long war with the French, and the islands became a crown colony of the British Empire in 1814. Like the Knights before them, the British used the islands as an important naval base and trading port, and spent substantial sums renovating the harbors and maintaining the British soldiers and sailors stationed there. However, these expenditures were never on the same order as those of the Knights, and could not meet the needs of the islands' growing population.[6] Unemployment increased, and for many, starvation was imminent. To make matters worse, the islands were hit by a series of epidemics and natural disasters, starting with a cholera epidemic in 1813 that killed nearly 5 percent of the population. As population growth continued unabated, the only hope, in the view of Malta's British governor, was to encourage emigration.[7] Many Maltese had come to the same conclusion, and they began to leave the islands in large numbers. By 1842, approximately 15 percent of the population of Malta lived outside the archipelago along the southern and eastern shores of the Mediterranean, with most settling in Algeria and Tunisia, and lesser numbers in Egypt and in eastern cities of the Ottoman empire, such as Constantinople, Smyrna, and the Ionian islands. Until emigration slowed in the 1880s, the shores of Africa and the Levant received more than 90 percent of the Maltese migrants (Price 1954, 189).

It may seem odd that the strongly religious Catholic Maltese rarely migrated to the Christian European states to the north,[8] preferring instead the Muslim territories to the south. This choice is all the more puzzling given the long rule of the Knights, during which these were the lands of the enemy infidels. Moreover, there was no recent precedent for European settlement in North Africa—aside from the hundreds of people enslaved there (including large numbers of Maltese; Ciappara 2001, 225–32), for the Mediterranean piracy that resulted in Muslim slave labor in Malta also led to Christian slavery in North Africa until the first decades of the nineteenth century.[9] The fact that so few Maltese left for the Knights' homelands in Europe suggests that the Order had remained so distinct from the Maltese that these places seemed foreign or less welcoming.

The Maltese preference for North African destinations may have been influenced by the similarity of the Maltese language to the locally spoken Arabic idiom, which allowed Maltese merchants to establish trading relationships with the local community. Another factor may have been cost; this was an emigration of the very poor, who may not have been able to afford longer journeys. The trip to Tunisia, less than two hundred miles to the south, could be made in small fishing boats for only a few shillings. There is also some indication that Maltese chose destinations closer to home with an ultimate goal of returning to Malta after having amassed some savings. Such a strategy is suggested by the extremely high rate of return migration, which Price estimates as 85 percent from 1840 to 1890 (1954, 189). That transportation costs were not the only limiting factor is further indicated by the regular failures of all free or subsidized emigration schemes developed by British officials and capitalists for more remote destinations like Jamaica, Cyprus, and Crete. Until the twentieth century, the Maltese had no interest in heading farther afield.

MALTESE DAILY LIFE

The picture of the indigenous Maltese that emerges from the latter years of the Knights and the first half century of British rule is of a hardworking, religious people strongly tied to family and their home villages, yet traveling with ease across the Mediterranean, and wily enough to retain a distinct identity and sense of pride despite centuries of foreign rule. By the mid-1750s, half of the Maltese lived in rural areas while the rest lived in the large fortified cities such as Valletta. Agriculture was a difficult undertaking in this rocky land of scant rainfall. Farmers managed to grow cotton, cumin, figs, melons, grapes, onions, and, in rotations, wheat, barley, and clover. As an inquisitor reported in the eighteenth century, "They break [the ground] into very little plots to produce any kind of crop. It is admirable how they endure the fatigue, always barefoot under a baking sun and sustained only by bread, barley and water" (in Ciappara 2001, 43). They kept rabbits, poultry, and goats, from which they obtained milk and cheese. They lived simply in flat-roofed houses made of limestone, sometimes with an upstairs room opening onto a terrace. The diet was frugal and people had few belongings, dressing simply in coarse cotton. Shoes were rare, even into the 1930s. Men wore a shirt, white pants, and a black cap, and sported moustaches. Fishermen often had gold earrings. Women wore long skirts and a jacket, but to church wore the traditional black *għonella* (or *faldetta*), a long veil with a starched brim (see Ciappara 2001, 14–15).

Religion was the central organizing institution in the daily lives of the Maltese. At the center of each village was the parish church. Church bells regulated village life, starting with *pater noster* at four o'clock in the morning and sounding throughout the day. Parish priests were held in great esteem and were deeply imbedded in the daily lives of their parishioners. People also were loyal to their village and its patron saints. Villages were reluctant to fully admit outsiders, and village rivalries were renowned (a continuing tradition; see Boissevain 1965, Mitchell 2002). By all accounts, the Maltese were courageous and did not blindly follow the will of the authorities. When inquisitors arrived in Malta in the eighteenth century, they found the Maltese less eager than most to report on their neighbors. Ciappara suggests that this means people feared reprisals from their neighbors more than the inquisitors themselves. Verbal insults were common, accounting for over 15 percent of the cases finally brought to the Inquisition tribunal. People also sang obscene songs, threatened each other with physical violence, and sometimes even denounced their parish priests (Ciappara 2001, 32, 33, 343, 367).

Compared to many of the inland French or Swiss peasants they eventually would encounter in Algeria, the Maltese were cosmopolitan and familiar with a whole array of cultural practices. Many Maltese men comfortably traversed the Mediterranean, working as skilled sailors, fishermen, or corsairs either for the Knights or on their own. In the nineteenth century they became formidable contrabandists, trading gunpowder and tobacco in the Regency of Tunis and even Algeria, leaving with illegal livestock, oil, and other raw materials (Clancy-Smith 1994, 159–67).

THE MALTESENESS OF
THE FRENCH SETTLERS

In what ways might the Franco-Maltese settler clubs reflect some connection to a prior, Maltese ethnic identity? Members of ethnic groups often share overt signs of distinction, boundary markers that identify them as members of a particular group, such as dress, hairstyle, and language, as well as basic value orientations, "the standards of morality and excellence by which performance is judged" (Barth 1969, 14). They may share an attachment to a place, representations of the past, and a belief in a common ancestry. The persistence and modification of an ethnic identity among an immigrant population will depend on forces encouraging integration and assimilation to the dominant population's ideologies and prevailing socioeconomic structures, as well as generation. The vast majority of the Maltese-origin former settlers I interviewed had grandparents or great-grandparents who left Malta for North Africa between the 1840s and the 1890s. Most of their parents, therefore, were members of the second generation at least, if not the third, and had long abandoned wearing the *faldetta,* going barefoot, and often even speaking Maltese. The people I interviewed were native French speakers who had been French citizens their whole lives. When we consider more overt expressions of ethnicity, we find that the Maltese settlers share far more features, such as dress, foodways, ideologies, and language, with other French settlers of Algeria or at least settlers of North Africa than with the Maltese of Malta, suggesting a complex relationship with Malta and their Maltese heritage. As one woman exclaimed, "Don't confuse the Maltese of Malta with us! We are two different cultures. The Maltese of Malta have a lot of British influences as well as indigenous Maltese culture, while us, we are basically French." Two different families illustrate well the varying degrees of affinity to Maltese traditions among former settlers.

The Sultanas, from Bône

The Sultanas lived in Bône (which is now called Annaba), a city in eastern Algeria known in colonial times for its high concentration of Maltese. The city is located in the eastern province of Constantine, where the majority of my interviewees had lived. In Algeria, the Sultanas were small-scale agriculturalists who sold milk and produce at market. Victor and Paulette Sultana went on the club's trip to Malta, and I found them to be vivacious and sociable. Victor had a particularly wry sense of humor. They now live in a villa on the outskirts of Aix, to which they retired a decade ago. They have a large family that Paulette describes as "typically Maltese": five children who live nearby. With the assorted grandchildren reaching their teens, this made for a very full household each time I visited.

Paulette Sultana was one of the best cooks I encountered, and clearly loved to entertain. She was skilled at arranging lavish meals for ever-changing numbers of guests, as her adult children sometimes stopped by unannounced only to be directed immediately to join us at the table. My first meal with them was a sumptuous affair. I arrived with a bouquet of flowers, and seeing them, Mrs. Sultana exclaimed, "Next time you bring flowers, I won't let you in the door!" She seemed delighted nevertheless. She had set the table with a white tablecloth, polished silver, and elegant glassware, and offered me some of her home-made orange blossom liquor. The meal was an elaborate blend of North African, Alsatian, and French cuisines: an "Algerian" salad with fennel, tomatoes, green peppers, cucumbers, and celery, followed by her own foie gras. A wonderful white wine was served that had no label; it had been made by their nephew, now living in Toulouse. Then a sauerkraut dish with sausage and ham. Throughout the meal, and each time I was at their house, I had a hard time following all of the conversations that occurred simultaneously. Everyone in the family seemed quite comfortable expressing his or her views, and quite loudly: "No, you don't like to eat that! What do you mean?" Or, "Well, you don't like to eat anything, so anything you say about the cuisines of different countries is really pointless!" When embarking on a story, Victor was often challenged by his children, and would shout back, "No! You weren't there, I remember. Let me finish my own story!" Sometimes the conversation seemed to be veering completely out of control, but later in my notes I wrote that this might be the normal tenor of a large family with people of different perspectives who aren't all compelled to accept the views of the patriarch.

The children appeared to be of modest socioeconomic status. A daughter in her early forties with two daughters is now divorced after a harrowing several years as a victim of spouse abuse. When I saw her the first time, she looked rather rough, quite thin, with short hair dyed dark red and shaved eyebrows drawn in. But five years later she was married again, to a kind man who worked the night shift at a Marseilles steel mill. The Sultanas' oldest son, Paul, has two sons, and is also divorced. Son Pierre has a daughter by a girlfriend whom he never married, and from whom he is now separated. He seems to spend much of his time in the Aix casino, and lives right next door; sometimes when I was visiting he would drop by in the late morning, seeming to have just woken up. Another son, Mathieu, appeared to be a manual laborer, for he had large, red, worker's hands, but I never learned his occupation, nor his marital status. He visited just one day I was there, and came alone, with his dog. Another daughter was still married. Looking at a photo of her and her husband, Paulette referred to them as the "perfect couple."

Victor was one of two people I interviewed who had parents who arrived directly from Malta. Some distant relatives, the Fenechs, were elderly and living in Algeria, and had run into difficulties managing their farm. They knew that their nephew, a Sultana, had four grown sons back in Malta and sent for one of them to help them out. This was Victor's father. The arrangement was short-lived, and he instead rented a small plot of land that he and his wife worked much of their life, raising cattle and selling the milk. In Victor's memory, his father worked incessantly: he came home at night at 10 P.M. and left at four o'clock the next morning to drive the vegetables to the market, so that he could be back in time to help out his worker who milked the cows. It was only toward the end of his life that he was able to purchase his own land, which was the farm that Victor inherited.

I learned most about their attachment to Malta and Algeria when I visited them a second time with Jeannette, François' widowed cousin who had grown up in Tunis, and with whom I had shared a hotel room during our trip to Malta. Perhaps on her account, the meal this time featured far more North African/Maltese dishes: *caldis,* cheese-filled pastries that were commonly eaten by Maltese in Algeria; *fèves,* or fresh fava beans that were steamed and then covered with olive oil, cumin, harissa (a red spicy paste), mint, and salt and pepper, which many people later told me to be their favorite snack during apéritifs at the "Maltese" bars in Algeria (I could understand why); grilled sardines; and finally French pastries for dessert. Much of the conversation that day was spent comparing *chez vous* with *chez nous,* what life had been like for the "Maltese" in Algeria versus what it was like in Tunisia. Even though Jeannette was the fourth generation in her family born in Tunisia, she too spoke Maltese fluently, like Victor, and they compared notes on language practices in the two colonies. Because his parents spoke Maltese at home, Victor grew up understanding it: his parents would speak to him in Maltese, and he would reply in French. But he was shocked when he went on the trip to Malta with us to learn that he could actually speak it. His wife, Paulette, also had parents of Maltese origin but she had never learned to speak that language. She was very curious about how it was, then, that Jeannette, whose family had been in Tunisia for about the same length of time, could. "When you spoke to your mother, did you speak French or Maltese?" she asked. "We spoke French." "Oh, French . . . because you speak Maltese so well, I wondered . . ." "Oh no, no. It was because when we were young, we heard Maltese at the cousins' house, they spoke Maltese, and they taught it to us. But among the sisters, no, it was French all the time. But what's funny is when we are together for Christmas, New Year's, or Easter, when the three sisters are together, a few words in Maltese always enter into the conversation." Paulette then explained that her parents only used Maltese when they had something very serious to say that they didn't want the children to understand. She elaborated then on her French skills: "We don't know how to speak French well. Because the *pieds-noirs,* well, at least me, I mix up the words a lot of the time. Why? Because there was Arabic, Maltese, Italian, and French. And often we mix them together. It's a crippled French that we speak! Even my boys will say to me, 'Mom, what are you saying?'"

When Jeannette and Victor then decided to speak in Maltese together, I asked them if it wasn't similar to Arabic. Victor's response was immediate: "Oh, now you're insulting us. That's an insult!" I suggested that sometimes Arabic and Maltese speakers could understand each other; at least, some Tunisians had told me they could understand people speaking Maltese. "Oh, OK, there are some words, just a few words, but it isn't Maltese. No, it is not Maltese." They went on to illustrate. "In Maltese, for example, there are a few words that are like Arabic. Bread, for instance, in Arabic, is *el-khubz, el-khubz.* But in Maltese we say *khobz.*" ("Yes, you see," Jeannette interjected, "it's not at all the same.") "And water, in Arabic, is *maa,* but in Maltese, we say *lelma.*" The conversation went on like this, with Victor demonstrating a rich knowledge of each language. Finally, I asked, "How do you know these languages so well?" "Because I am Maltese and I was born surrounded by Arabs," he responded. His wife retorted, "Well, I was born surrounded by Arabs and I don't speak Arabic." "But I was a farmer," he replied. "Well, I guess I understand it," his wife admitted, "I just don't speak it." "I even speak Kabyle," Victor added. "Well, at least some words," and he was off, detailing differences between Maltese, Berber, and Arabic, and comparing terms one might know as an agriculturalist, such as "plow," "bread," "tomato," and so on. He later explained that in the countryside surrounding Bône, "90 percent" of the Maltese were agriculturalists who hired indigenous laborers. I asked if there were Maltese workers on these farms as well, and he said no, that there had been plenty during his father's generation, but by the time he was a young adult, most of the Maltese had finally purchased their own lands. Although, he added, he knew several Maltese families who still rented, and did not own, their farms.

This family illustrates well a primary attachment to Algeria, but a familiarity with aspects of Maltese culture as well. Other settlers described them as a "typical Maltese family," referring, I thought, to their numerousness. Despite their matter-of-fact self-presentation as "Maltese," however, and their cooking dishes eaten typically by Maltese in Algeria, Victor and Paulette had never thought of traveling there until they went on the trip with the *Amicale France-Malte*. The example of the Sultanas is also noteworthy because it illustrates a certain cross-colony connection with other former settlers of the same heritage, and a basic knowledge of, if not fluency in, Arabic among the smaller-scale agriculturalists in eastern Algeria. A very different connection to Malta is illustrated by the next example, a family in which only one of the parents had Maltese ancestors, and lived in the franocentric city of Algiers.

The Mifsuds, from Algiers

Mr. Mifsud is a tall, thin man in his mid-seventies, of mixed origins, with thick white hair, blue eyes, and skewed teeth. His mother's ancestors came to the colony from Provence, while his father's father came from Malta. He grew up in Algiers, and, until recently, he told me, he had had "no connection with his Maltese heritage whatsoever." My first meeting with him, at his home in the suburbs between Aix and Marseilles, occurred in midsummer, during the months leading up to our trip to Malta. I met their daughter Catherine and her friend Juliette at the town hall after my bus ride from Aix. Catherine is quite pretty. She is thin, relatively tall, with thick, nicely cut dark brown hair and intelligent dark eyes. That day she was wearing thin strappy gold sandals, tiny pink terry cloth shorts, and a skin-tight white top with spaghetti straps that showed off her tan. Her friend is a few years younger and shorter, with permed brown hair in an unfortunate cut with bangs. Catherine's husband had just left her after nineteen years together, and she was only then breaking a habit of biting her nails down to the quick. The friends smoked as we walked through the old part of town, with its narrow cobble-stoned streets, honey-colored stone buildings and fountains, and typical Provençal blue shutters and window pots full of pink and red geraniums. We stopped at an ancient local bakery to pick up a loaf of bread.

We arrived at the family's villa in the suburban subdivision, in which each home was surrounded by a five- to six-foot stucco wall enclosing lush gardens. Mrs. Mifsud was in the kitchen putting last-minute touches on the meal. Like her husband, she was born in Algeria, but while he is of Maltese and French heritage, she is Corsican and Sardinian in origin. She is a jovial woman in her mid-seventies, with shoulder-length brown hair, quite tanned and with a warm smile that lights up her face and her brown eyes. She is usually joking and laughing, and seems to be the true center of the household, entertaining everyone with stories of her adventures—looking after her grandchild, or the stray cat that had made himself at home. Still vigorously taking charge, she would direct her daughter and me to help her set the table or take orders for apéritifs before the meal. Her husband, in his upper seventies, seemed to do considerably less around the house, at least in my presence. That day he was constantly leaping up to pull an encyclopedia off the shelf to pinpoint some date in the rapid conversation I was having with him and his well-informed daughter, or to locate an old map of Algeria to show me where in Algiers he had grown up.

"I discovered Malta just six years ago!" he announced right away. He tried to explain why it was he had never been interested in Malta before: "The people who immigrate are not all from the upper classes, you know," he told me; "in fact, it is usually the opposite. So you can get a distorted view of a country from its immigrants. It wasn't until I went to Malta and saw just how industrious the people are, how much they've accomplished with that little stone [*caillou*] in the middle of the ocean, that I began to be proud of my Maltese roots. Before, I had never thought of Malta. I went to visit six years ago with the *Amicale France-Malte*. My neighbor Xuereb talked me into going."

Mr. Mifsud claimed that his participation in the local club could be explained by the charismatic personality of the organization's founder, François Xuereb, who happened to live in the same town:

> It's Xuereb. I don't know when we first met him, and I can't remember why either . . . Back then he was in politics, he was in the RPR [Rally for the Republic, a Gaullist central-right political party]. So he said to us, "Well, we're taking a trip to Malta." We said, "Well, OK, well, Malta; me, I'm of Maltese origins, Mifsud, we'll go to Malta." And it's just since that day then that I felt Maltese. My wife can tell you, before then, I didn't talk about it, I didn't talk about Malta. I had forgotten that I was of Maltese origins. It's since I discovered Malta that it really interested me, that I can tell you how much I feel Maltese, but . . . well, I hadn't ever denied my Maltese origins, but I just never talked about it.

There are many interesting elements in this testimony. First, Mr. Mifsud uses his surname as evidence of his Maltese heritage. Many other former settlers also relied on their last names as proof of their connection to

THE MALTESE ISLANDS

Figure 4. Settler hospitality. Photograph by the author.

Malta. What is especially interesting in this case is the fact that Mr. Mifsud on other occasions used his distinctive last name as evidence of his French heritage as well. I elaborate on the polysemic nature of Maltese surnames for many North African repatriates below. Second, he discovered Malta late in life, practically by chance, and is himself surprised at his now strong ties to the place. Third, much of this reawakening (or initial awakening) of a connection to Malta seems to have occurred following his trip there with a Franco-Maltese club. Finally, he knew the club leader not through some active involvement in the *pied-noir association* milieu, but through other so-cial ties: in this case, through their involvement as rivals in local politics.

Our meal that day was a wonderful hybrid celebration of the family's North African heritage and the husband's Maltese roots. Mrs. Mifsud served a lamb couscous, and they passed around harissa, which she explained they used to always serve in Algeria, and which she had to locate in specialty shops in Marseilles. She served no overtly Maltese dishes, which is under-standable considering the strict division of labor in families of this genera-tion, and the fact that her own heritage was Corsican and Sardinian; how-ever, the meal was served on festive placemats that Catherine had purchased for her parents on one of her many postcolonial Maltese vacations, and which I imagined at the time were featured especially on account of my presence (see fig. 4).

Despite the many differences between these two couples—one looking back to Algiers, the other to Bône; the mixed background of the Mifsuds; and the lengths of time their forebears had been in Algeria—they share many features as well. In both cases, the family's involvement in the Maltese clubs is a recent, post-Algerian phenomenon. While the Sultanas had a much stronger attachment to a Maltese identity, they had not traveled there during the past thirty-five years in France, nor had they visited when they were based in the colony. Many such people, including François Xuereb, explained why it would never have occurred to them to travel there:

> Never did anyone in my family, neither my parents nor my grandparents, ever travel to Malta. Why? Because they had cut the umbilical cord. It was finished. The culture is different, generations have passed, and my children have no interest. They don't even know one word of Maltese and when they hear it, they laugh. It's like the United States. You have some Irish ancestry, right? Do you think about your relatives back there? For us it is the same thing. Why? Because our grandparents were not born in Malta.

In fact, over the course of my time in France, I met only two people who had traveled to Malta from colonial North Africa. People in the early part of the twentieth century were preoccupied with their livelihoods and voyaging overseas was an extravagance few could afford.

The idea of forming Franco-Maltese social clubs seems to have developed spontaneously in France. People told me repeatedly that such clubs had never existed in Algeria or Tunisia. I learned later that they were wrong; through archival research, I found evidence of a few social activities uniting people of this background, such as the newspaper *Melita* that served the Maltese in eastern Algeria, and the enigmatic *Société amicale Franco-Maltaise La Vallette,* based in the town of Constantine, which by 1938 was rapidly losing members. However, these were local and short-lived groups,[10] and were either defunct by the time my interviewees were young adults, or else attracted people of a different generation. Certainly, nobody I met remembered ever encountering such organizations in the colony.

TUNISIA VS. ALGERIA

An intriguing feature of the Franco-Maltese clubs that seems to indicate a deeper, prior, connection to this lost homeland is the fact that they unite people from both Tunisia and Algeria, unlike other settler clubs that tend to organize more strictly along colonial and even regional lines. Uniting residents from these two settings is notable, because contrasts between Algeria and Tunisia were great. Not only was Tunisia a smaller colony with a less important French presence, but its juridical relationship to France was markedly different. Several of the elderly repatriates I met had been born in one colonial setting and moved to another, so that they had real grounds for comparison. When I asked them how life differed in Algeria and Tunisia, the reactions were unanimous: "Oh—it was completely different in every way!" France's tenure in Algeria (1830–1962) was far longer than in Tunisia (1881–1956). Because Algeria was considered a part of France, many settlers living there did not view it as a colony, an ideology that persists among many *pieds-noirs* today. The European immigrants there were all naturalized through laws enacted in the late nineteenth century. This had an impact on the degree to which immigrants could feel comfortable maintaining ties to their previous ethnicities. A Tunisia-born man told me that, since Algeria was a French department, it was practically France. "Thus the immigrants tried to assimilate?" I asked. "No," he corrected me, "they tried to suppress anything that wasn't French."

Tunisia, on the other hand, was a protectorate and was ruled indirectly. In fact, the French allowed the Tunisian monarch to stay in power, albeit with greatly restricted authority. Settlement of French, Italian, and, in lesser numbers, Maltese immigrants had been underway before the establishment of the protectorate, but even with the advent of French rule, the numbers of European immigrants increased slowly and they never amounted to more than 7 percent of the total population (Perkins 1997, 9). Tunisia had its own legal institutions, unlike Algeria. For example, naturalization was optional there until 1923.[11] Many Maltese opted to maintain their *statut britannique,* their British subject status (which was also a source of considerable prestige), even though doing so meant that they could not hope for careers in French colonial administrations. Tunisian cities often comprised discrete and self-perpetuating communities of foreign-origin Europeans, including Sicilian, Maltese, and Greek neighborhoods.

Language politics also varied between the two colonial settings, as is suggested by my conversations with the Sultanas and the Mifsuds. In Algeria, with French citizenship came education in French schools and a real pressure to speak French. The "Algerian" settlers like the Mifsuds discussed at length their desire to speak perfect French, and to thus blend in with their "true" French classmates. By contrast, due to the ethnic enclaves that persisted in Tunisian cities, many interviewees from Tunisia, such as Jeannette, spoke some Maltese and a few spoke it fluently.

As a result of these contrasts, people who had grown up in Tunisia were more comfortable than their Algeria-born counterparts in claiming a double Franco-Maltese identity. Mr. Azzopardi explained that he and his friends were both Maltese and French: "We are good French men and women. And we serve France, perhaps better than the French do themselves. But we are Maltese too. We don't forget our origins." On the other hand, the Algiers-born Mr. Grech explained that in Algeria, "we became *hyper Français.* They [in Tunisia] saw themselves as Maltese first, and French second, while those of Algeria wanted to see themselves as French before all else." Despite these major differences in their personal connections to

French and Maltese identifications, club members were uniting, ostensibly around prior, precolonial commonalities. This paradox leads us to consider again the question of whether or not a knowledge of Malta persisted for decades in French North Africa.

MALTA REMEMBERED?

For many settlers, it is their initial journey to Malta that sparks an interest in all things Maltese. Many have since made multiple return trips, often bringing with them other relatives. As I noted at the outset of this chapter, I initially wondered if these journeys were tapping into a lingering memory of Malta that had been sustained for generations. This would have helped explain how it is that people from two very different colonial settings, Algeria and Tunisia, are able to bond around this common background. But as I continued to interview informants I found that, just as the club leaders had predicted, people did not discuss such stories spontaneously. I began to ask people directly about this question, and what I found added another fascinating dimension to the Maltese enigma.

When I met repatriates alone or in small groups, they talked about the colonial past whether I introduced the subject or not, and whether or not I was taping the meeting. Conversations about that past ceased, however, when members of the next generations, the children or grandchildren of the *pieds-noirs,* entered the room. The elderly informants returned to the question of the colonial past only once their younger relatives had left. While generation mattered a great deal in these discussions, however, colony of origin did not. Interviews proceeded in a similar way whether I was talking with repatriates of Maltese origin who had grown up in Tunisia or Algeria. Most interviewees began by outlining their family's migration histories. They told me which ancestors first came to the colony, from where, and when. Often they did not know which towns these ancestors came from, but they knew the countries. These highly structured narratives were in many cases illustrated by genealogical information that they had collected, including handwritten or typed genealogies they or other relatives had prepared, and photocopied birth and death certificates that were stored with their family papers. Some showed me copies of their *blazon de famille,* the coat of arms associated with their Maltese surname that they had obtained in Malta or from association leaders. Many expounded on the roots of these surnames: surprising numbers of people claimed to have names with early Swedish, French, Dutch, Russian, or other European origins, due, they presumed, to the multinational origins of the Knights of Malta. The formality of this initial "genealogical" portion of the interview may stem from the nature of the material outlined. People often read to me from photocopied archival documents, and, if I was not taking notes, they directed me to do so. They spelled out names and birth dates of the most distant relatives, working down through the generations, usually through the male line. My fieldnotes and tapes contain a wealth of such details about my informants' great-grandparents and grandparents, the first generations to arrive in North Africa.

The formal nature of this introductory narrative was also reflected in its presentation style. One elderly gentleman in particular liked to hold the tape recorder's microphone in his hands, speaking to me like a reporter at a sporting event. He said this was to ensure that my recording had the best sound quality possible, but this practice, coupled with his donning a tie for the occasion, suggested that he took the interview seriously. This formality suggests that the interlocutors felt that we were now engaged in a different kind of interaction, and it should be noted that the very existence of my project may have shaped the interviewees' relationship to their own pasts in subtle ways. The second part of these discussions was more variable, however, and the accounts were not structured chronologically. I sometimes heard tales of the speaker's mother, then of a great-uncle, then comments on the lifestyles of the earliest migrants, followed by more stories about the mother, and so forth.

Over the course of these conversations, it was becoming clear that François and Michel had been right: despite the fact that people talked at length about their ancestors, they never discussed their lives in Malta. Their ancestors' migration histories had a definite North African orientation: even the stories that people recounted in detail about their earliest relatives were set in North Africa (for instance, "My great-great-grandfather first worked as a stonemason in Constantine"). Clearly, neither stories about motivations for leaving Malta nor stories about Malta itself had been passed down the generations. When I finally asked people directly what they had been told by their grandparents or parents about the place, and if they knew where in Malta their ancestors were from or how they got to Algeria, the results were astounding. Most did not know which island their ancestors were from, let alone which town; or that town's patron saint; nor why their ancestors had decided to leave; and they had been told few if any details about life there. This is apparent in the following excerpt of a taped interview with a husband and wife in their mid-seventies.

AUTHOR: So, your parents . . . didn't speak too much about their pasts in
           Malta . . .
HUSBAND: Never.
WIFE: No.
AUTHOR: So . . .
HUSBAND: We didn't talk about it.

AUTHOR:	Yes.
HUSBAND:	We talked about *us,* us in Algeria.
WIFE:	No.
HUSBAND:	We spoke about our lives in Algeria. We didn't speak about our . . .
AUTHOR:	So, you didn't have . . . any images of Malta, ideas of . . . churches, other family members, anything like that?
HUSBAND:	No.
WIFE:	No.
HUSBAND:	No, and along with other Maltese, we socialized with Spanish, Italians . . . and they didn't . . . they didn't speak about their origins either . . .
WIFE:	We were French, and that's that, you know?

Silence regarding Malta was total. Some of my informants had thought about this a great deal and had developed theories as to why this might be so. The common belief was that their ancestors were working so hard that they had had little time to maintain contact with their relatives back in Malta. One woman knew about illiteracy among the Maltese, for, as she pointed out to me, her grandparents' marriage certificate was signed with an X. It would have been difficult, she noted, for those who could not write to keep in touch with their relatives during the previous century. Others seemed embarrassed by this "problem," for here was a researcher who had come all the way from the United States to interview them and they knew so little about their purported homeland.

Viewed from this perspective, the genealogical introductions of most interviews and the proud display of the family coats of arms take on new meaning. These presentations may have been motivated by a desire to demonstrate a link with Malta, and thus the relevance of their particular family story to my study. The following excerpt from an interview with Mr. Grech illustrates such an attempt to link family with Malta as well as a complete silencing of Malta in Algeria. Mr. Grech, a former leader of the Paris Franco-Maltese club and a retired lawyer who is actively involved in *pied-noir* literary endeavors, was proud of being entirely Maltese in origin, and outlined his family migration history in detail. He, his parents, and all but one grandparent were born in Algiers:

> Thus, I'm one of the rare cases, and there are others in my family, where I am Grech, paternal, and Pisani, maternal, of Maltese origin. Thus, I am really, at heart, at the heart of Malta. OK. And yet! I'll tell you one thing: as far as I can remember, we never spoke of Malta.

He then talked about his paternal grandfather, who had migrated to France directly from Malta:

OK, so he, he was the immigrant. But we, we never talked about Malta. Even though we spoke about the past. But my father . . . well, my mother didn't tell me much of anything . . . Well, yes, she talked about . . . we talked about *people,* but not of the country. So, which people? Well, my parents spoke to me about their own childhood . . . but, well, this childhood was already in Algiers! So, at the level of Malta, what does this mean? We didn't speak about Malta proper. But my father spoke about his parents, his father and mother. He must have told me that they came from Malta, because I couldn't have made that up.

In his narrative, Mr. Grech first tries to tell me that he heard his mother mention people back in Malta, but then cannot come up with any examples, and realizes, midnarrative, that his parents mainly talked about people already in Algeria, not those back in Malta. He then tries to explain his lack of knowledge about Malta despite his unusual, pure Maltese heritage. It is clear that Malta was rarely if ever addressed.

The apparent paradox of an ethnic revitalization movement among a people lacking clear memories of the land of their ancestors is resolvable if we consider both the exigencies of French identity politics today and the possibility that their ethnic identity is rooted not in Malta, per se, but in the colony. The members of Franco-Maltese clubs today cling to their family coats of arms and photos of these voyages, tattered copies of birth and death records of their grandparents and great-grandparents, family genealogies, and their inventive stories of the origins of their surnames as key symbols granting them access to this forgotten homeland. These symbols do not derive organically or in an unbroken fashion from an attachment to Malta, and seem to have been resurrected recently, perhaps even because of the current exile in France. We should not view this phenomenon as entirely a postcolonial movement, however. Over the course of interviews with dozens of people of this background, I found that they shared something more: a collective memory, not of Malta, but of their experiences in the colony of discrimination and suspicion due to their Maltese heritage. This seemingly paradoxical mass movement, this heritage tourism in the absence of a developed heritage consciousness, becomes more explicable when we return to the colonial context and the creation there of a colony-based "Maltese" identity.

THREE

A Hierarchy of Settlers and the Liminal Maltese

The existence of the Maltese clubs is our first indication that settler assimilation to French culture in Algeria was not as thorough or complete as many historical sources would lead us to believe. As I spent time with the former settlers at their social gatherings, I encountered additional clues indicating that a wealth of ethnic and other distinctions continue to be meaningful to them today. Michel Pisani was the first to instruct me about the great gulfs between settlers in the colony. One afternoon while at the *Amicale France-Malte* office at the Maison, he regaled me with stories about his father, a humble man who had been a baker in their small rural village in eastern Algeria. Life in the countryside, the *bled,* was so very different from that in the big cities, he explained. There was a high concentration of Maltese and Italian immigrants in his village, and most of his father's friends and neighbors worked long hours with little to show for their labors. They were members of the rural *petite bourgeoisie* who ran small hardware and bakery shops, and who aspired one day to be able to purchase plots of land. In contrast to the French elite—owners of the growing enterprises and *grandes domaines* (large estates) who lived in urban centers, especially in the capital, Algiers—the rural settlers lived quite modestly. A play on words summarized this contrast in lifestyles perfectly, Michel said, and he wrote it down to make sure I understood: they, the inhabitants of Algiers, the *Algérois,* were kings (*rois*). We, on the other hand, the inhabitants of the country, Algeria, were the *Algériens,* or nothings (*riens*). Michel found this wordplay wickedly funny.

Michel's joke suggests that there were significant status distinctions between the settlers who lived in the capital and those who lived in the rural hinterlands. As I continued to meet with the elderly *pieds-noirs,* I was struck by the fact that, despite the dominant ideology that settlers of different origins had "melted together" in the *creuset algérien,* the Algerian melting pot, *pieds-noirs* of all backgrounds still identify each other today according to ethnicity or former place of residence. A woman might be referred to as Renée, *la Souk-Ahrasiènne* (Renée, the woman from Souk-Ahras), or Renée, *la Maltaise* or *la Corse* (Renée, the "Maltese" or "Corsican" woman, indicating ethnic heritage). People employed a whole array of ethnic labels. At first I found this usage confusing, for the people referred to in this way were not Maltese, Spanish, or Italian nationals, but French citizens of these backgrounds; to acknowledge the distinction between these *pied-noir* labels and nationality, I place the ethnic labels here in quotation marks.

Class is another important distinction in the *pied-noir* way of speaking; and class and ethnicity are often linked. The "Spanish," "Italian," and "Maltese" *pieds-noirs* are sometimes referred to as *le petit peuple,* the lower or humble classes, or as *Français du deuxième zone,* "second-class French." The conflation of class and ethnicity was never more pronounced or telling than in discussions among the "non-French" about "the real French," however. The elderly Franco-Maltese regularly identified the individuals in their stories who were "pure" French (*pur Français*), "real French" (*vrai Français*), of "French stock" (*Français de souche*), or "French French" (*Français de France, Français d'origine*). In school, as Mr. Missud explained, the goal both socially and educationally was to try to reach the same level as the *Français de souche,* that is, *les vrais Français.* On another occasion, Michel's wife, Rose, recounted how her mother and grandmother had worked in Algeria as house-cleaners for a lawyer's family, who were "*des gens riches et tout*" (rich people and all) and, she added with reverence, "*des Français de France,*" as if this specification of the family's ethnic background would immediately communicate to me their elite social standing.

These speech practices are reflections of the salience of ethnicity and class in colonial classificatory systems and of the speakers' membership, at least at one time, in a common speech community (Duranti 1997, 72). They also suggest that we need to further explore the question of settler homogeneity and French assimilation in the colony. As we will see, status differences understood as ethnic in origin developed early on, and were grounded in access to land. This land, taken from the indigenous populations, was granted to the settlers, although unequally, and largely according to nationality. As the indigenous population experienced rapid pauperization, a status hierarchy based on ethnicity and class developed among Europeans. In the process, the Maltese immigrants soon found themselves in the lowest of settler ranks.

LAND AND SETTLER COLONIES

Some scholars now reject distinctions between settler colonialism and "its Other," citing the fuzzy boundaries between this and other forms of colonialism (Krautwurst 2003). It can be argued that each colonial setting was in fact unique; even the term "settler" may apply to different social groups at various historical junctures. However, some striking parallels remain between many "settler" colonies, particularly in their dependence on the exclusion and exploitation of indigenous peoples through coercive, ideological, and other measures, and in the efforts made to "maintain indigenous peoples in various states of labor indenture or servitude," processes facilitated by the appropriation of their lands (Stasiulis and Yuval-Davis 1995, 4, 11; Weaver 2003). As Krautwurst writes, "the colonizers desire to take the place of the colonized"—not to become colonized, but to substitute themselves for them (2003, 58).

This was certainly the case in French Algeria. Before the arrival of the French, most indigenous Algerians lived in rural regions where land was the foundation of the agropastoral subsistence economy. The country is divided into three main ecological zones by two great mountain chains roughly parallel to the coast. The Tell Atlas chain to the north encloses rich narrow coastal plains that enjoy a moist Mediterranean climate. To its south are mountainous highlands, vast semiarid steppes that have long served as a grazing zone for livestock. In the eastern Tellian highlands live Kabyle highlanders, and south of them the Chaouia, two important Berber-speaking populations. To the south of the Saharan Atlas lies the vast southern desert, broken by oasis towns.

Before the French, land use and ownership varied across the vast region according to geography, availability of water, and local political arrangements. Properties of large latifundia were farmed by sharecroppers, while other producers owned the means of production. Pasture lands were often held in common, with various land tenure arrangements and classifications. In the valleys and the foothills of the Tell, a typical political and social unit was a tribe of several thousand people sharing use rights over thousands to tens of thousands of hectares of grazing lands (*arsch*), often held in common, while arable fields were often subdivided. Tribes were subdivided into semiautonomous subunits such as lineages, often living in encampments of dozens of families. The members often alternately cultivated the common lands and used them for pasture. Some tribes held in common vast agricultural reserves, dwelling sites, and woods. Other plots were subdivided and worked by families in accordance with *mulk* (or *milk*), a form of individual use rights, sometimes reallocated periodically according to family needs and the condition of the land, and in other cases akin to individual property rights. In Kabylia, in contrast, people lived in permanent villages and farmed intensively. Most lands were in *mulk*, and common property was reduced to threshing areas, marketplaces, and water sources. In the south, the economy was more tied to pastoralism and lands in *mulk* declined. Great north-south seasonal migrations of nomads persisted in Algeria into the twentieth century. Oasis towns represented important "mediating centers" between peoples and lifeways, goods and political rivals (Clancy-Smith 1994, 15–21; Gallisot 1975; Bennoune 1988, 25–26).

Under colonization, these lands were wrested from indigenous collectivities through a protracted process marked by everything from outright battles to the imposition of new legislation. Because a clear governmental consensus regarding France's future use for the colony had not preceded invasion, initial official land grabs were carried out more to achieve immediate military objectives than to prepare for eventual large-scale immigration. The French military in the 1830s was preoccupied by conquest operations and had no funds set aside for colonization projects, for colonization policies had yet to be articulated. Military operations often develop a dynamic of their own, however. While politicians in France debated whether or not to maintain a French presence in the area, military leaders, in their efforts to "secure" key port towns or to repel Algerian counter-attacks, continued to occupy ever-expanding portions of Algerian territory. The French conquest, starting with the occupation of the former Regency's urban coastal centers, proceeded in stages and with great difficulty (see map 3). The fertile coastal plains were seized only after a long and brutal war. During his tenure in the colony (1841–1847), General Bugeaud instituted a policy of total conquest, and his troops carried out raids with the goal of ravaging all territory not yet under French control. They massacred people and livestock, and burned crops, fields, and dwellings. The next eight years saw the defeat of local Algerian leader Abd al-Qadir, devastation and acute economic crisis for the indigenous population, and the definitive alienation of the Algerians from the French (Ageron 1991, 18–21). The final phases of French conquest were similarly brutal and involved the subjugation of sedentary and nomadic groups in more remote, mountainous areas and in the desert and oasis areas to the south. The army met resistance at every step: between 1830 and 1871, only one year passed without major armed conflict in some part of the country (Ruedy 1992, 55). Algerians were dispossessed of their homes, farms, and grazing lands, and thousands perished in epidemics and famines as well as in raids by French troops.

THE GREAT MIGRATION

The Maltese arrived in Algeria soon after the first installations of French troops, as part of a great trans-Mediterranean migration. Despite the general insecurity caused by near-constant warfare during the first decades of French occupation, people from throughout Europe were drawn to the place. The first to arrive were temporary migrants who returned home once

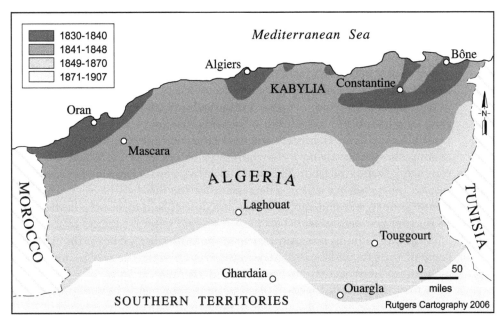

Map 3. Stages in the French conquest of Algeria.

they had secured sufficient profits.[1] Early migrants also included traders, café and bar owners, and prostitutes, who all saw in the French army a wealthy new client. More permanent migrants followed. Over the next century, nearly half of these were French nationals, particularly from the regions bordering the Mediterranean[2] and Corsica. However, French nationals were outnumbered by migrants from across southern Europe, along the Mediterranean and from the islands of Sardinia, the Balearic Islands, Sicily, Malta, Pantelleria, and the Lipari Islands, and in lesser numbers from Portugal, Germany, Russia, and Greece. Many of these immigrants were impoverished peasant farmers and agricultural laborers forced to migrate by widespread land reform movements that swept across Mediterranean Europe in the eighteenth and nineteenth centuries, leading to cataclysmic changes involving the privatization of common lands and the commercialization of labor (Gilmore 1982, 188). Spain, ruined after the War of Independence and in a depression for the first half of the nineteenth century, was undergoing a dramatic shift in land ownership in the 1830s (the *desamortización*). This process of land reform, contrary to the reformists' intentions, primarily benefited the latifundian estates at the expense of the peasant laborers (Malefakis 1970, 61–64). The first Spanish nationals to arrive were ruined peasants and day laborers, many of whom came from the Balearic Islands. They were quite poor, hence the derogatory ethnic term *escargots* (snails), because many arrived with all of their possessions on their backs (Jordi 1986, 206). Many *Mahonnais* (residents of Majorca) settled near Algiers, where they worked as market gardeners and sold produce to the army and to city residents. Spanish peasants from provinces with high concentrations of large estates, such as Alicante, Albacete, and Valencia, began emigrating soon after (Crespo and Jordi 1991).

Most migrants from the Italian peninsula were also members of the poorer classes fleeing impoverishment. Approximately half were agricultural workers from the south, especially Sicily and Sardinia. Sicilian sharecroppers had suffered earlier in the century from competition with Russian and New World grain imports. Here too, land reform policies that called for the partitioning of feudal lands, followed by the division of communal properties in 1838–1841, had left the peasant farmers in a precarious state (Schneider and Schneider 1976). Miners, masons, and artisans from northern Italy, particularly from the Piedmont and Tuscany, followed later in the century. Some crossed the Mediterranean annually to find work in large construction projects, building roads, bridges, and canals, clearing swamps, or laboring in mines (Prochaska 1990, 150). Sardine, anchovy, and coral fishermen from Naples and the islands of Ischia, Sicily, and Pantelleria who had been fishing annually along Algerian shores even before French conquest began to settle on a more permanent basis (Crespo 1994, 29).

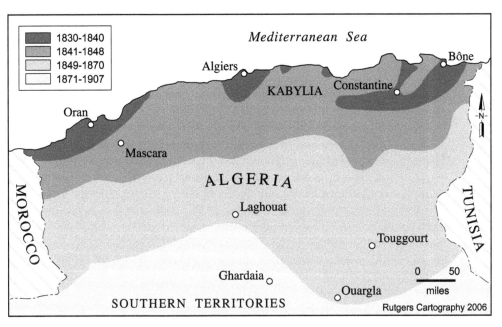

Map 4. Divisions and principal towns of French Algeria.

The Maltese were certainly among the poorest of the immigrants to arrive. As we have seen, their poverty stemmed from many factors and increased with the advent of British rule. Because of Malta's proximity to North Africa and the desperate circumstances faced by many of the migrants, the Maltese emigration to North Africa was characterized by minimal planning and transience, and the Regency of Tunis became an integral element of the Malta-Algeria migratory flow. Not only was the Regency closer than Algeria to Malta, but until 1881 it was a remote province of the Ottoman Empire where Europeans were under the jurisdiction of a handful of consular agents, and thus subject to significantly less surveillance. Many Maltese landed first in Tunisia and then made their way to Algeria overland or by boarding one of the small trading vessels that followed the coast. They often traveled without any documents whatsoever, to the great frustration of French bureaucrats in Algeria.[3] Men searching for work sometimes landed first in a Tunisian port, only to head on to Algeria and later to Alexandria and ultimately return to Tunis, while stopping off in Malta once or twice in the process.[4] In Algeria, they were concentrated in areas closest to their home.

By 1840, there were over twenty-five thousand European immigrants in the former Regency, most of whom inhabited urban centers, with over half in Algiers. The rest had settled in the regions of Algeria closest to their countries of origin: migrants from Spain stayed primarily in the western region, later the department of Oran, while most Maltese and Italians became rooted in the east, in the department of Constantine (see map 4). In general, more men than woman migrated in these early years, and there was much return migration, suggesting that the first to arrive were predominantly temporary migrants prospecting for work.

The Maltese made up only a fraction of the total European population of Algeria, reaching a high of 15.5 percent in 1833 and diminishing to 4 percent in 1876.[5] Although they represented a small proportion of the overall settler population, they outnumbered other settlers in the eastern department of Constantine for the first decades of French rule, and constituted at least half of the European population of Bône and Philippeville through the middle of the century. Maltese also settled in large numbers in smaller towns and villages of the Constantinois, in Guelma, Jemmapes, Souk-Ahras, and Philippeville, where many of my interviewees had been born and raised. Early Maltese migrants found work in Algeria as day laborers on construction projects or farms, and as porters unloading goods from ships. In the growing towns, they held such low-capital occupations as juice peddlers, and ambulatory fish, vegetable, and milk salesmen. In later years, some women worked as housekeepers. Maltese also arrived in Algeria with their goats, and people told me they remembered them traveling door to door with their herds, selling fresh milk and cheese. Those able to obtain small plots of land were noted to be masters of intensive cultivation.

A FRENCH LAND GRAB

During the first decades of conquest, colonial land surveyors followed the army to help delineate and record titles (Bennoune 1988, 43). Speculators and soldiers claimed properties through mere occupation or by purchasing them at cut-rate prices from their fleeing owners. By far the most powerful new landowner in the region, however, was the French state itself. Land that had been held by Turkish rulers was simply declared state property during the first years of conquest and held in the public domain. This was not an insignificant development: the economically productive lands alone of the *dey,* the ruler based in Algiers, and his three *beys* (provincial governors), including *hubus* (*waqf,* religious endowments) totaled approximately 1.5 million hectares in 1830 (Ruedy 1967, 9). Property was also taken from local tribes through sequestration (confiscation), a policy often employed as a form of punishment for tribes deemed uncooperative.[6] By 1843, religious, or *hubus,* lands were incorporated into the domain, and a law passed in 1844 declared these lands alienable to Europeans (Julien 1964, 240). Also in 1844, uncultivated lands not claimed through officially prescribed procedures requiring titles predating July 1830 were deemed vacant and transferred to the state. These included hundreds of thousands of hectares crucial to the pastoral economy, which were classified as *terres mortes* or "dead lands." Land policies of the 1850s and 1860s, during Louis-Napoleon Bonaparte's rule, further dispossessed the autochthonous peoples by restricting tribes to smaller pieces of land (a policy termed *cantonnement*).

The end of the Second Empire, following Louis-Napoléon III's defeat in the Franco-Prussian War (July 1870–January 1871), and the establishment of the Third Republic in France mark a major break in the history of colonial Algeria. The new French government began to issue decrees in that fall and winter while Paris was still under siege, ending the military's unrestricted power in Algeria and shifting the balance of power to the colonists. The indigenous population watched these developments with increasing concern. A civil regime meant settlers' rule, further confiscation of Algerian lands, government by European-elected officials, and even subjection to trials with European juries (Julien 1964, 464–67). By this time, Arabs and Berbers of all classes were suffering greatly from warfare and the subsequent loss of their property as well as a recent drought and failed harvests that had triggered widespread famine and epidemics.[7] Just at this time, many of the French troops that had been based in Algeria were transferred to Europe to fight the Prussians. This confluence of events provided an opening for those willing to resist the occupation. A massive revolt erupted in January of 1871.[8] After a call for holy war, nearly a million people joined the insurrection (Ageron 1968, 1–66). It took the French seven months to suppress the revolt, and in its wake followed a terrible repression of the revolutionaries. French authorities deported many of the leaders as far as New Caledonia, imposed war reparation penalties, and confiscated more of their land.[9] The total cost of the war to the Algerian revolutionaries approached an impossible 65 million francs. Most of the tribes concerned were ruined, and it took others twenty years to repay the debt (Ageron 1979, 14–16).

The impact of this first half century of French rule on the indigenous population was extreme and lasting. Urban elites had fled, and the former traditional craft economy had all but collapsed. Extensive agriculturists found it increasingly difficult to produce decent harvests since they were restricted to smaller and smaller parcels of land. These trends were compounded by the closing of forests to pastoralists, leading to a serious decline in livestock numbers. Peasants were further burdened by the *impôts arabes,* a discriminatory tax regime, and in 1881, the *code de l'indigénat,* a set of laws developed exclusively for the indigenous population that curbed many remaining freedoms and imposed collective fines, prison sentences, and individual and collective confiscations (Ageron 1979, 23–26). The establishment late in the century of regulations allowing the purchase of indigenous property led many poor farmers to sell their remaining lands to Europeans at reduced prices in order to pay off their debts.[10] Finally, in the late 1880s, the state started a massive survey of the remaining domain and common properties, the first step in yet another wave of appropriations.[11] As one Algerian noted, "Once again, settlement of property law seems to have been undertaken only to grant without charge to the state as much land as possible" (Ageron 1979, 202). The impoverished indigenous population started to swell the ranks of a growing proletariat. Men migrated to the cities seeking work and increasingly, starting in 1907, to the metropole itself to work in industry (Ageron 1979, 526–32). Meanwhile, land grant programs were underway, initiating the process by which newcomers themselves would become rooted to the land.

INEQUITIES IN LAND DISTRIBUTION

At first, because the ever-expanding French army was in constant need of foodstuffs, officials welcomed *Mahonnais* and Maltese agriculturalists, who sold their produce to the military. However, when state-sponsored programs were established to grant lands *en masse* to new immigrants beginning in the 1840s, they privileged French nationals, although they were ostensibly open to settlers of any background. Such pro-French policies can be partly explained by a demographic imbalance that would persist for decades in the colony: to the great consternation of French administrators, French immigrants were outnumbered by the non-French. The governor-general of the colony expressed this displeasure in 1853 when he wrote about the "very real concern at seeing the foreign European element become predominant in Algeria, causing problems one day for the colony as well as the French administration."[12] Hoping to encourage an improved balance between French and foreign settlers, French administrators established preferential policies regarding land ownership, employment, and, later on, business concessions and bank credit.

The first colonization program, in 1841, provided land to immigrants who could provide the minimum capital required of 1,200 to 1,500 francs. Candidates submitted their applications to the minister of war, who made the final selection. Prospective colonists received building materials, oxen, temporary loans, and seed, as well as free passage to Algeria. In 1843, fourteen thousand concessionaires settled in Algeria, of whom nearly thirteen thousand were French; the rest were from Germany, Ireland, and Switzerland. Italians, Maltese, and Spanish were not encouraged to apply (Peyerimhoff 1906, 21–23).

A second wave of official colonization followed the 1848 revolution. The French government was confronted with widespread unemployment, and officials decided to send some of these families overseas. The state's announcement of a program of free concessions in Algeria had the desired results: over a hundred thousand individuals applied, from which twenty thousand were accepted, including fifteen thousand from Paris. After a difficult journey across France, the *quarante-huitards* ("forty-eighters") were settled in forty-two hastily created villages. This project was only a partial success, however, and many concessions were abandoned. A third wave followed the loss of Alsace and Lorraine after the Franco-Prussian War. Concessions were restricted to French nationals, and a program was developed to settle residents of Alsace and Lorraine in particular.

These official land concession programs were not a resounding success, and there was considerable return migration during the mid-nineteenth century (Julien 1964, 250). Despite the availability of cheap or free land, life in the colony was not easy. Many migrants had not been agriculturalists in France, and even those who were had to adapt to new agricultural conditions. They were stricken by a series of epidemics,[13] and discouraged by the long wait necessary to obtain land titles. Immigrants who had arrived with little capital often had to borrow at usurious rates in order to survive. If they experienced too many poor harvests in a row, they could be ruined. Despite these obstacles, after a half century of colonization, the landscape of this part of North Africa was becoming profoundly transformed. Rectilinear colonist villages were superimposed over preexisting social and political boundaries, while indigenous inhabitants were displaced.

The terms of official colonization programs changed throughout the nineteenth century, but they reflected overall the policy-makers' images of the ideal farm and farming techniques, notions based on a northern European intensive agricultural model. Despite the fact that much of Algeria, aside from the immediate coastal strip, had been under extensive cultivation or used as pasture for generations, land uses that many would argue are most appropriate for the region's climate and low population density at that time (Boserup 1965; Netting 1977, 69), French officials envisioned an Algeria covered with small, intensively farmed homesteads, and they divided the lands seized accordingly. The fact that French nationals received a much larger share of the concessions during this time than did the more numerous Spanish, Italian, and Maltese migrants suggests that an unofficial pro-French policy may have been practiced. In the province of Oran, where Spanish migrants far outnumbered the French, a minute number applied.[14] Jordi suggests that the capital requirements for concessionaires may have proved discouraging. While this may have been the case, a close look at internal documents of eastern Algeria provides evidence that the administration went to great lengths to ensure that French and German nationals received the lion's share of the property, as we find in the town of Guelma, in the province of Constantine, where several of the Franco-Maltese club members were raised. In this instance, even when officials had difficulty finding applicants for a newly created settlement, they expended time and money seeking French, German, and Swiss candidates still in Europe instead of placing individuals of other nationalities who were already there on site.

Officials wanted to develop a settlement between Bône and Constantine, and selected Guelma, which one administrator described in 1845 as "an old Roman site, and nicest 'camp' in all of Algeria . . . in the center of a *cercle* that includes rich and friendly Tribes with whom one could enter commercial relations."[15] It was also an Arab town with an important regional livestock market. A large French military camp was also established there, as were some three hundred European migrants who had arrived spontaneously to work as masons, bakers, shopkeepers, and farmers. The first European civilian in town was a Maltese butcher who arrived in 1837. Once the proposal to create a colonization center at this site was approved, officials made plans to grant farming and building lots to the first hundred families to arrive. However, they soon found that few in France were interested in settling there, and those families designated for that location requested to be rerouted to Algiers, despite the absence in that city of available concessions. According to one local official, colonists didn't want to settle "isolated in the middle of Arab tribes, far from Bône," where there were few resources for cultivators and where foodstuffs and other goods were available only at elevated prices due to high transportation costs. Although there were many Maltese, Italian, and Spanish migrants in Guelma already, and hundreds of their countrymen and -women crowded in the nearby city of Bône who could have filled the ranks of the concessionaires to the desired numbers, no attempt was made to recruit settlers from these populations. Instead, the official submitted a list of fifty other families who had not yet arrived in Algeria and "who thus might not have fixed ideas about where they want to go and who thus may be persuaded to go to Guelma."[16] All of these prospective settlers were French and still lived in France.

At the same time, the thirty-eight families already living in Guelma were granted titles to the urban lots they occupied for free or for a nominal fee. To accommodate an evolving town plan, officials decided that several buildings had to be demolished. None of the properties owned by the twenty-six French families were slated for demolition, while half of the twelve foreign families' houses were to be torn down to accommodate roads or other public works. The local mosque was viewed as the only public building "badly situated," and officials determined that it should be moved to an area "isolated and surrounded by trees" near the town gates.

Over the next year, forty-five families were placed on newly created lots. They were all from France or the "German" regions of Bavaria, Baden, and the Grand Duchy of Hesse, save one family from Spain. Most of the newcomers received ten-hectare rural lots, while a few received three or four hectares. The Spanish family, however, received only half a hectare of land. One might assume that lots were being granted in proportion to the amount of capital a migrant brought to the colony, as Jordi suggested for the department of Oran. However, this was not the case, for in 1847, twelve more families from the Grand Duchy of Hesse were sent to Guelma,[17] and fully half of the families told officials before embarking on the ships that they had no resources whatsoever, while most of the remaining families had half or less of the funds officially required to be a concessionaire. It would appear that government officials were going out of their way to place families of certain nationalities on the newly created concessions.

Similar processes were underway across the colony.[18] While pro-French policies may have been motivated by a desire to right demographic imbalances that were placing the French at a disadvantage, this cannot explain why Germans and Swiss were encouraged to settle on land concessions in Algeria, while Spanish, Italians, and Maltese were not. The selection of migrants was ostensibly based on prior farming experience and capital,[19] but documents such as letters and reports by colonization officials contain re-vealing statements about immigrants of different nationalities that are re-plete with value judgments; their image of the ideal candidate was informed by their conception of model settlers and Europeans, who for these officials were certainly not Maltese or Spanish, but French, German, or Swiss na-tionals.[20]

The effects of these practices on the developing colonial division of labor were great. While French nationals received most government-granted concessions, many of these concessionaires had no farming back-ground and needed laborers. Non-French Europeans such as the Maltese, renowned in their homeland for their skill at reaping great harvests from the tiniest of terrains, were unable to obtain their own properties and re-sorted to working as day laborers on the French-owned concessions. This was the case in Philippeville (Skikda), as we shall soon see, as well as in Oran, where, by the second half of the nineteenth century, 70 percent of the European agricultural day laborers were Spanish (Jordi 1986, 235). People were forced into other occupations that required minimal capital, which helps explain the large numbers of Maltese who started out as ped-dlers, selling fish, lemonade, or milk door to door in the larger towns, only later to open up shops as butchers, bakers, or café owners. On the death certificates of the Maltese who died between 1840 and 1858 in Bône and Philippeville, the most common occupation listed was day laborer (*jour-nalier*), which appeared sixty-five times. Twenty-one were identified as gar-deners, fifteen had been in transport, ten were in the building trades (car-penters, masons, and so forth), and twenty were in businesses offering food and drink (such as butchers, bakers, *cafetiers* [café owners], waiters, and ambulatory vegetable, fruit, and fish merchants). Smaller numbers did other sorts of work. Only one individual out of 149 was listed as a landowner (*propriétaire*).[21]

French capitalists, meanwhile, were receiving massive concessions de-spite their not meeting the basic requirements.[22] Capitalist involvement in-creased dramatically with Louis-Napoleon Bonaparte's coup d'état and the return of military rule in 1851. The emperor's new concession system facil-itated the concentration of land into fewer, larger estates.[23] Forest products such as wood, charcoal, and tannin had been important in Ottoman Alge-ria, and in eastern Algeria great tracts of forest lands comprising mostly cork trees had been held in trust by the Turkish state (Prochaska 1990, 47, 73). Upon arrival, the French state claimed these lands, and French capital-ists soon benefited from the state's largesse here as well, receiving thousands of hectares of forest lands with forty- to ninety-year leases.[24] Mining was another important resource, especially in eastern Algeria with its great de-posits of iron and phosphate. The most important mines were conceded to

French elites, who sometimes gained further advantages by using their political influence to convince the state to build infrastructure such as railroads in locations particularly convenient to their new acquisitions.[25]

As the colony grew and became more closely modeled after the French state, French nationals benefited from expanded civil service employment and political rights. The colony's three administrative units became three departments of France in 1848—Oran, Algiers, and Constantine—and three types of municipalities were developed according to the ratio of settlers to indigenous people, with *communes de plein exercise* ostensibly modeled after communes in France and *communes mixtes* that allowed limited self-government for settlers.[26] New towns were proliferating rapidly as well, resulting in a brisk increase in administrative positions, since each municipality needed secretaries, judges, lawyers, postal workers, sanitation experts, and so forth, jobs unavailable to non-French Europeans. Settlers began to receive more political and civil rights in 1848. These too were unevenly distributed by nationality. Communal residents now could vote for municipal council members: French citizens could vote at age twenty-one, while foreigners and indigenous populations were granted restricted voting rights at age twenty-five, after meeting "certain conditions." They could never elect more than one-third of the municipal council, and could never constitute one-half of the electorate of any voting district.[27]

While the state continued through the 1840s and 1850s to settle French and German migrants on free concessions in the hinterlands, other migrants were arriving in the larger cities looking for work. State officials began to monitor foreign populations, and this surveillance accelerated in both France and Algeria after the 1848 revolution. Legislation designed for Algeria outlining the way in which people could gather specified that this right was held only by French citizens; the law expressly stated that foreigners and Algerians had no right to gather whatsoever.[28] Despite the fact that foreigners did not enjoy the same political rights as French citizens in Algeria, they did share in many of the obligations. By the 1850s, non-French Europeans could be called up like any French citizen to serve in the national guard, and, by the end of that decade, service in the militia was obligatory for all foreigners. Only those who had received special immunity through consular channels, were able to avoid this obligation.[29]

A SETTLER HIERARCHY AND
ITS RATIONALIZATION

Policies and practices discriminating between French and non-French settlers had lasting effects. In Guelma in 1845, French nationals were granted the largest rural and urban estates, and owned several businesses, including the town hotel. Other French nationals had more modest occupations, working as masons, butchers, carpenters, and day laborers. Maltese, Italians, and Spanish supplied foodstuffs or worked as gardeners and shepherds. Once the town was officially established and more families settled, this pattern was elaborated. From 1852 to 1880, a full 23 percent of French men enumerated were in the military. The other French nationals were concentrated in governmental and administrative positions, such as in the tobacco and telegraph administrations. All people in liberal professions, such as schoolteachers, doctors, and lawyers, were French. Most food shops were in French hands, including bakeries, butcher shops, and restaurants. The French were prominent landowners, building entrepreneurs, and skilled artisans. In contrast, the Maltese had small shops and groceries, and served as gardeners, porters, and stable hands. Fifty-eight percent of the Italians were day laborers or masons. The rest were mostly skilled artisans such as ironsmiths and carpenters.[30]

The development of a hierarchy of nationalities is not uncommon in a colonial setting; the British colonies of North America are a case in point. In multiethnic British Guyana in the nineteenth century, the British were the elite and controlled the plantations. The other immigrants, such as the Portuguese, East Indians, Africans, and Chinese, had to develop different adaptive strategies for subsistence and social mobility according to changing circumstances. As Brackette Williams demonstrates, practices conducive to the consolidation and improvement of each group's economic well-being were, over time, "strengthened and 'traditionalized,'" becoming symbolic of their identity and place in the socioeconomic order. Once adaptive strategies were developed, the elite rationalized them as the "natural outcome of cultural differences and of differences in ethnic/racial groups' innate intellectual and physical capabilities." Thus, after manipulating the allocation of occupations, the elite "justified the successes (or failures) of different ethnic groups by their alleged relative racial (physical and intellectual) and cultural (value orientations and institutional forms) inferiority" (Williams 1991, 149, 151).

We can observe a similar process in French Algeria. By garnering the means of production, as well as administrative and political positions, the French secured elite status for themselves as the dominant group in this newly emerging society. The other migrants worked around the limitations that were set for them, and each wave of migrants adapted to a changing field of opportunities and constraints. By the late nineteenth century, observers regularly reported on the distribution of ethnic groups into specific occupational niches, as we see in the following passage from the demographer René Ricoux: "Sicilians and Neapolitans live near the sea; they are fishermen and sailors . . . Sardinians are farmers . . . The public work sites are frequented by Italians. Those from the north are generally masons . . . The Maltese works as fisherman and market gardener . . . he also works as a grocer, innkeeper, and café keeper" (Ricoux 1880, 12).

Associations between ethnicity and occupation were so consistent that specific occupational niches became emblematic of the different ethnic groups, and increasingly fixed ethnic stereotypes emerged. While the migrants arrived in the colony with their own linguistic, religious, and cultural traits, as well as the ideologies prevalent in different parts of Europe that helped them interpret this diversity, these would evolve and be imbued with new meanings in the colonial setting (Comaroff 1987, 304). Value judgments developed by the elite to understand the evolving hierarchy of ethnicities were also shared. As Barth notes, in complex multiethnic societies where there is a differential control of resources, the cultures of the component ethnic groups are integrated in at least one important way: they begin to share specific value orientations on which they can arrive at "judgements of hierarchy" (1969, 27). Such judgments are obvious in the following passage by the Vicount de Caix de Saint-Aymour, a member of the French elite who owned an estate in the Constantinois:

> The Italians, Spanish, and also the Maltese are, for the most part, people of very low origins, taking on jobs for which one would have a hard time finding a French man. They are almost always workers, and thus compete with the indigenous population as manual laborers. The French, in contrast, if they work with their hands, usually own vineyards or are managers; landowners trust them naturally in watching over other workers and looking out for their interests, with a feeling of national solidarity. (1987, 98)

Colonial authorities and, later, French historians highlighted the capital and skills the migrants brought with them to the colony as prime determinants of their place in the local economy, implying that rational economic principles were at work in the evolving ethnic stratification. In this view, workers were assigned to the tasks deemed to be most suited to their experiences and training. Of course, in some instances, we can imagine that education and other forms of human capital were factors. However, some models of the formation of a labor market split along ethnic lines discount skill altogether (Bonacich 1972). In the case of nineteenth-century migrants to French Algeria, both French and non-French immigrants often had similar expectations, standards of living, and information about work prospects prior to arrival; few knew even the most basic details about the climate or their economic prospects. Their political resources, however, diverged sharply, and it is here that we must look to understand the formation of an economic and status hierarchy among colonists. As Silverblatt writes, class formation is an inherently political process: "Creation of class entails the institutionalization of the means to facilitate, ensure, and regulate the appropriation of surplus" (1987, xixn2).

That the assignment of tasks was not based entirely on individual interests or skills is best illustrated by the distribution of land. The vast majority of nineteenth-century non-French migrants, such as the Maltese, had worked in agriculture in their home countries, and it is puzzling that people known to excel as market gardeners would decide instead to embark on an unknown career with uncertain prospects. In fact, many did not farm because they could not obtain land. This argument is further supported by the fact that, when they could purchase lands, many did, as many of my interviewees relayed (see also Solal n.d.). With farming all but closed off, migrants of other nationalities had to look elsewhere for work.

As ideas about the ethnic segregation of labor became more widespread and began to crystallize into distinct stereotypes, these ideologies helped further the existing occupational segregation. People would more easily find work in the area in which they were publicly acknowledged to excel. A Sardinian migrant, for instance, would find work more readily on a fishing vessel than as a carriage driver or innkeeper, due to widespread stereotypical associations between ethnicities and occupations. As Comaroff reveals, ethnicity in this way seems to determine an individual's predicament, and can assume the character of a "prime mover" in peoples' destinies (1987, 312).

Once an ideology of ethnic difference is elaborated, it also serves to rationalize the ensuing structures of inequality. The occupational choices of the European immigrants were described as representing their "natural" domains or prior inclinations, even by prominent French historians such as Charles-André Julien. Julien describes the Spanish as "the best agriculturalists and also excellent terrace-builders," who, he writes, did not ask for concessions. The Maltese "could have been good farmers, but preferred to concentrate in the raising of goats and pigs, and commerce: first as ambulant merchants and then in stores . . . The Germans and Swiss adapted poorly to the new country . . . People described their men as drunks and their girls as loose." He adds, "The Italians didn't like to work the earth. Hardworking masons, they responded to the demand for construction workers, sometimes without complaint, and then they sought *petits métiers* as maids, boat-builders, owned canteens, brothels, restaurants, or pasta shops" (Julien 1964, 250–51). Occupational segregation is explained here as emerging from group preferences, skills, and innate characteristics; the structural impediments that made only certain choices possible are ignored. Julien seems to have forgotten that the Spanish, Maltese, and Italians, who he says did not want to work the land, could not at first, and, finding this occupation inaccessible, sought out other means by which to support themselves and their families.

Ethnicity, occupation, and class were meaningful grounds for differentiating settlers, and we can better understand why ethnic labels held such salience in the colony. When we consider the fact that Algiers, the capital of the colony, was also the city with the largest concentration of French nationals, and of French born in France in particular, Michel's joke linking place and class is further elucidated. The (French) *Algérois* were kings. In the rural hinterlands, disproportionately peopled by subaltern non-French settlers, lived the "nothings." While ethnicity is not explicit in Michel's joke, the close linkages between ethnicity, class, and place were such that place and class often served as proxies for ethnicity in this colonial setting.

COLONIAL LIMINALITY

Thus far, I have argued that an evolving hierarchy of settlers, understood as based in ethnicity, had its origins in the initial distribution of land concessions and the resulting colonial division of labor. It is now time to consider in greater detail the especially difficult status position of the settlers at the bottom of this hierarchy, the Maltese. It may never be possible to determine which came first, Maltese liminality or the Maltese placement at the bottom of this class/status hierarchy, for we find evidence of both conditions during the earliest years of the colony. What is clear is that the Maltese were noticed early on by other, mostly northern, European observers, and anti-Maltese stereotypes and discrimination were widespread. In the mid-1850s, French observers such as Bard described them as a hybrid or transitional people bridging Africa and Europe:

> Let us do justice to this half-Italian, half-Arab people from Malta, a real transitional and moral link between the East and the West . . . he is a brother to the Europeans, and a friend and almost comrade of the Arabs . . . they are a type of hard-working Moor. (Bard 1854, 99)

One French official in the 1840s dedicated a paragraph to each European immigrant group in his town, but allocated four whole pages to a discussion of the Maltese, and we will visit his text shortly. Writings such as these expressed the prevailing uncertainty as to whether or not the Maltese should be included in the colonizer or colonized categories, and whether or not they were European.[31] Outright negative assessments of the Maltese can be found in letters and publications up until the end of the nineteenth century. Narcisse Faucon wrote in 1893, "The Maltese who arrive from their island still have a semi-barbaric allure. They are ignorant, crude, and argumentative, but they clean up fairly quickly" (1893, 301). Although the conditions of the Maltese migration and settlement in Algeria did not differ substantially from those of other southern European migrants, many people saw the Maltese as particularly noteworthy.

Liminal peoples are those who elude "the network of classifications that normally locate states and positions in cultural space"; examples include monks, nuns, and hippies, who live stripped of possessions and other symbols of social distinction (Turner 1969, 95). Such boundary-defying peoples may be credited with magical or religious properties, but are also often viewed as polluting, as Mary Douglas discussed (1966), or otherwise threatening to authorities.

In colonial societies, shaped by the rule of a foreign minority over an indigenous majority, concerns about the maintenance of prevailing social divisions were amplified. As Balandier wrote, "the colonials fear, more or less consciously, that group size alone will become the criterion of hierarchy" (1951, 64) thus supplanting their own dominance. In societies characterized by extreme power differentials, the boundaries between those with power and those without were and still are often based on various fictions that must be developed, articulated, and maintained publicly as a "public transcript" (Scott 1990). It was of the utmost importance that social categories remain clearly drawn, and people within them easily definable. In many colonies, phenotypical difference or race was employed by the ruling strata as the most expeditious means by which to divide populations, and racial ideologies often became highly elaborated. However, because race is a social construction, it was not always obvious just where to draw the boundary lines. As a result, social boundaries were sources of constant anxiety in colonial contexts, and governments spent considerable effort developing and retooling membership criteria. As historians Frederick Cooper and Ann Laura Stoler explain, "A large colonial bureaucracy occupied itself . . . with classifying people and their attributes, with censuses, surveys, and ethnographies," as regimes tried to "*define* the constituents of a certain kind of civil society" (Cooper and Stoler 1989, 611).

Populations situated at the margins of social categories, in "contradictory colonial locations," threatened the stability of dominant rule (Stoler 1989, 154). As a result, they were targets of official attention, and experienced considerable status anxiety. Stoler has shown (1989, 1992) how poor whites and interstitial "racial" groups, such as *métis,* the offspring of mixed marriages, who confounded colonial classification schemes, created concern in several colonial contexts, such as the Dutch East Indies.

In Algeria, phenotypical differences between the majority of the Algerians and the members of the colonizing power were not great, and the French relied less on race as a rationalization and criteria for difference than they did in other colonies. The underlying logic informing the distinction between colonists and colonized was an evolving social construction rooted in a contrast between "civilization" and "barbarism,"[32] not unlike that de-scribed by Alonso for colonial Mexico (1995, 56). Rationalizations for the subjugation of the Muslims and Jews, as well as Kabyles, Arabs, and other indigenous groups, were complex and evolved over time.[33] In general, how-ever, their subaltern status was understood to be based on their inferior "civilization" and technology. The civilization/barbarism dualism was both informed by and conflated with religious dualism, the opposition of Chris-tianity and Islam. The centuries-long antagonism between the adherents of these faiths served members of each side in drawing the boundaries be-tween self and other, in outlining the extent of the European continent and that of Islam, and in determining the criteria according to which cor-responding social boundaries should be drawn. It is thus no surprise that the French conquest of Algeria was sometimes described as a "reconquest" or the liberation of lands once Christianized but suffering ever since under centuries of Muslim rule. Religious affiliation served French officials when first sorting peoples in North Africa into colonist and colonized: non-Christian indigenous populations—Muslims and Jews—were at first uni-formly viewed as "colonizable," while European Christians, no matter how inferior in economic and educational standing, immediately gained higher social status upon crossing the Mediterranean because of their membership in the faith of the colonizing power.[34] The different European settler pop-ulations were further evaluated according to the degree to which they ex-hibited modes of behavior and degrees of civility similar to those of the French elite.

The Maltese posed problems for this evolving social classification sys-tem, for they shared many features in common with North Africans. The occupations they held, their language (so close to the locally spoken Arabic idiom), their last names, and their poverty placed them in close propin-quity with North African natives, whom the French at the time were dis-possessing of land and property, influence, standing, and even humanity. Although many Maltese themselves considered their Christianity "proof" of their Europeanness, other observers found the fervor of their Christian-ity alarming. Their religiosity was viewed by many colonial-era observers and even descendants of the early settlers as placing them closer cultur-ally to Muslims than to the comparatively secular French (Camilleri 1985, 496–97). Faucon reported bluntly, "Regarding their faith, they are as intol-erant as Arabs" (1893, 301). Elements of Maltese folklore, such as the evil eye, were also discomfitingly close to beliefs of indigenous Algerians.

More than any other trait, the language of the Maltese was grounds for questioning their Europeanness and placement in the colony. One French observer wrote, "As for the Maltese language, we know that this kind of pa-tois is just a corrupt Arabic" (Charmes 1888, 13). According to nineteenth-century accounts, Maltese was nearly mutually intelligible with the North African Arabic dialect, and in archival sources I found many examples of Maltese using Arabic-speaking translators to negotiate with French officials, such as Laurent Antoine Augustin André Salvator Teuma, who married in Algiers in 1838.[35] Settlers of this background remain sensitive about the Maltese language today, as we have seen, and the Phoenician-origin language ideology has persisted. When we consider what was at stake for the Maltese immigrants, it is easy to see why.

In the end, their Christian heritage, with its links to the Knights of Malta, served the Maltese well, and they were not classified by state officials alongside the indigenous populations. The Europeans were Christian; as Christians, then, the Maltese had to be Europeans. However, questions about this placement would resurface often, even to the present day.

LIMINALITY AND THE STATE

State officials sometimes treated the Maltese immigrants as a potent source of anarchy and a threat to the public safety. Already in 1831, the British consul general, responsible for his country's subjects in Algeria, complained that Maltese were habitually arrested and punished without being judged or having been granted the right to first see their consular agent. In 1832, he reported, "The French do not like the Maltese at all, and never lose an opportunity to punish them."[36] Maltese who had not obtained the proper signatures in their passports were refused entry by the marine police.[37] Writing about the drunkenness, theft, and nightly brawls in Bône in 1838, an officer described the need to create order "in the midst of these Maltese, natives, loafers and thieves."[38] In 1839, the director of the interior requested that twenty to thirty "Maltese of bad character" in Bône, who were "presumed thieves," be returned to Malta.[39]

During the first decades of the colony, French and non-French Europeans alike who were convicted in Algeria of serious crimes were sent to France to serve their sentences. In sending them to France, however, local authorities soon found that they were not rid of them forever, for many of these ex-convicts returned to Algeria once they had completed their sentences. Local authorities perceived the return of Maltese ex-convicts as a special threat, and, over time, a stereotype of the Maltese as potentially violent criminals emerged, not unlike that which Michel and François encountered sometimes at the Maison. In fact, several laws were designed specifically to mitigate the danger immigrants of this nationality allegedly represented. The most significant was a decree of 1843 stating that all Maltese who had completed prison terms of a year or more were forbidden in perpetuity from returning to Algeria. This decree is striking in that it singled out one ethnic group. The measure was viewed by the Ministry of War as "nicely resolving" a delicate matter, and the minister of the interior wrote that the law provided the administration "a natural means of *purification* against which nobody can complain, and, furthermore, promotes the development of the colony by further guaranteeing its security."[40] Such language suggests that the Maltese ex-convicts were viewed as polluting, and the minister's letter also indicates that the administration had been engaged previously in discussions about how to go about limiting Maltese migration. While an overt prohibition on Maltese immigration to Algeria may have been untenable for political reasons, the new law was viewed as a politically shrewd move that could arouse little formal complaint.

Fears of Maltese migrants were such that the acting director of the Ministry of the Interior sent a frenzied letter to the governor-general in 1845 stating that he had heard from the police commissioner that two British vessels full of escaped Maltese prisoners were on their way to Algiers. The letter is summarized in its margin: "We pray that you refuse admission to Algiers of 200 Maltese bandits."[41] As late as the 1850s, after receiving a letter from the prefect of Constantine, who was concerned about maintaining these regulations against the return of Maltese prisoners, the secretary-general replied that, contrary to the prefect's opinion, "the Maltese emigration [was] still too active" and consisted in large part of an element "*trop mauvais*" (too bad) not to maintain these regulations, which would ultimately keep all of the Maltese in Algeria on the "right path."[42] Furthermore, according to this official, if the Maltese arrived with the intention of staying, it would be easier to repeal these "severe and unjust measures," but this was not the case: "The Maltese come to Algeria only to make money, and they then return home with a considerable amount, earned with a greediness that does not stop at illicit and illegal measures."

ANTI-MALTESE PREJUDICE
IN PHILIPPEVILLE

As the attribution of greed and criminality to the Maltese by the French official indicates, antipathy toward the Maltese was prevalent in the colony soon after the first French victories in Algiers. This problem was discussed openly in a report by a local official, Mr. Lapaine.[43] Lapaine was then acting *commissaire civile*[44] of Philippeville (now Skikda), a town in eastern Algeria where many Maltese immigrants first settled, and where interviewees such as Joseph Zammit were raised, and it is worthwhile to consider the rise of this prejudice in greater detail.

Soon after capturing the regional and trading capital, Constantine, the French took the small coastal fishing village of Stora in October 1838 and

Figure 5. The port at Philippeville, 1840s. From Bettinger, *Vues et costumes de l'Algérie, 1846–1847: Vues prises au daguerreotipe par Bettinger et lithographiées par Mrs. Champin et H. Walter* (Paris: chez Wild), Archives d'Outre-Mer, Iconographie, 8 fi 11. Used by permission.

renamed it Philippeville, after King Louis-Philippe. Immigrants began arriving in increasing numbers soon after the garrisoning of French troops within the newly constructed city walls.[45] Over the next few years, the city developed in an "astonishing" manner (see fig. 5). Maltese were among the first civilians to arrive and soon made up approximately one-third of the European settler population.[46] As elsewhere in Algeria, the first European immigrants found employment in services catering to the military establishment. Traders brought foodstuffs from overseas, or served as intermediaries between the army and the local indigenous population. Liquor shops were set up, and prostitutes arrived. By 1842, Philippeville was an unusual town featuring 110 cafés and liquor stores, but only ten bakeries, ten butcher shops, and not a single church (or mosque). Clearly the town's economy revolved around the sizeable military installation there. However, commerce was increasing. Ships were arriving in the port from France, England, and other European countries to trade with the townspeople and the nearby indigenous population, and imported goods such as cloth and hardware were being transported to the internal trading cities of Constantine and Souk-Ahras.

French civilians were in charge of most of the business, and they controlled two-thirds of local agriculture and all commerce with Marseilles. Italians, on the other hand, worked as masons, gardeners, and retailers (*marchands de détails*). The small number of Spanish and Portuguese worked as gardeners, terrace builders, and cigar makers. Apparently most of the prostitutes originated in these two countries as well. Smaller numbers of Germans, Greeks, and Russians worked as gardeners or set up brasseries. According to Lapaine, the Maltese were hired for "the most difficult jobs": as porters and as manual laborers for construction projects. Others were grocers, food suppliers for the army, or field hands. The few Jews living there worked as merchants or brokers for commerce with indigenous peoples in the interior. The remaining people were "Moors and Arabs," which in Lapaine's report included indigenous peoples from Biskra[47] and Kabyles, numbering in the hundreds.

The Porter Affair

During this early period of Philippeville's development, some Maltese became embroiled in a porter labor dispute. International trade in nineteenth-century Algeria relied on shipping and thus on the porters (*portefaix*) who loaded and unloaded the vessels. Prior to French conquest, this work was carried out by ethnic organizations under the control of *amins,* who negotiated contracts and took a percentage of the earnings. By all accounts, it seems that this arrangement continued during the first decade of French control.[48]

After the French troops arrived in Stora-cum-Philippeville, a French entrepreneur, Mr. Dobignard, established a company of Biskri porters. Dobignard's company worked primarily for the troops and the military administration. He boasted that with the arrival of his company in Philippeville, the military's transportation expenses were reduced by 30 percent. Traffic at the port was so heavy that in April 1840, he requested permission to bring an additional twenty Biskris from Algiers to Philippeville, to double the size of his crew. But in August of the next year, troubles rocked Dobignard's operation. For reasons that remain unknown, his porters refused to make a requested delivery, and Dobignard called on the local authority, Commissioner Fenech, to settle the dispute. But Fenech found fault not with the porters but with Dobignard, who he determined had became so abusive to the porters as to have almost caused a riot. During Fenech's investigation, Dobignard only made matters worse by verbally abusing the commissioner. The fact that Fenech was a French citizen of Maltese origins may be relevant here.[49] This interpersonal squabble did not end there. Dobignard, who was also under-lieutenant of the local Philippeville militia, participated in a militia parade in a drunken state later that evening and verbally assaulted Fenech in public. Because the chief of his militia battalion had previously lodged complaints about Dobignard,[50] he was removed from his position for two months and sent to Bône to be tried, and his Biskri company was dissolved,[51] although individual porters continued to work on an independent basis.

A group of Maltese immigrants took advantage of Dobignard's absence and formed their own porter company. The Maltese and Biskri porters were now in direct competition, and, surprisingly, it was the company of Biskris that foundered. The Maltese porter company carried on with no intermediary, and soon had a monopoly on this thriving business, essential to local trade and military activities. Commissioner Fenech's difficulties were far from over. After only a few months, the Maltese company had caused so many problems that Fenech contacted his superiors to request that the "leader" of the company be permanently expelled from the colony. According to Fenech, the offences of the Maltese were the following:

> They are the sole individuals in charge of commercial and military transportation and use this advantageous situation to make others grant their constantly increasing demands. Just yesterday, merchandise was dropped in the mud in the middle of the street under the pretext that it was not their responsibility, but that of the owners, to bring it inside the stores.[52]

Fenech acknowledged that abolishing the Maltese company altogether would be undesirable, for it would result in considerable disruption to local trade. Instead, he requested that his superiors deport the main "instigator," whom he identified as Vincent Vella. Vella was a risk, he felt, for he had apparently been trying to organize his fellow workers into a "coalition" to demand higher wages.[53] The military, he felt, should not be forced to comply. The local officer expelled Vella and four other Maltese porters to nearby Bône, and Vella was eventually deported in perpetuity from the territory of Algeria on March 2, 1842.[54] The Biskri company was reorganized and the Maltese company formally dissolved due to its "intolerable pretensions."[55]

The *portefaix* affair provides an unusual example of a European immigrant group competing in a labor market formerly dominated by indigenous people. In this instance, Maltese immigrants were willing to work at wages so low that they could compete with the existing indigenous porter company. By working alongside Biskris at the docks, the Maltese were "crossing over" in the colonial imagination from "European" to "indigenous," and thus confounding the evolving ideologies about ethnicity, occupation, and status. While we do not know for certain, it seems that the Maltese, criticized for their "impossible" attitude and "outrageous" pretensions, also may have been less compliant than previous porter corporations, and certainly were positioning themselves for improved wages.

Dissecting Anti-Maltese Prejudice

By 1842, the *portefaix* affair had died down and the most "disruptive" members of the Maltese organization were expelled from the colony. It was at this time that Fenech's successor, Commissioner Lapaine, reported on the deeply rooted anti-Maltese sentiments of the townfolk. He was alarmed by the widespread ostracism of the Maltese: they were considered "just barely European" and were treated by some of the colonists with the same mistrust and contempt that the indigenous population suffered. They responded by segregating themselves from the wider community, and Lapaine was fearful of the long-term consequences of this. He devotes part of his report to dissecting the roots of this prejudice. He states that the Maltese have a temperament dominated by their "African blood," and are degraded by their poverty and lack of education. According to Lapaine, the other colonists did not like the Maltese in part because of their "fierce" character, "their lack of good faith in their relations with other Europeans[, and] their greed, which brings them to be seized by an irresistible competition." However, he also describes them as motivated, industrious, and gifted with an entrepreneurial flair:

> The most difficult occupations, the most tiring work, the most minute sales which can yield a profit only through the practice of strict thrift and rigorous savings, become their sole domain; little by little, their modest investments become more extensive; their earnings, prudently invested, multiply . . . their sobriety and their patience thus result in their monopoly of almost all branches of local retail.

Lapaine determines that the prejudices of the townspeople are rooted in professional jealousy: merchants especially are frustrated with the ability of the Maltese to undercut their prices. He condemns the townspeople for their hypocrisy, for although they "shower the Maltese with disdain," they nevertheless frequent their shops, which offer reduced prices for almost all necessities.

From Lapaine's detailed description, it appears that these strong anti-Maltese sentiments derive at least partly from Maltese willingness to work for lower wages or at a smaller profit margin than other European-origin populations, a willingness that has spawned ethnic conflict in other settings. In her work on split-labor markets, Edna Bonacich writes (1972) that animosity from a higher-priced labor force will emerge when its status is threatened by the arrival of a population willing to accept lower wages. Faced by such a threat, the higher-priced labor group will attempt either to exclude the migrants altogether, as in the 1882 Chinese Exclusion Act in the United States, or will attempt to create a permanent, hereditary split-labor market that will protect the jobs of the higher-priced workers. In the process, the lower-waged group tends to be racialized and blamed for the ills of the society as a whole. This model applies well to the anti-Maltese prejudices outlined by Lapaine. The Maltese arrived in Algeria already extremely poor and accustomed to terrible conditions. In Malta, they had been accustomed to day laborer wages that were considerably lower than those prevalent in Algeria (Donato 1985, 106). Furthermore, between the 1830s and 1850s, they had endured epidemics, rampant unemployment, and famine. One imagines that their expectations were low indeed, and that the first Maltese to arrive would have been willing to accept wages and working conditions that migrants from other parts of Europe might not have accepted. Their access to information was limited: they did not speak French and some studies suggest that they had the highest illiteracy rates of all the colonists (Ricoux 1880, 107). They had few political resources: indeed, in Malta, they were a subject people. In Algeria, they had few political rights and could be deported without a trial by the military officials. As the porter affair illustrates, their ability to organize was vigorously monitored by French officials. Their one major advantage was their language, yet even this asset proved a source of suspicion.

Lapaine's report and other early sources demonstrate that French authorities and settlers singled out the Maltese, whom they saw as situated at the boundaries between colonized and colonist. In his discussions of liminality, Turner states that any manifestations of "communitas" would appear "dangerous and anarchical, and have to be hedged around with prescriptions, prohibitions, and conditions" (1969, 109). This was certainly the case for some Maltese, who were viewed as an impurity to be expelled. There was another liminal population in colonial Algeria that was also treated with suspicion: indigenous Jews. It is no surprise that in colonial Algeria, the Maltese and the Jews were often viewed by French observers as similar or symbolically related.

MALTESE AND JEWS

A tale about the origins of the Maltese people that I heard from a Swiss priest who had spent many years in the Maghreb depicts the Maltese as a hybrid, boundary-defying people closely related to Jews. According to his story, the Maltese were created one day when Jesus was overtired. Once his skill at performing miracles had become widely known, Jesus was in demand, rushing to and fro to help out those in need. On the day in question, two men got into a tremendous fight, a Jew and an Arab. They both drew their swords, and, in an instant, cut off each others' heads. People gathered around, horrified. Somebody went to find Jesus, saying, "Please sir, can't you do something? These men have families, and they have left their wives and children with nobody to support them." Jesus agreed, but he was exhausted from working so many miracles. He put the heads back on the men and healed them, but made a mistake—he put the heads on the wrong bodies. "These two men," the priest told me, "were the first Maltese!" The priest's anecdote challenges the Maltese self-presentation of solidly Christian and European origins, exposing them as being derived from "no more than" Arabs and Jews. The implication is that they have Oriental non-Christian origins, and that they are hybrid Orientals at that.

Jews had been living in Algeria for hundreds of years when Arabs and Muslims arrived in the seventh century,[56] and, by the time of French conquest, they spoke the local Arabic dialect or closely related Judeo-Arabic and shared culinary, dress, and other cultural practices with the surrounding populations (see Bahloul 1996, 17). Some French Jews who arrived in Algeria in the early decades of the colony were shocked at the standard of living of their Algerian Jewish brethren and actively engaged in a mission to reform them (Laloum and Allouche 1987, 19), a process later scholars have termed their "colonization."[57] This project culminated in the naturalization of the Algerian Jews as French citizens en masse by the Crémieux decree of 1870. Their naturalization, and the wholesale transfer of a subset of the indigenous population of Algeria into the colonizer category, has been linked by many scholars to the later widespread and virulent anti-Judaism that characterized *pied-noir* society in the 1880s–1890s and 1920s–1930s. This movement was manifested in violent anti-Jewish rampages, largely carried out by settlers.[58] The decree, in shifting one subset of the indigenous population into the "colonizer" category, "upset the social classification scheme," heightening colonists' anxieties about their status and stability (Friedman 1988, 23–25). In reviewing the writings of some of the anti-Semites, Friedman finds a shift after 1870 from a condemnation of Jewish *actions* to a vilification of their essential *nature,* with Jews portrayed as dirty or "polluting." Not unlike the Maltese, Algerian Jews became another boundary-crossing, liminal people in the colony.[59]

This liminality persisted. In her discussion of the Jewish community of Sétif in the 1930s, Joëlle Bahloul writes about the Jewish community's intermediate socioeconomic status between native Muslims and European Christians. Even though they now enjoyed the status of French citizens, they were excluded from Christian society by that society's extreme anti-Semitism. Bahloul writes that this anti-Semitism created a tremendous gulf between Jews and Christians: "Despite their strong desire for Frenchification and emancipation, the Jews of Sétif, like those of other Algerian small towns . . . remained on the margins of European society" (Bahloul 1996, 12, 47).

The associations drawn by contemporary non-Maltese settlers between the Maltese and the indigenous Jews underscore the awkward social position both groups inhabited.[60] During the same decade in which the Maltese porter company was dissolved and their leader deported, indigenous Algerian Jewish traders were also expelled, ostensibly for monopolizing scarce goods. It seems clear that the ultimate source of disruption in the local economy was the arrival of the French (see Nouschi 1961, 160–87); however, the alleged *speculateurs avides* (voracious speculators) were nevertheless deported in perpetuity from their homeland.[61] No doubt the army, the biggest purchaser of goods and services, was frustrated by the ability of Maltese porters, on the one hand, and Jewish traders, on the other, to hold their ground in the fluid wartime situation. By expelling them, the army demonstrated its hegemony and secured a better position from which to negotiate with remaining traders and suppliers.

Overt links between the two groups can be found in demographer Ricoux's writings, in which he asserts that the "mercantile spirit of the Maltese brings him very close to the Israelite" (1880, 12). Given the status anxieties associated with liminality, I assumed that the Maltese in Algeria would have been major actors in anti-Jewish rioting, and I searched the historical records for evidence of this, to no avail.[62] I found instead that Maltese were sometimes the victims of such riots, mistaken by the rioters for Jews, as in the case of a Charles Xicluna who was *pris pour un juif* (taken for a Jew) during anti-Jewish riots in the Jewish quarter of Constantine in September 1899.[63] Other French settlers I met, like the priest, made similar connections between the Maltese and Jews. In a strange attempt to challenge dominant stereotypes that nevertheless incorporated and thus reproduced dominant terms and ideologies, contemporary Maltese *pieds-noirs* sometimes proudly explained to me that in the colonies, especially in their business dealings, they had been a kind of "super Jew."

SOCIAL SEGREGATION, RACE, AND COLONIAL LIMINALITY

Over the next several decades, despite discrimination by French officials and townspeople alike, Maltese continued to arrive in Algeria and settle, especially in the east. The cities of Bône, Philippeville, Guelma, and Constantine soon had hundreds of Maltese. They lived in Maltese-dominated neighborhoods and married other Maltese. Most were still not French citizens. Others lived in the hinterlands without any consular authorities to protect their interests. In the 1870s, the large Maltese community in the inland town of Constantine petitioned British authorities for a vice-consular officer, like those installed for the Spanish and Italian immigrants there. Without such an official, they were at a disadvantage, and had to hire independent lawyers for assistance in all civic matters. Their legal intermediaries, like the ministerial authorities, were not trained in their language, and French magistrates had to request that additional people serve as interpreters.[64] This was not to be. The British consul general of Algeria at the time, R. Lambert Playfair, in forwarding the petition to his superiors, added that he thought that having an additional consular employee in Constantine was unnecessary. While the Maltese were "a most valuable part of the population of this country," he found them "too illiterate and not of sufficient social position to [merit] a Vice Consul."[65] Even their own consular authorities found them too marginal to merit real attention.

The social segregation described by Lapaine in 1840s Philippeville continued across the colony, though whether it was predominantly in- or out-group motivated, we do not know. This can be best seen in the marriage choices of the settlers. Between 1854 and 1878 in Philippeville, not only did the different European nationalities represented prefer in-group marriage, but the Maltese in particular were socially isolated. In 1878, Philippeville's European population was half French, and included 3,000 Italians, over 2,000 Maltese, and only 1,000 Spanish and 157 Germans. Although the Maltese were the third most numerous European nationality in Philippeville at this time, they intermarried with other Europeans the least. French from France sought each other out: looking at the marriages of French men, Ricoux found that 804 per thousand of them married French women, 68 married Spanish women, 48 married Italians, 38 married Germans, and only 28 married Maltese (Ricoux 1880, 95). French males were apparently excluding the very sizeable pool of Maltese women, and selecting women from much smaller pools, such as that of Germans or Swiss. French women for the most part avoided Maltese men as well. In addition, place of birth mattered a great deal in individuals' willingness to marry Maltese. The vast majority of French men and women who did marry Maltese had been born in Europe, while those born in Algeria rarely if ever took Maltese spouses.[66] This suggests that the latter group had been shaped by attitudes toward the Maltese they learned in the colony. Ricoux felt he knew why Maltese women were so rarely selected by the French: it was due to their "harsh" or "crude" behavior, their practice of religious superstitions, and their lack of elegance and charm compared to other European immigrants. He even attributed the extremely low number of illegitimate births among Maltese women not to the intensity of their Catholic faith, but to their appearance:

> The truth is that the Maltese woman has nothing seductive about her . . .
> with a wild appearance, squalid dress, she is seldom sought after for marriage
> by the French, or even the Italians and Spanish. The same reasons can re-
> duce the number of extramarital relations. (1880, 121)

It is at this time that observers began to highlight Maltese racial differences. While the suspect racial origins of the Maltese had been addressed
briefly by Lapaine in 1842 ("their African blood"), he had focused princi-
pally on such cultural traits as attitudes, behavior, and work ethic. By the
1880s, however, many began to suggest, like the Swiss priest cited earlier,
that their Arabic language was a clue to a more lasting failing, one rooted in
biology. Ricoux, for instance, raises the question of the race of the Maltese
in his 1880 study. Unlike the French, Spanish, Italians, and Germans,
whom he details only according to their region of origin and occupational
choices, Ricoux feels compelled to say a few words about racial background
in his passage on the Maltese. The Maltese cultural affinity for North Africans, in his view, can be explained by their racial origins: "Of Carthaginian
origin, their race [or 'their stock'; *leur race*] is strongly steeped in the Arab
'type,' of which they have preserved physical traits, and, mentally, the
crudeness of their customs" (1880, 12). Similarly, Faucon addresses the
purported underlying Maltese racial affinity with Arabs: "Their build, physical features, language, temperament, customs, all reveal their Arab blood"
(1893, 301). Even former settlers today sometimes make reference to their
own *peau matte* (swarthy complexion). Mr. Costa told me that he was sure
that there had to be a lot of "Arab blood" in Malta, for in his family photographs, his grandfather had "very very dusky" skin. Even his father used
to always say that the Maltese were "85 percent Arab."

In my own interactions with descendants of *pieds-noirs* of Maltese and
other backgrounds, I could see no clear-cut phenotypical distinctions, and
early photographs from Algeria of Maltese, Sicilian, Spanish, and other
southern Europeans depict individuals distinguishable only by dress and
hairstyle, as a photograph of a Maltese family in 1930s Guelma attests (see
fig. 6). Immigrant groups are often racialized in a new setting, however,
particularly when consigned to low-wage, low-skill employment (Brodkin
1998). That the Maltese would be racialized is thus no surprise, especially
in the late nineteenth century when race became such an important theme
and dimension of difference for French social scientists and the general
public alike. What is especially interesting here is that the Maltese were
continually associated with "Arabs" some sixty years after they first arrived,
and that a contemporaneous racialization of the Algerian Jews was highly
elaborated at this time as well. It is further revealing that in some key texts,
such as that by Ricoux, race is never mentioned in regard to the other European immigrants, implying a purported racial continuity between French,
Italians, Spanish, and Germans. Even in the 1970s, when the historian
Charles-Robert Ageron surveys the settler population, he writes that the
Spanish were "so well integrated morally and socially that few characteristics allowed them to be distinguished from the *Français d'origine*," and the

Figure 6. A Maltese family in Guelma, 1930s. Photograph courtesy Lucette Juliano-Lafranque.

"Italians never posed any problem with assimilation." However, "only per-haps the Maltese . . . conserved their characteristics" (1979, 478–79).

LIMINALITY, DISCRIMINATION, AND ETHNIC SOCIAL CLUBS

Over the course of a generation or two, many Maltese families began to ex-perience considerable upward mobility in the colony. Some became traders or shopkeepers, others became quite wealthy as middlemen in the cattle trade or as millers, or began to purchase small farms. As one French settler told me, "On the tiniest piece of land, they had everything. After a while, they threw themselves into commerce, and in my village, when they got a lot of money, they bought some beautiful properties."

Most interviewees told me that there were no Maltese or Sicilian "colonies" in French Algerian cities, no distinct neighborhoods in urban areas, unlike in neighboring Tunisia. However, the same people could list the Maltese-dominated occupations and even the regions where most of the Maltese families lived, such as the outskirts of Algiers, in the Tagarins, populated by Maltese shepherds. Louis Arnaud described such a neighbor-hood in Bône. His memoir, *Bône: Son histoire, ses histoires* (1960), is a nos-talgic look at his natal city as he remembered it in 1956, before the exodus to France. He describes a *quartier des chèvres* (a goat herders' neighborhood) in the city outskirts:

In a real city of wooden barracks, all the same, one story high, separated by tiny gardens meticulously kept where only those vegetables essential for cooking were cultivated . . . lived families of Maltese goat-herders. On the top level, which one accessed with stairs or an outside ladder, were the bedrooms, with a balcony across the entire façade. While walking down the road in the afternoon, it was pleasant to see the women sitting on the wooden balcony, sewing . . . while inside, the men and the children tended the goats, whose stable was formed by the ground floor. Everyone in the household worked. What struck the passerby, aside from the originality of this village of pink and pale blue whitewashed boards, was the quality of cleanliness and order apparent to anyone looking in. This exemplifies the characteristic of the Maltese families who lived together outside the city and its noise. These Mediterranean islanders were happy to have been able to create, in their forced exile, an atmosphere that reminded them of some corner of their natal island. (Arnaud 1960, 55)

Despite the difference in building materials, the housing styles described here resemble the traditional Maltese homes outlined by Ciappara (2001, 5). Their agricultural skill also seems transplanted directly from Malta. Arnaud describes the rich gardens of onions, greens, carrots, and other vegetables, and the expanses behind the houses where the goats found pasture. He reminisces about the goats coming into the city:

You had to see these little quadrupeds . . . leaving for the city, with the first light of dawn, in all seasons and in all kinds of weather. They left, leaping and trotting, and their bells rang without respite, waking the inhabitants still asleep in their homes. In the city, the herd would divide into little groups of five or six goats, each which would occupy part of the street, always the same, in different neighborhoods.

Arnaud also describes the *halle aux légumes,* a large central market that was destroyed in 1942, where Maltese market gardeners would bring their carts laden with fresh vegetables, arriving well before dawn, a schedule that sounds much like that of Mr. Sultana's father. Before the market doors opened, they sold their goods on the sidewalk, going to the nearby cafés to negotiate prices. Next to the market were five of these cafés, "all held by Maltese-origin patrons. These rough workers, who lived alone during the rest of the day, were happy to find themselves together, at the counter, in front of a cup of steaming hot coffee, . . . or even around a marble table, spending a moment after having negotiated their sales, having a snack, with bread, cheese, an onion, a hot 'caldi,' or a spicy piece of 'fougasse' . . . It was their sole pleasure of the day." Arnaud explains that between three and six o'clock in the morning, these cafés were frequented by an almost exclusively Maltese clientele, primarily gardeners and produce brokers (1960, 178). While gilded with a nostalgic hue, Arnaud's recollections reveal the persistence well into the mid-twentieth century of "Maltese" neighborhoods and the consolidation of a North African–Maltese vernacular architecture, occupation, cuisine, and even rhythm of daily life.

Long after the immigrants had begun to gain French citizenship in the late nineteenth century, "French," "Maltese," and "Italian" were salient terms despite the fact that the individuals thus characterized shared a common nationality. This is because they shared in this nationality unequally. "French" was a label that denoted wealth, "proper" speech, manners, and other forms of cultural capital limited to the very privileged. People living at the bottom of this socioeconomic hierarchy, such as the "Maltese," were in an especially precarious position. Not only were the Maltese marginalized economically, but in confounding existing cognitive maps of the social universe, they were viewed as a special threat in the colony's early years. Some were deported, and others were subject to prejudices and stereotypes. A people thus targeted cannot be oblivious to that fact, and we must assume that these experiences will have been retained in family stories, shaping understandings of Malteseness and Frenchness in that and subsequent generations. How long do people recount and retain in the collective repertoire stories of discrimination, the experience of liminality? It is in regard to their social position and the attitudes they endured that the Maltese experience differs from that of the settlers of other non-French backgrounds. Their especially vulnerable social position as "subaltern settlers" is an important dimension of the colonial past that fostered a distinct Franco-Maltese identity and memory, and which granted a unique tenor to their experience of exile following decolonization.

FOUR

The Algerian Melting Pot

The initial awkward liminal status of the early Maltese immigrants in French Algeria was complicated by their confrontation of contradictory forces in the evolving settler society. Through legislation governing access to land and other concessions, they and other "foreign" settlers were relegated to a lower class status, that of subaltern colonists, and yet, as the nineteenth century came to a close, they were also invited to become full-fledged members of the colony as French citizens through a series of naturalization laws. It is this latter process that was highlighted in French school texts and that is celebrated in the dominant memory. However, the people who were subject to these opposing processes remembered both, as we can see in their narratives today.

The stories the elderly Maltese former settlers shared with me were often ambivalent or contradictory. Nowhere was this ambivalence greater than in their accounts of assimilation, their ethnic identity, and their relationships in the colony with other settlers, particularly the French. They proudly proclaimed the Maltese immigrant's aptitude for assimilating to new cultural norms, but then told me how this assimilation was necessary to avoid the discrimination that had plagued them and their parents and grandparents. They bristled when I described them as anything but French, but then referred to each other as "the Maltese" or "the Corsican." They proclaimed their Frenchness without question, and itemized for me just how many men in their immediate family had served in the French military, underscoring in particular which relative(s) had been killed during World War I or II, while at the same time referring to a distinct group in the colony, "the French," and discussing this group with awe and reverence.

This ambivalence can be viewed as reflecting both their liminal social position in the colony and the ambivalence inherent in processes of cultural assimilation and change more generally. The discourse of the elderly Maltese on assimilation in Algeria both reproduced and challenged the official melting pot narrative found in mainstream texts on colonial Algeria. In what follows, we will take a closer look at the dominant, albeit highly simplified, narrative of the Algerian melting pot, and then turn to additional sources to better understand the processes by which the Maltese, Spanish, and other immigrants became French in this colonial setting. In the subsequent chapter, we will take a closer look at the ways this ambivalence is reflected in narrative multivocality.

FRENCH AND ALGERIAN
MELTING POTS

The melting pot metaphor, a powerful and enduring image used to describe the integration of immigrants in U.S. society into a new "American" amalgam, also serves as a potent, multivocal symbol in France. Less known is its application to Algeria, where it became a remarkably widespread way of discussing the creation of a new settler society there. As a powerful visual image, the metaphor screens from view the lived assimilation experience, and its meaning is ambivalent enough that it can be deployed by people who hold very different positions on immigration and the assimilation of foreigners. The metaphor's ambivalence reflects the contradictions and tensions inherent in the assimilation process itself, a process that necessarily involves loss and the death of one lifeway as well as the adoption and creation of new ones.

Ambivalence is apparent in the many ways the metaphor has been deployed to describe U.S. society. In an early, progressive variant, the U.S. is depicted not as built upon reproductions of English institutions and cultural forms, but rather as a completely new society involving the mixture or melting together of the cultures of peoples from across the globe (Gordon 1964). This model has been promoted since the eighteenth century, although the language used has varied. In 1782, a French immigrant, J. Hector Crévecoeur, wrote in his *Letters from an American Farmer*, "here individuals of all nations are melted into a new race of men" (quoted in Green 1991, 72). By 1845, this new society was described by Emerson as a new alloy formed in a "smelting" pot. The metaphor that we know today entered mainstream U.S. culture with the popular 1908 play by Israel Zangwill, *The Melting Pot*, which has been described as a "hymn to the power of assimilative forces in American life" (Thernstrom 2004, 48). Zangwill and other progressives sought to celebrate the creation of what they perceived to be a completely new society free of the prejudices and strictures of the Old World. Even at this time, however, some felt that the notion implied a necessary renunciation of one's ethnic heritage, and Zangwill himself felt compelled to add a statement to later editions of his play explaining that this was not his position (Green 1991, 72). With the increase of xenophobia and extreme nativism at the turn of the century, the phrase was used to refer to the adoption by newcomers of American cultural practices, or "Anglo-conformity."[1]

In contrast to the U.S., where scholars, politicians, and the public alike have long debated the pros and cons of assimilation and cultural pluralism, these questions have only recently begun to reach similar levels of national concern in France, as Noiriel so clearly describes in his 1988 *Le creuset français* (*The French Melting Pot,* 1996). Despite the fact that, especially since the nineteenth century, the two countries have been built on immigration, this past has yet to fully enter French national consciousness, and a remarkable collective amnesia persists about the role played by immigration in shaping French society (xii). With heightened interest in immigration questions in the past several decades, the phrase has been imported. As in the U.S., however, the French usage is contradictory and dependent on the users' political beliefs and understandings of the assimilation experience. People may employ this metaphor to argue that France is homogenous and thus is not a melting pot, or that it is homogenous because of the melting pot. It can also be used to present the extreme image of the *modèle Anglo-Saxon,* of a society composed of distinct ethnic groups battling it out in urban centers, an image often summarized as "ghettoization" (Green 1991).

The melting pot metaphor also appears in accounts of colonial Algeria from the late nineteenth century to this day. Algeria is described as a "melting pot" (*creuset*) in which the various European ethnicities "melted together" (*se sont fondues*), underwent "fusion" (*la fusion*) or "blended together" (*se sont amalgamés*). Demographer Victor Demontès, writing about "a new people forming on the sunny shores of the Mediterranean," discussed the "mixing, or better yet fusion" of different European races in the "African melting pot" (*creuset africain*) (1906, 8, 9). A 1960s publication describes Bab-el-Oued, a neighborhood of Algiers, as "a miraculous melting pot at the bottom of which are slowly melted . . . all of the ethnicities of the Mediterranean" (Gignoux and Simiot 1961).

In classic French historiography, the metaphor provides a simplified shorthand, a way to discuss the immigration and integration of foreigners without getting into the particulars. This is the case even in the most thorough and respected histories of the colony, *Histoire de l'Algérie contemporaine,* volume 1 (1827–1871) by Charles-André Julien (1964), and volume 2 (1870–1954) by Charles-Robert Ageron (1979). It should be noted outright that the settlers rarely appear in this literature except in the most perfunctory manner.[2] As historian David Prochaska has noted, "It is almost as if their presence in the Algerian tragedy was a fact too big to be seen"

(1990, 4). Because settlers barely appear in these works, it is not surprising that the fate of the foreign, non-French settlers has been almost entirely overlooked. Their assimilation to French culture in the colony is more implied than explained, or is glossed with the melting pot metaphor. In the first volume, which covers the most important periods of European migration to Algeria, Julien outlines the most basic demographic details of the European immigrant populations and provides brief and stereotyped profiles of the different immigrant groups, as we have seen (1964, 250–51). We learn little more about the migrants' experiences once settled in Algeria, or how or when they became politically or culturally French. In volume 2, the foreign settlers are again discussed briefly in one section (Ageron 1979, 118–31). The "fusion" of the non-French in the Algerian "melting pot" is presented as a nonissue, or at best as a straightforward process not worthy of historical examination or focus. Ageron notes this process at various junctures with statements such as the following: "These European communities didn't just cohabitate in Algeria, they began very early to mix together." Complete assimilation is assumed to have occurred through involvement with such French institutions as obligatory military service for men, public school, and the electoral and legal systems, and through intermarriage and daily interaction with French citizens. As he concludes, "In sum, the mixture occurred on its own through the school, the street, and the barracks" (1979, 131). The end of World War I is often presented as the turning point after which ethnic distinctions were blurred and a unified colonist population was formed (Baroli 1967; Crespo and Jordi 1991; Crespo 1994, 133).

A dominant memory has been forged through these accounts. This simplified representation of the assimilation process tells only part of the story, however. The melting pot metaphor serves here as almost a formula of erasure, a figure of discourse that aids in the production of silences in historical narratives (Trouillot 1995). We will now turn to the various "stages" that the dominant narrative identifies in the process of foreigners' becoming French, starting with their naturalization. As we will see, only a subset of those living in Algeria were invited to join the dominant elite in the "melting pot," and the assimilation process proceeded in fits and starts, with uneven results.

MAKING THE FOREIGNERS FRENCH

One of the most important stages in the assimilation process was the forced naturalization of hundreds of thousands of non-French Europeans, including the Maltese. This occurred as the final stage of a long process, and in response to two growing concerns: the striking demographic imbalance between settlers and colonized peoples, and the unfavorable French/non-French settler ratio. Such anxieties were heightened following the defeat of the French in the Franco-Prussian War and the 1871 Algerian Insurrection, which came close to marking the end of the colony. Despite pro-French land grant programs, the French showed less interest in the colony than did their Mediterranean neighbors. The naturalization of Algeria's Jews in 1870 temporarily assisted in correcting the balance, for it had the effect of increasing the size of the French settler population by over 34,500 (at a time when 95,500 French faced 115,000 non-French European settlers).[3] The foreign presence was striking in some regions of the colony. By 1887 in the department of Oran, there were only 67,000 French civilians but at least 100,000 non-French European civilians, and 92,290 Spanish (Leroy-Beaulieu 1887, 52–53). Even the Spanish consul described the department of Oran in 1868 as follows:

> There are streets and neighborhoods that are completely Spanish. From the interior until the Oran coast, somebody traveling across the countryside would hear no other language more than our own . . . The same language, the same practices and customs make the Spanish impermeable to French influence. They marry, are born and live amongst other Spanish. I believe that if things continue in this way it will be easier for the Spanish portion of the population to absorb that of the French than for the latter to eliminate the Spanish influence.[4]

In eastern Algeria, Italian migration had increased over the course of the century, and similar concerns were raised there about the maintenance of French cultural influence. With so many foreigners, would Algeria remain French, or would other nations steal this prize colony away? How could it be assured that Algeria would remain *culturally* French with so many foreigners present? Because the settlers were already so outnumbered by the Muslims and the French hold on the colony was never sure, it was important not to alienate any portion of the settler population. Deporting the non-French was thus unthinkable. Since programs encouraging French immigration had limited success, naturalization emerged as a logical next step.

A mechanism allowing foreigners to request French citizenship on an individual basis had been in place in France and Algeria since the late 1840s, and included a ten-year residence requirement.[5] Napoleon III's *Sénatus-Consulte* of 1865 reduced the residence requirement to three years.[6] Published with the law was a report stating that a goal in reducing these requirements was to facilitate naturalization of the burgeoning number of non-French Europeans in the colony:

Today, foreign emigration makes up approximately one half of the African colony . . . don't we sense how important it is to prevent Algeria from losing its French character to this mixture of foreigners, by transforming as fast as possible these foreigners into Frenchmen? (Dalloz and Dalloz 1865, 117)

This bill did not have the desired effect, however. From 1865 to 1874, only 293 Spanish, 313 Italians, and 601 Germans obtained French citizenship in this way (Jordi 1986, 129), out of total populations of approximately 92,500, 25,800, and 5,700, respectively.

It is unclear why the European settlers were not requesting French citizenship. Citizens' benefits included greater civil and political rights, the possibility of obtaining administrative positions, and decided advantages in obtaining land concessions. The negative consequences were few. In France at the same time, foreigners were avoiding naturalization in order to avoid the mandatory military service there. But this could not be a motivation in Algeria until after 1875, when French recruitment laws were applied there. Moreover, the requirement to serve in local militia units was applied equally to French and non-French alike throughout most of this period.[7]

Pro-French economic policies were established in Algeria at this time. Motivations for these policies were complex, and while they clearly reflected a desire to secure the more profitable enterprises for the French, another motivation may have been to encourage non-French settlers to naturalize or to leave. Measures established in 1836 and 1843 had granted foreigners complete freedom in all trades in Algeria, and bilateral trade agreements had been set up with neighboring European countries. But, toward the end of the century, foreigners faced a reduction in these rights. Land concessions were targeted first and were restricted to French citizens in 1871.[8] Foreign fishermen were targeted next. Fishing during the early decades of the colony had been dominated by foreign fishermen and vessels. Sardinians specializing in tuna arrived seasonally, and fishermen came from Sicily, Genoa, and Naples to La Calle, Stora, and Philippeville in the 1870s for sardines and anchovies. Fishing camps were established all along the Algerian coast, and the road between Philippeville and Stora was soon filled with sardine and anchovy canning and preserving factories (Crespo 1994, 66–69). By 1880, the maritime population of the colony was predominantly Italian (50 percent), while French and indigenous fishermen constituted only 30 percent of the total (Spaniards made up 15, and Maltese, 5 percent). A British source reported that "this state of affairs caused serious anxiety to the Algerian authorities, who desired, by every means in their power, to force foreigners residing in the colony to abandon their nationalities, and to accept naturalization as French citizens." This situation changed in 1886, when a new law restricting navigation was established.

From this point on, the crews of fishing vessels in French Algerian waters had to be at least 75 percent French. Even more significant was the law of March 1, 1888, which prohibited fishing within three miles along the coast to all but French citizens (Lacoste 1931, 34). This law compelled "all fishermen not of French origin, to abandon their nationality or quit the colony."[9] Many Maltese and Italians left at this time, either to return home or to resettle in neighboring Tunisia. Foreign fishermen wishing to stay in the colony were required to apply for citizenship through the 1865 *Sénatus-Consulte,* and many chose to do so, with naturalizations leaping from 34 in 1885 to 545 in 1887. By 1901, the vast majority of the fishermen of Algeria were naturalized French citizens.[10]

Despite these measures, the non-French population continued to dominate numerically. Concern in France and Algeria regarding the relative sizes of the French and non-French settler populations grew into an obsession, and several demographic studies of the European populations of Algeria were published.[11] Demographers such as Ricoux and Demontès analyzed in detail comparative birth, death, and fertility rates for the different European nationalities in Algeria, noting anxiously the higher fertility rates of Maltese, Italian, and Spanish couples relative to the French, and demonstrating their concern at the relentless increase in the size of these populations (see Leroy-Beaulieu 1887, chapter 3). A French school textbook reports the relative proportions of the colonist populations as if describing a sports match: "The following years, the French triumphed. In 1861, they were 112,000 against 80,000 foreigners . . . then they lost this lead a little" (Bernard and Redon 1936, 78). Writers like Leroy-Beaulieu began to argue for the resolution of the "foreigner question" through naturalization (1887, vi).

MASS NATURALIZATION LAWS

It was becoming clear that widespread naturalization of Europeans would not be achieved unless the element of choice was removed (Jordi 1986, 132), a strategy articulated openly by some prominent French politicians (Leroy-Beaulieu 1887, 54–55). A precedent had been set in Algeria just a few years before with the mass naturalization of Algerian Jews through the Crémieux decree of October 24, 1870, discussed briefly in the previous chapter. This law was the culmination of a long process in which coreligionists in France organized to help pull Algerian Jews out of their situation of "ignorance and poverty" (Laloum and Allouche 1987, 18–19) and to reform their schools and religious practices. Rabbis were sent as instructors from France, and some French organizations tried to encourage indigenous Jews to adopt European clothes and the French language. In 1839, a commission was formed to help "regularize" the educational system and religious practices of the Algerian Jews so that they would more closely correspond with those of the Jewish community in France. Parisian lawyer Adolphe Crémieux, the author of the Crémieux decree, became involved in this project in the 1840s. The commission recommended the complete incorporation of Algerian Jews into the French consistory system. Since French Jews in France had full citizenship status and thus were undeniably "Europeans," it was awkward at best that Jews in Algeria remained *indigènes,* and this incongruity threatened to raise dangerous questions about the "Europeanness" of the Jews in France.

Even when in 1865 Jews, like Muslims, were granted the opportunity to become naturalized French citizens, with Napoleon III's 1865 *Sénatus-Consulte* legislation, few applied (Julien 1964, 467). The Crémieux decree settled the matter. While traditional scholarship claims that Algerian Jews first reacted enthusiastically to French citizenship, Friedman notes that Crémieux had been to Algeria seventeen times and knew that the Jewish community there was conservative and that legislation offering the choice to become French would not work. The decree thus appears to have been a final attempt by frustrated supporters of the consistory system to "encourage" assimilation by formally requiring Algerian Jews to conform to French Jewish practices (see Schwartzfuchs 1980).

The Crémieux decree is often cited as the key to explaining the widespread and violent anti-Jewish agitation among Algerian colonists in the 1890s. Prochaska writes that in granting Jews the right to vote, the decree unleashed an electoral crisis in Algeria, for the Jewish vote subsequently became a swing vote in certain regions (1990, 202). He also states that the decree would set off a time bomb: "The veneer of French citizenship could not hide the fact that the Jews resembled the Muslims more than the Christians" (1990, 138). I believe that to fully understand the extreme anti-Semitism of the Europeans of Algeria, we need to consider the changing statuses of the key actors in the anti-Jewish movement, the non-French Europeans. The worst anti-Jewish riots occurred during a period of heightened concern in Algeria regarding the foreign presence there, concern not alleviated but exacerbated by the mass naturalization of non-French Europeans.

Mass naturalization was applied to non-French European settlers with the citizenship law of June 26, 1889. This law automatically naturalized all foreign children of a foreign father who himself was born on French soil, and, as long as they did not refuse French nationality in the year following their majority, children born in Algeria or France to a foreign-born father, if they were still residing in France. It was applied to "France," which in-

Table 1. Changing Proportion of French and Non-French Europeans, 1886–1901

	Total French	Naturalized French	Non-French
1886	219,000[1]		211,000
1896	318,000	50,000	212,000
1901	364,000	72,000	189,000

Source: Ageron 1991, 62.

[1] Of the total French population in 1886, approximately 43,000 were naturalized French Jews (Leroy-Beaulieu 1887, 50–51).

cluded the Algerian territories, and was responding in part to concerns about the rising numbers of foreigners in the metropole and their possible development into "a nation within the nation" (Brubaker 1992, 106). In France, the question of military service was paramount, and comparisons made between French and German naturalization rates (Noiriel 1996, 55) demonstrated an underlying concern for relative troop strength. Demographic concerns were critical factors in the 1889 law's application to the colony as well. In his report to the Senate on June 3, 1889, Senator Delsol presented figures from the Algerian censuses of 1865 and 1886, and stated that the foreign population had been increasing there at a faster rate than the French due to higher birth and migration rates. He predicted that soon it would surpass that of the French, and added, "In such circumstances, isn't *jus soli* imperative, and doesn't it even become the only way to assure the predominance of the French over the non-French population in the future?" (Dalloz and Dalloz 1889, 65). The procedure established for those wishing to refuse naturalization was extremely elaborate and reveals that those writing the law intended to prevent most from choosing this option.[12] Consequently, the 1889 naturalization law had the effect of almost immediately elevating the size of the "French" portion of the colonist population (see Table 1). However, the "Frenchness" of these newly naturalized Europeans would be challenged, as we will see.

NATURALIZATION LAWS AND THE "JURIDICAL PROBLEM"

Naturalization laws first invited and then forced hundreds of thousands of people—Algerian Jews and foreign Europeans—into the melting pot. French citizenship was viewed as the first step in turning them into loyal French men and women, and patriotic defenders of a French Algeria. By assimilating outsiders legally into the colonial body, naturalization laws initiated a process that, ideally, would be carried on by the other great assimilating institutions of the state: the school, the military, and the political and legal systems that would assist in their assimilation to the aspirations and ideals of the dominant group. Gramsci highlighted the role of law in winning the consent of subaltern groups and thus creating the social conformity that "is useful to the ruling group's line of development," which he termed the "juridical problem" (1971, 195). The assimilating function of law is most obvious when the laws in question are those determining citizenship status. By forcibly moving one group of people into a new social category, that of the dominant class, naturalization laws in colonial Algeria paved the way for other assimilating forces and facilitated the acceptance by the subaltern settlers of the dominant group's conception of the world.

In a colonial setting, however, domination of the colonized usually is achieved by coercion, not consent, and no parallel mass naturalizations of Muslims occurred. Instead, Muslims were effectively excluded from the "melting pot." While Napoleon III's *Sénatus-Consulte* law of July 14, 1865,[13] had also established a mechanism for the naturalization of Muslims, they were required to abandon their *statut personnel,* which meant forsaking their rights and obligations under Koranic law and thus practices integral to their religious practice and to their identity as Muslims. Many viewed naturalization with such conditions as a form of social suicide, and others undoubtedly did not want to abandon their religion. Between 1865 and 1899, only 1,309 requests for naturalization were filed (with only 178 of the applications rejected) out of a population of approximately 4 million Muslims by 1901 (Ageron 1968, 1118). Until the last years of the colony, French policy concerning the assimilation of Algerian Muslims was fraught with contradictions. Metropolitan politicians increasingly called for reforms that would improve the condition of the *indigènes,* especially following their conscription in 1912, and the engagement of approximately 174,000 indigenous Algerian troops in World War I (Michel 1984, 119). But each reform movement failed, in part due to categorical opposition from the Algerian settlers and their representatives in France. Political assimilation of the indigenous population, especially in later years when this would be accompanied by an extension of voting rights, was a direct threat to the settlers, who were all too aware that their own enjoyment of political and economic domination in Algeria would quickly come to an end if even a tenth of the Muslim population was granted full and equal voting rights. The offering of French citizenship to Muslims only when coupled with a denial of their personal status may have been presented as a compromise solution, but it was a "compromise" designed to fail. This seemed to be the opinion of many journalists writing for the indigenous press in the early twentieth century. As Gosnell reports, "Virtually all of the newspapers formed a consensus on this point. A naturalized Arab or Berber continued to be Muslim while assuming all rights and duties of being French. Islamic identity did not in any way negate one's capacity to become French" (2002, 114).

It was only after World War II that Algerian Muslims were able to receive French citizenship and still retain their *statut personnel.* This became possible with the law of May 7, 1946, which granted French citizenship to all subjects of the French colonial empire in conjunction with the formation of the *Union française,* a federation of former colonies established as a means to grant partial autonomy while keeping the empire together (Ageron 1994, 71–74). But this liberal gesture on the part of the French state was too late. While it resulted in a shift in the French relationship to the colonies from which there would be no return, many of the reforms proposed got bogged down in debate, and Algerian nationalist leaders had already determined that they would have to pursue a different path altogether.

Both failed and successful naturalization laws had lasting effects. The nonassimilation of the Muslims would become one of the main complaints of the Algerian nationalists, who found this especially galling in the case of the veterans of the two world wars. The conversion of hundreds of thousands of foreign Europeans to French men and women also had important consequences. This mass engineering of the social universe was not immediately embraced by everyone in the colony or in France, and with the laws' enactment, concerns spread regarding the "Frenchness" and the patriotism of the new French citizens.

NÉOS, THE "FOREIGN PERIL," AND ANTI-SEMITISM

Third Republic politicians were confident in the assimilating power of their nation, and believed that through their service in the military and participation in the educational system, the children born and raised on French soil would soon become assimilated to French culture and ideals (Brubaker 1992, 108–109). Not everyone in Algeria had such faith in this process, and people began to distinguish between the "pure" and the naturalized French: *néo-Français,* or *néos,* as they were called until the 1930s (Jordi 1986). Pejorative terms denoted individuals from mixed marriages, even between "native" and naturalized French (Sivan 1980). The loyalty of the large numbers of *néos,* ultimately representing at least half of the French population of Algeria, was questioned, and by the end of the nineteenth century, fear of a *péril étranger* (foreign peril) was widespread and foreign-origin colonists faced subtle but real discrimination (Ageron 1979,

121–24). The editor of the journal *Le temps,* for example, wrote in 1896, "The French-origin portion [of the population] is swamped . . . if things continue, it will be drowned . . . if we aren't careful, Algeria will soon be in the hands of the foreigners" (Crespo 1994, 130). During a hearing in December 1898 in the French Chamber, the "Frenchness" of Algeria's naturalized French citizens was questioned. The president of the council, M. Charles Dupuy, stated,

> Take the naturalized of yesterday, who profited by the law of 1889—were they old Frenchmen of France, these Italo-Frenchmen, these Neapolitan fishermen, perhaps ignorant of their duties toward France, but well acquainted with their fishery rights? These Spaniards of Oran, who had to be harangued in Spanish because they were ignorant of French—were they thorough Frenchmen?[14]

In 1899, members of the Algiers Masonic Order debated this and other laws conferring automatic naturalization and called for a modification of the electoral policies. According to the majority of those in attendance, individuals should not be allowed to vote unless they had solicited this right through formal channels, and only after *une enquête minutieuse* (a careful inquest). Many also felt that the electorate should be required to demonstrate ten years' residence in the colony and knowledge of spoken and written French (Dazet and Dupuy 1900).

The anti-Semitic movement of the late nineteenth century occurred in the middle of the "foreign peril" furor, and can be attributed in part to the status anxiety of the large *néo* contingent. In their desire for acceptance as full-fledged members of the elite status group, and sensitivity, no doubt, to challenges of their Frenchness by the "true" French elite, many naturalized colonists shifted attention away from themselves and onto the naturalized Jews. There is even evidence that more naturalized French than native French participated in this movement (Prochaska 1996, 696). Among them was Max Régis, a *néo* of Italian descent who became one of the leaders of the movement, and who was even elected mayor of Algiers in 1898. *Néos'* involvement in this movement is indicated in the following account of late-nineteenth-century anti-Semitism by a British traveler:

> Do the Spaniards and Italians that clamour in broken French or in their own vernacular against the Jews imagine that their own status will be benefited by the expulsion of the first of the non-French elements? Let them cherish no such illusion. (Wilkin 1900, 261)

The terrorization of the Jewish community by the more recently naturalized non-French can be seen as an attempt to deflect attention away from themselves and to demonstrate their Frenchness. Anti-Semitic attacks became proof in the eyes of some anti-Semites that they were even "more French than the French," one of their rallying cries.

The legacies of the *péril étranger* were lasting, and can be found in the settlers' participation in right-wing political movements in the 1930s, and even beyond. Mr. Caldi, a man from Philippeville of French, Spanish, and Maltese ancestry, talked to me one day about upward mobility in the colony and the process of becoming French. His paternal grandfather was from the Balearic Islands and arrived in Algeria as a young man. He volunteered for the World War I to gain French citizenship, and later became an ultranationalist, even joining the ultra-right party, the *Croix de feu*. Mr. Caldi thought it somewhat comical to remember this man shouting out of his window during parades and demonstrations in his thickly accented French, *"La France pour les Français!"* (France for the French). Such contradictions were widespread in the colony, he explained. One of his aunts used to always say, "I will never marry anyone who doesn't have a very, very French family name," but in the end married a man of Italian descent. "This is the strange thing about Algeria," he mused; "the most nationalist cities and neighborhoods were those with large working-class populations, mostly *étrangers,* like the Maltese or the Spanish. Oran, for instance, was really for maintaining a French Algeria." It is interesting, furthermore, that in recounting this pattern to me, he still shifted to the colonial usage associated with the *péril étranger,* describing these neighborhoods as made up of foreigners, when clearly, during the periods he was discussing (into the era of the French-Algerian War), naturalized French citizens would have predominated.

NOUS, LES ALGÉRIENS:
THE FUSION COMPLETED?

Migration from Europe to Algeria slowed considerably during the twentieth century, and every year more settlers were born in the colony. The late-nineteenth-century naturalization laws continued turning foreigners into French citizens: in 1886, the colonist population of Algeria was almost equally divided between French and non-French Europeans, but, by 1961, the non-French proportion had been reduced to 6 percent.[15] By then, 83 percent of the French in Algeria had been born there.

These naturalization laws had some immediate consequences: as French citizens, the *néos* were now able to participate in French institutions and apply for jobs in the constantly expanding civil service sector, the postal service, the railroads, public works, the prison system, and the police. Most of the people I interviewed had some relatives, either parents or grandparents, who had held such positions. They were also required to attend French public school and complete military service.

Education

The Ferry Laws of 1881 and 1882,[16] which made primary schooling free, mandatory, and secular in France, are often cited as one of the most important steps in turning France's diverse rural populations into French men and women (Weber 1976), although more recent research has shown that regional identities have persisted nevertheless (Reed-Danahay 1996). In a similar spirit of optimism, a decree of February 13, 1883, extended these laws to Algeria. Fanny Colonna points out that while these laws had emerged slowly in France, in Algeria the situation was quite different. Algerian schooling had been developed primarily for the European populations, but not very systematically, while education for Algerians had been a haphazard and largely neglected enterprise. Republicans in France wanted not only to extend these laws to Algeria, but to apply them uniformly to all children. From 1883 to 1890, moreover, they wanted to employ the same curriculum as primary schools in France. This policy was difficult to put into practice, because schools had to be built first, teachers trained, and an administrative structure put into place (Colonna 1975). Ultimately, separate school tracks emerged for the peasants and working classes and for the bourgeoisie, and most of the Arab and Berber children who participated in the French school system attended "indigenous" schools emphasizing practical and vocational education (Gosnell 2002, 47). This two-tiered system was in place until the fusion of the European and indigenous school tracks in 1949.

The results of this educational system were mixed. Like the naturalization laws, education was provided systematically only to the European populations, for a deep-seated ambivalence persisted regarding the education of "colonized" peoples. For the indigenous peoples, mandatory schooling came during the most intensely assimilationist period in Algerian history (1881–1896), involving a coherent set of laws that proved very destructive to the indigenous population.[17] Colonna suggests that it was in part in reaction to this era of increased repression that the indigenous Algerians engaged in passive resistance to colonialism by not sending their children to school until the 1920s (1975, 26). But even then, attendance continued to be extremely low: only 8.9 percent of Arab and Berber children were in school in 1936, and this number would increase to only 15.4 percent in 1954 (Gosnell 2002, 48).

A similar but far less marked gap in school attendance appeared between French and foreign settler children during the first decades of the free public school system. While many foreign settlers sent their children to primary school, few continued their education after that. In 1920, only two hundred foreigners were pursuing secondary education, although in the preceding years an average of thirty thousand had attended primary school. Clearly, many children quit school so that they could enter the workforce (Crespo 1994, 143–44), such as Joseph Zammit, who started working at age eleven following the death of his father. Because statistics do not separate students by ethnic origins, we cannot know if these differences persisted between "original" and "naturalized" French, but most of my elderly interviewees told me that their parents supported their education in primary school and often beyond.

Many see the Ferry laws as having an effect in Algeria similar to their effect in France, in that they helped to turn Italians, Maltese, and other foreign Europeans into French men and women. The two main emphases of the colonial educational program were the French language and French history. History textbooks often were the same as those used in France, and presented a sweeping overview of French history, highlighting especially the prerevolutionary period. Additional texts, prepared specifically for schoolchildren in Algeria, emphasized the intersection of Algerian and French histories, and outlined Algeria's geography in detail (Gosnell 2002; Bernard and Redon 1936). These texts instructed students in patriotism and love for France. However, Gosnell writes that "the distinction between the country where one lived and the *patrie* to which one was devoted was not always clear" (2002, 63).

To what degree did the educational system succeed in fostering a feeling of inclusion in the imagined French national community among naturalized French settler children? The *pieds-noirs* that I met in France had attended this colonial school system in the 1920s and 1930s. They told me about their powerful emotional attachments to France, which was for them the community of central concern, not Malta. Mr. Grech remembers in especially vivid language wholly embracing a sense of French national belonging that he learned early on in school. For him, France "eclipsed all else":

> OK, so, me, what did I learn . . . for me, Malta was really very, very far. Remember, it's far from Algiers! Hey, when you see Algiers, across from Marseilles, Malta is a thousand kilometers to the east. But what I mean is it was far geographically, but far in time, and also far psychologically. Because here, and I think I'm telling you something that isn't true only for the Maltese . . . When we were in Algiers we looked north, we looked to France. You see? And, I'm not saying that we weren't interested in our country, but we weren't taught very much about our . . . our country. We were taught a bit here and there, but on a very superficial level. We weren't taught about our origins, but, on the other hand, we knew, . . . this, this is the strength of the French

educational system. Here, I'll give an example which is . . . everything I'm telling you is true, huh? OK. I was a very sensitive little boy, who cried easily, and, in 1940, when I was five, I would cry while singing "*Je vais revoir ma Normandie; c'est le pays qui m'a donné le jour.*" I was crying because it's a song . . . well, it was during the war, we had lost, all that, and there was a very sad atmosphere, and so forth, but, this is to show you that I sang that mechanically, like a child, but it moved me, I had tears when singing "I am going to see *my* Normandy . . ." But I had *never* seen Normandy—well, I had never even crossed the Mediterranean! This example is . . . it's a little like when, they say, the little black kids used to sing "Our ancestors the Gauls." In my case, I could have been saying "My ancestors the Normans," even though I had never been to France. But we were brought up to *worship* France. France, for us, was . . . was . . . a *divinity.* You see? And, so, France eclipsed all else.

Despite Malta's physical propinquity to Algeria, Grech viewed Malta as remote compared to France. Whether this view stemmed primarily from their contact with French pedagogical materials or from other factors is difficult to determine. Yet a strong connection to the *patrie,* the fatherland or national community, was widespread among the *pieds-noirs* I met, and is also evidenced by their pride in their own military service and in the strong service records of their ancestors.

Military Service

In the official melting pot narrative, military service is identified as one of the principal elements of the "fusion," with World War I service presented as a turning point in this process. Certainly, practical aspects of service during this time, as in any other war—the mixing together of recruits from different regions and ethnic groups of Algeria as well as their exposure to France—helped reduce the gulf between the various European ethnic groups in Algeria. War service in 1914–1918 also served as a psychological turning point for both the *Français de France* and the *néos,* particularly so soon after the *péril étranger* crisis. The French had the evidence they needed of the real loyalty of the recently naturalized. In turn, the *néos* now had the best proof possible of their true fealty to the nation: their military service. It may be in part for this reason that during World War I, the newly naturalized French of Algeria accepted their enlistment and there were few problems with recruitment, proving wrong the xenophobes in Algeria and France. In addition, many non-French Europeans volunteered in large numbers to fight for this nation which was not yet theirs. Meynier estimates that 60 percent of the foreigners of draft age in Algeria who could have avoided the war decided to serve and in the process become French. Overall, approximately seventy-three thousand European-origin troops from Algeria were mobilized (Meynier 1981, 601), of whom twenty-two thousand perished (Heggoy and Haar 1984, 40). The extreme patriotism of those settlers who remained behind can be viewed as their own expression of their Frenchness. After the battle of Verdun, for example, parades and demonstrations went on for weeks even in the remotest villages of Algeria, and funeral processions and mass commemorations of the dead were elaborate (Meynier 1981, 603). School textbooks linked foreigner assimilation to military service overtly, as we see in a passage from 1936:

> There is reason to add that a large number of foreigners, born in Algeria or permanently settled there, have become French thanks to the naturalization laws. They are sincerely attached to their new *Patrie*. All behaved valiantly during the great war of 1914–18. Already French by law, they have become even more so through the common experience of perils and spilled blood. (Bernard and Redon 1936, 192–93)

What is of special interest here is the fact that several decades after the naturalization laws and the "foreign peril," the authors still felt a need to demonstrate to French Algerian schoolchildren that the naturalized French were really and truly French. Their French citizenship was not enough; *néos* had to risk the ultimate sacrifice to demonstrate that they deserved membership in the national community.

Popular Culture

Newspapers, like primary school texts, both reflected local sentiment and helped produce ideas about France and Frenchness. As Gosnell reports, "In doing so, the French-language Algerian press participated in the formation of French men and women" (2002, 74). Readers of the colonial presses would encounter stories about trivial events that typified metropolitan daily life, accounts of sporting events such as the Tour de France, political developments in France and across Europe, and even the celebration of national holidays on both sides of the Mediterranean. As a result, they would be subtly guided into imagining a world in which France was the centerpiece, and a degree of cultural assimilation undoubtedly occurred in this way.

Novelists also helped construct an image of the colonial universe. Already by the 1870s, writers were exploring the possibility that a "new race" was being forged in the "crucible" of Africa, and this idea became widespread by the 1880s. In part as a reaction against the Orientalism of much French literature concerning North African topics, French writers in Algeria began to write novels that illustrated Algeria as they experienced it. Louis Bertrand is one of the best known (and most infamous) of these authors promoting *algérianité,* or Algerianness. In works such as *Pépète le bien-aimé* (1904), he promoted the idea of a Latin Africa, popularizing the idea that the French colonial mission in North Africa was a continuation of the Roman conquest, and therefore that Latin civilization was the first, true civilization of North Africa (Lorcin 1995, 201).[18] The novels of this movement celebrated especially the poorer classes of settlers, depicting Maltese, Neapolitan, and *Mahonnais* masons and cart-drivers sitting around drinking after work. While the figures in Bertrand's texts are in many ways caricatures, his writings clearly describe a world rife with real economic and social disparities. They also reproduced to a certain extent the spoken language of the period, called *pataouète.*[19] Already by the 1880s, authors were noting the formation of a new language from the mixture of the languages and dialects spoken by the European and indigenous people of Algeria (e.g., Ricoux 1880, 276). Not unlike the "Native American" political parties of the early-nineteenth-century United States, *Algérianiste* writers claimed a new identity, that of the *Algériens,* positioning themselves as the true "natives" of the new land. In this brazen claim that *Algériens* were a new people forged under the Mediterranean sun, they symbolically wrested Algeria from its owners. Many of these works were also overtly anti-Semitic or relegated Jews to the indigenous category.[20] Through cultural productions and their widespread dissemination, a distinct consciousness and identity were developing.

Upward Mobility

Finally, economic assimilation is sometimes identified as yet another stage in the "fusion" of the foreign Europeans into the French settler contingent (Jordi 1986, 276). Certainly immigrants' adaptation to a new economic system is one of the first important changes they must make. It is quite another matter for them to attain economic parity with the ruling elite, however. Many sources from the twentieth century provide anecdotal evidence of the rapid ascension to considerable wealth of some settlers of Spanish, Maltese, and Italian origin. By the turn of the century in Oran, Spanish laborers were no longer being employed in difficult manual jobs; Moroccans had by this time replaced them. The community was no longer mired in poverty, and Spanish-origin settlers were working as artisans, businessmen, sailors, carpenters, and even doctors and lawyers, and those naturalized often held positions as police officers and teachers (Jordi 1996). In eastern Algeria at the dawn of independence, many Italian-origin French men and women were also moving out of extreme poverty and some were even becoming wealthy, although scholars find that most still lived modestly (Crespo 1994, 163–66). The Maltese in this region were starting to purchase plots of land from concessionaires,[21] and many of the parents of my informants were establishing themselves with private businesses in the 1920s and 1930s: as dairy farmers, bakers, or livestock traders; in the latter profession they could become quite wealthy. This upward mobility is alluded to in a 1920s geography text, which states that while the Maltese were "pretty crude in their behavior upon arrival, they adapted fairly fast . . . they arrive at a comfortable living, even fortune; in Algiers and in the Department of Constantine some Maltese commercial businesses are among the most sound" (Allain 1923, 291).

Despite the attainment by some people of great wealth, there is considerable evidence that the bulk of the non-French-origin settlers remained a distinct subaltern group. In his landmark work, *Making Algeria French,* Prochaska has demonstrated the persistence of marked social and economic distinctions in the city of Bône (now Annaba) between French and non-French colonists well into the twentieth century, even between "original" and naturalized French (Prochaska 1990). In this town, a hub of Maltese settlement, Italian and Maltese migrants outnumbered the French until the naturalization law of 1889. While the official documents Prochaska uses do not distinguish between different European ethnicities, they do identify French, naturalized French, non-French European, and Jewish settlers, allowing for revealing comparisons. Regarding occupational segregation, Prochaska found that Algerians were more likely to work the land than Europeans, while Jews were less likely to work the land, and were underrepresented relative to their numbers in some fields, such as food preparation, building and construction, and home furnishings. Native French had a virtual monopoly on jobs in government, the military, and the liberal professions, such as medicine and law, as we saw in Guelma previously. They were more likely to work in commerce than naturalized or non-French Europeans, and were less likely to work in menial jobs. They dominated in "modern," technically advanced trades. All mines, and industries such as flour mills and transportation companies, were French-owned. In contrast, in 1904 and 1907, Maltese and Italians were less likely to own a business than were the native French. The ones that did carved out their own niches: Italians were in construction, and Maltese were in farming, sold foodstuffs, and were peddlers. There was unequal pay for equal work, with Italians and Maltese earning less than French did across the board from 1904 to 1907, but more than Algerians. Finally, non-naturalized Europeans were closer to the indigenous population than to the French in terms of their relative proportion of white and blue collar workers (Prochaska 1990).

Marked social segregation between French- and non-French-origin settlers persisted in Bône, despite the fact that increasing numbers of both populations by this time had been born there. This can be seen in continued residential segregation. Jews were segregated longer than any other group, in an area surrounding the synagogue. Among the European immigrants, Prochaska finds an overrepresentation of the native French in the newer and more select neighborhoods. In sum, the "non-French," which included large numbers of naturalized French citizens, constituted a large "European colony within the French colony." While the "non-French" were certainly closer to the French in socioeconomic status than to the Algerians, Prochaska writes that the "Algerians were not the only ones whom the French colonialized" (Prochaska 1990, 124). Prochaska's findings correspond with eyewitness accounts from later in the twentieth century, which indicate continued distinctions between settlers based on ethnic origin. Residential segregation, for example, persisted in many cities: many children of the Italians, Spanish, and Maltese lived in working-class neighborhoods along the coast. In the late 1920s, the Italian quarter of Algiers was still the Marine, which was referred to as *le petit Naples* (little Naples), while Bab-el-Oued was *la petite Espagne* (little Spain). We have already seen Arnaud's descriptions of the neighborhood of Maltese shepherds in Bône. Writing about Algiers in 1955, Pelletier says, "The social classes are not mixed, because there exists a fairly rigid residential segregation of the population" (quoted in Crespo 1994, 170).

EXCLUSION, INCLUSION, AND IMMIGRANT AGENCY

It remains to be seen to what degree the newly naturalized French of Maltese origin embraced their new nationality, and if this new identity allowed them space for a continued connection to their ethnic heritage. This is a question of more general concern. In France today, the risks posed to traditional notions of Frenchness by some citizens' maintenance of distinct cultural practices is hotly debated. As Noiriel writes, "the question posed is whether immigrants can succeed in integrating into a national society while at the same time preserving their culture of origin" (1996, xix). Dominant ideologies of host countries or colonizing powers are not necessarily adopted wholly, or imposed only by force. In her study of Navajo language and culture, Deborah House highlights the ways Navajo society exhibits a simultaneous attraction to and repulsion from elements of the dominant culture. Yet Navajo adoption of practices of the dominant society often go unrecognized: "it is clear that long-term and persistent hegemonic incorporation has taken place," she writes (2002, 24). This adoption has been motivated in part by an attempt to gain access to the more attractive aspects of the dominant society. The simultaneous mimesis and alterity that House describes for the Navajo seems particularly apt for understanding the position of immigrants as well. For many immigrants, assimilation becomes a crucial choice, and instances abound of children's rejecting their culture of origin to avoid stigmatization, evidenced by name changes, hypercorrect language skills, and suppression of other ethnic boundary markers. This is not merely a question of coping with prejudicial attitudes: newcomers and marginalized groups at the bottom of a socioeconomic hierarchy often shed the most obvious markers of difference to escape from grinding poverty. As Steinberg writes, "When ethnicity is associated with class disadvantage—with poverty, hardship, a low standard of living and so on—then powerful inducements exist for the members of such groups to assimilate into the mainstream culture, since this will improve their chances for a better life" (1989, 256). Perhaps moving out of poverty was the primary motivation for the Maltese to become *assimilationistes extraordinaires.* The question remains as to what degree adoption of such norms represented a conscious choice that has remained a public transcript (Scott 1990), and to what degree complete hegemonic incorporation ensued.

FIVE

The Ambivalence of Assimilation

THE MELTING POT METAPHOR
IN FAMILY NARRATIVES

A group's social memory develops not in a vacuum but in relation to other representations of the past generated by an array of sources, such as professional historians, school texts, public discourse, popular culture, family members, and religious organizations. Some of these representations are promulgated by organizations closely related to the government or hegemonic status groups, while others may remain confined to a neighborhood or even a few families. The dynamic interaction between dominant and subaltern, and public and private, representations of the past is especially apparent when we turn to the colonial assimilation experience. The assimilation of the non-French-origin settlers to French nationality and culture in the colony is represented by a remarkably consistent and well disseminated dominant narrative summarized by the melting pot metaphor, as we have seen, and elements of this narrative even emerge in oral accounts of the Maltese-origin former settlers. In fact, some ways of talking about this experience are so similar to those found in printed texts that they likely involve an incorporation of the dominant memory, a narrative perhaps first learned at school, into the subaltern repertoire. Underlying and contradicting this version of the past, however, is another version of this same past, based more on private, family stories of difficulty and discrimination. These memories of discrimination sometimes surface only obliquely as a counter-narrative undermining the speaker's main point. On other occasions, the difficulties of assimilation became the overt topic of discussion as the elderly settlers grappled with their sometimes internally inconsistent views of the past. At least two distinct and even mutually exclusive perspectives can be identified in these narratives, and may be articulated by the same person in the same speech event: French Algeria was a melting pot that blended all of the colonists of different origins into a new colonist culture, one "voice" asserts, while the other claims that ethnicity and class were prominent social categories that divided the colonists into distinct, identifiable, and ranked subgroups.

My taped interviews with family members often followed a similar narrative structure that I call the "immigrant family narrative." This is an optimistic tale of the assimilation process as illustrated by family stories. Once people had established with genealogical data exactly when their first ancestors migrated to Algeria and from where, they followed with stories of their hardships. They informed me at length about the difficult lives of the early "pioneers," describing the hazards of disease, deaths during childbirth, and, above all, the relentless hard work required to survive in this difficult environment. "My father's father never took a day off in his life. He was a *petit agriculteur*. He worked every day from three A.M. until sundown until the day of his death," one woman told me.

Tales of the upward mobility of the succeeding generations followed. Rapid assimilation was a feature particular to the Maltese, as Michel told me: "The first to arrive were day laborers who worked extremely hard. They pushed their children to work hard at school so they could move into high-level administrative and other positions." To illustrate the rapid integration and assimilation of the Maltese, many of my informants enumerated the occupations of the men of each generation of their families, usually starting with their Maltese grandparents. Mr. Grech, the former club leader and retired lawyer, stated,

> It's important to know that the Maltese have a real capacity for assimilation, in just two generations. Yes, they have an ability to . . . to progress. OK, now I get to brag a little . . . My grandfather, huh, he had a grocery store, he made anchovies. OK! And the . . . well, I won't talk about the girls, because the girls during that time didn't go on to higher studies . . . My father was a broker. His brother was a broker. Another brother had a wholesale grocery business, and another was in banking. Already, that's one generation. The second generation, that's mine. OK, lawyer, doctor of law. And I have a cousin who is a *polytechnicien* . . . another is a pharmacist, another was a military general, another is an engineer . . . In, in, in, in *two* generations!

Since Mr. Grech grew up in Algiers, the occupations he outlined were those more characteristic of urban areas. Families who had settled in rural regions delineated a different trajectory: goat herder, milkman, head of a dairy enterprise; or itinerant farm worker, truck farmer, vineyard owner. Mr. Caldi's grandfather was a Philippeville porter; his son became a wine salesman and later ran a hardware store. His son, in turn, was a pharmacist. "*Voilà* the social progression," he concluded. By the time of their own arrival into the world, many told me, their "bed was already made." While they too worked hard their whole lives, my interviewees had been born into a more economically secure environment than their parents or grandparents.

In the process of recounting these stories, elderly former settlers of all backgrounds glossed their history through the use of the "melting pot" metaphor. After talking about the different European immigrant populations and their concentrations in specific occupational niches in Algeria, they would turn to me and say, "Well, you know, it was a melting pot, like your country." The first few times I heard this, I thought that the speakers were resorting to this famous metaphor for U.S. immigration history primarily in response to my presence: in trying to illustrate their ancestors' pasts in a way that I could understand, they were taking advantage of a widely shared perception of the history of my part of the world. But this image came up so often that it soon became clear that this was their way of depicting the history of French Algeria as well. They explained that over the decades, the boundaries between the various European populations slowly began to dissolve, the cultures began to merge together, and a new culture arose. Like the historical texts reviewed previously, speakers also used the melting pot metaphor directly by talking about assimilation in the Algerian melting pot (*le creuset*), or indirectly by using verbs such as *fondre,* to melt, as in "we all melted together." Colonial Algeria was described as a *mélange des races* (a mixture of races/peoples), a *fusion* (fusion). Sometimes a "stock pot" variant was used, and people discussed how they were all "mixed together" (*mêlés*) as if in a large cauldron.

The use of this metaphor conjured up a narrative that, in its telling, doubly bound together the former settlers from all parts of Algeria, and of all origins. They shared not only a common past, but also a particular orientation to that past. This iteration of the colonial past was especially prominent during conversations at large and more formal gatherings of *pieds-noirs,* and at the earlier stages of long taped interviews. At the annual meeting of former residents of Bône (now Annaba) at the Maison one cold February afternoon, I found myself seated at a table with people of various ethnic origins who were meeting me and each other for the first time. Mr. Frendo, a man in his early seventies, was telling me about his efforts to trace his family back to Malta. A younger woman who had traveled there by motorcycle with her non-*pied-noir* husband joined in. I asked Mr. Frendo about Algeria. Were there any ethnic neighborhoods, or Maltese communities there? "Well," he answered, "Bône was a wonderful small city. The people came from all over. Such a range of religions and races. But we were all mixed, we were French first and Maltese second. We went to French schools, of course, and that is how we were mixed, how we melted together" (*nous nous sommes fondus*). The chic younger couple began to take part in the discussion, and the young woman concurred. "Yes, we were all mixed (*mélangés*), that was the beauty of Algeria."

One conclusion that could be drawn from the close parallels in the spoken and written accounts is that this version represents the primary "truth," with the written "official" and spoken "subaltern" representations corresponding nicely. The elderly former settlers I met were all native French speakers who were also French citizens at birth, as were most of their parents and many of their grandparents, so one could easily imagine that assimilation had never been a difficult issue for them. However, in recounting these stories, they sometimes presented clues, such as the use of ethnicity as a primary social category, which suggested otherwise. These clues within the standard official narratives alert us to the existence of another, quite contrasting, representation of the same past.

CLUES TO A CONTRASTING MEMORY

The standard immigrant narrative, summarized by the melting pot metaphor, was optimistic, uncontroversial, and, I soon found after listening to several iterations, somewhat uninteresting. However, in narrating the very stories meant to illustrate how thoroughly everyone had "melted" together to form a new French culture, one in which former distinctions between colonists were no longer relevant, people used terms that indicated that this colonial society was understood as organized by ethnicity and class. The marking of the social universe by individuals' national origins was a feature even of stories meant to illustrate how little these distinctions mattered, as in the following conversation with Mr. Mifsud. I had mistakenly started this conversation by asking him how it felt to be Maltese when he was growing up in Algiers, thus eliciting a long monologue in which he first made it quite clear to me that he was, and always had been, a French citizen. Furthermore, he added, nobody cared about ethnic origins in Algeria; they were completely irrelevant:

> You see? Between Italians, French, Maltese, Greeks, uh, I never heard . . . There was a real cohesion. And during the war, in '42, in '40, well, '42, we were all mobilized, we all served in the war . . . Italians, French, well, French, of course, but of French, Italian, and Spanish origins, without difficulties. We served . . . without even know—without even *thinking* that we were of foreign origins.

This passage is interesting because Mr. Mifsud twice backtracked to revise his story. In the first sentence he used the national origins of the individuals, e.g., *Italiens, Français* (Italians, French), as I had, as a shorthand to refer to individuals of these ethnic heritages. Technically, this usage is incorrect, for the people he was referring to, as enlisted men in the French army, were undoubtedly French citizens. This is not an insignificant error. Since the French Revolution, there has been great disapproval in France of distinguishing "groups" of people by religion, ethnicity, or race. Even today, plural identities such as "Italo-French" or "Portuguese-French" are rare and viewed with suspicion (Gross, McMurray, and Swedenburg 1996, 128; see also Blum 2002), in contrast to the United States, where such labels as "Italian-American" appear frequently and without overt negative valence. French society officially comprises only citizens and foreigners, and the latter are further distinguished by their nationalities, if at all. Viewed in this context, settlers' use of ethnic labels in this way is doubly aberrant: not only are they choosing not to identify people by both labels (as in "Italian-American" or "Maltese-French"), but they are choosing the ethnic heritage as the only label of note, a speech practice analogous to referring to "Italian-Americans" as simply "Italians." Perhaps Mr. Mifsud recognized that he was employing nonstandard usage, for he corrected himself to more closely match official usage, referring to them instead as people of French or Spanish origins, as we see in the next-to-last sentence. But he then corrected himself a second time. After beginning to tell me that they did not even know that they were of foreign origins, he altered his statement to indicate instead that they did not even think about these origins. To further illustrate this point, he exclaimed further on in the same interview, "There were Spanish who did not even speak Spanish anymore!"

Mr. Mifsud's statements are internally contradictory. If ethnic distinctions had been thoroughly erased, he presumably would not have known the origins of the people in these stories. If the individuals who he says did not speak Spanish anymore were so thoroughly "blended in," for instance, how could he possibly know that they were Spanish in origin? Did he instead know at some level, perhaps in further consideration of their last names, and was able to acknowledge this fact only later in life? As we have seen, the ethnic marking of the colonial social world was widespread, suggesting the continued salience of ethnicity in the colony. Former colonists of all backgrounds—elite, middle, and lower socioeconomic class status, "French-origin" and "foreign-origin"—identified each other in this ethnically marked way. Even the naturalized French, such as the military recruits in Mr. Mifsud's story, remained identifiable as members of distinct European ethnicities.

A SUBALTERN SETTLER MEMORY

People discussed additional aspects of the assimilation process that indicated a less optimistic counterpoint to the melting pot iteration. These narratives suggest that assimilation was not automatic. Instead, it was a process that the interlocutors observed, and one in which they and their ancestors played very active roles. Most were proud of the efforts made by their ancestors toward greater social, economic, and cultural integration, but at the same time their narratives express considerable ambivalence toward this process, what it required of them or their relatives, and their reasons for making such great efforts in this direction in the first place.

Arriving in Algeria extremely poor, many Maltese came to quick conclusions about what it would take to advance. While some undoubtedly focused on improving their social or linguistic capital, the majority seem to have worked first on improving their economic status. Mr. Grech invited me to come visit when his eighty-seven-year-old uncle was in town, whom he thought I should interview. Mr. Farrugia told fascinating stories of the twenties and thirties in the colony. Orphaned at a young age, he was raised by elderly grandparents, and explained his early decision to become "successful":

> When I was thirteen or so [in 1921] I was walking in Constantine on the Boulevard de Bésillon—it's near my house, next to the town hall—and I was looking at night, there, the balconies were open, at a dining room with chandeliers. For me, it was like that. I said to myself, "I am going to work hard so one day I can have a chandelier at my house." It isn't much, but it is progress. I wanted . . . wanted to be somebody.

Many explained that their grandparents' lives were dominated by work. The Maltese were tireless, "*increvables*" (impossible to defeat), one man emphasized. "They worked harder than anyone," his wife added. "If you needed some physical work done, you hired a Maltese." Many confessed that they never got to know their grandparents because they were always working. The earliest ancestors were all *morts à la tâche,* they said (had all died on the job).

These indefatigable workers succeeded as well through incredible thrift, and many perhaps apocryphal stories indicated this "Maltese" trait. I heard more than once the story of the Maltese man who went to his wedding in Algeria wearing the shoes he had worn at his communion; he had been too cheap to buy another pair. Another tale was that of the poor Maltese couple who arrived with nothing, worked incessantly, and died at an early age. Upon their deaths, in putting their parents' meager belongings in order, their children found to their amazement a stash of gold coins they had saved, buried in the wall of the home. Interestingly enough, the hoarding of money in the home was common in early modern Maltese society (see Ciappara 2001, 265). Another man told me that even after achieving considerable wealth, his father continued to work in the fields, right in front of the hired workers. This way, his father had told him, he could get more work out of his laborers, for they had to keep up with their tireless boss.

But it was not enough to become wealthy. The awkward place of the Maltese who had achieved wealth at the cost of investing in any cultural capital was beautifully illustrated by a story I heard one day at a settler cocktail party. Michel Pisani told us about a Maltese man he knew in his rural village. This man had worked a tiny plot of land year after year, first clearing the brush, then fertilizing the soil, and eventually managing to grow vegetables for the market. He and his wife worked day in, day out. They finally bought adjoining lots and soon had a handsome estate. Even into his old age, he spent his days working in the fields, wearing a big straw hat. One day some French people came over to his land, asking to speak to the owner. "Where is the patron?" they shouted out to the man. The old man shouted back in broken French, "*Le patron au village! Le patron au village!*" ("The owner in village"). As Michel explained to us, the man did not want the visitors to know that he, in fact, was the owner of the fine estate, and pretended that he was a simple worker in order to hide his poor French language skills.

I heard a similar story from Mr. Raynaud, a settler of French heritage who grew up near Mr. Pisani, and who had worked for years for the local Department of Agriculture. One of his research projects entailed interviewing vineyard owners in the area surrounding Guelma to determine which species of plants were being developed successfully and where. He told me he remembered arriving at a very large farm, with beautiful rows of vines, and asking to be directed to the owner. Mr. Raynaud was astonished to find that the man, of Maltese origin, who owned and operated this successful estate could barely speak any French at all. When Raynaud asked him which roots he had on his vines, he replied "*cinq sous, cinq sous*" (five pennies) instead of the correct "*cinsault.*" For another part of the plant, instead of the proper term "*mourvedre,*" he had memorized and responded "*mars verts*" (green March). When Raynaud asked him what kind of fertilizer he was using on the fields, the owner had to ask one of his Arab workers to translate the question for him. This wealthy landowner could barely speak French, let alone read or write it, but had managed to run the entire estate thanks to his fluency in Arabic and by memorizing simple phrases in French for terms essential for his work.

These tales of wealth at all costs suggest a particular kind of upward mobility. Many Maltese obviously felt that attempting to assimilate through the channels highlighted in the dominant narrative of French colonial assimilation, first politically through naturalization and then socially through the educational system and military service, would yield uncertain results. They may have been sensitive to the racism inherent in the early French anti-Maltese attitudes, and perhaps felt too "marked" either racially or culturally to attempt political or social assimilation. Instead, they calculated that they could more reliably attain a certain level of comfort through economic success.

ERASING SIGNS OF DIFFERENCE

In many of the stories I heard of wealthy ancestors, the efforts of these forebears were described as extreme, and one gets a sense of a desperation underlying all this hard work. The Galeas told me that many Maltese, including Mr. Galea's aunts, were motivated to earn more than a moderate income by the anti-Maltese discrimination they faced daily:

MR. GALEA: So, at the beginning, this kind of distrust, little by little, turned into contempt [*mépris*] for the Maltese. So these Maltese *had* to go to school, learn, evolve, or otherwise have money, and become *very* rich. And in these cases, the French, due to the fact that they were rich . . .

MRS. GALEA: . . . accepted . . .

MR. GALEA: . . . that these were good people. That they were decent people. And the *Français de France*, those working in the administration, married these Maltese girls because they had dowries and lots of money.

MRS. GALEA: Your grandfather's sisters, that's exactly what happened . . .

MR. GALEA: It's what happened to all of grandfather's sisters . . . So, naturally, the sisters of my grandfather, who were among the elite, got rid of their language, and spoke only French. Saying, we are French . . .

MRS. GALEA: . . . and anyhow, they became French citizens . . .

MR. GALEA: . . . and they got rid of their origins . . .

AUTHOR: I see. They never . . . taught their children [Maltese].

MRS. GALEA: No, no, no.

MR. GALEA: They were sophisticated, part of the *bourgeoisie*. You see?

Here, Mr. Galea and his wife present another facet of the experience. Mr. Galea's great-grandparents had to accumulate a certain amount of wealth to marry off their daughters to French men; this was apparently their strategy for familial upward mobility. These women, then, embraced their new nationality practically with a vengeance. We can see, too, the linkages made between class status and ethnicity, and how becoming French was equated with attaining elite status. A foreign—or Maltese—ethnic heritage was a stigma that could prove quite damaging to one's social standing.

Other families followed similar strategies. Surnames were immediately recognizable markers of Maltese ethnicity, and while women such as those in Mr. Galea's family would shed such liabilities upon marrying French or other non-Maltese men, Maltese men could not do so. Some were so embarrassed by their names that they "frenchified" them. Reversing the letters was a common strategy among those with last names beginning with an X, such as "Xuereb"; in reverse, it becomes a "respectable"-sounding "Bereux." People who didn't change their names sometimes developed elaborate explanations for their origins. Echoing the oppositional linguistic ideology that helped define them as European, many Maltese-origin settlers today subscribe to equally fanciful invented traditions that may stem from a similar desire for respectability. I was told that "Borg," for instance, was Swedish in origin, "Micalef" was Russian, and "Cauchi" was French, and that these surnames derived from the multinational Knights of Malta, recognized members of the European nobility (while, according to scholars, the names "Borg" and "Micalef" predate the arrival of the Knights; see Wettinger 2000). Especially revealing of this group's negotiation between multiple identities is the polysemy I sometimes encountered in such explanations, a polysemy that surely stems from their limited social status and the stigma associated with all things Maltese in some circles. A few people proposed more than one origin for their surnames, such as Mr. Mifsud, whom I have taped asserting once that it was Maltese, and on another occasion that it was derived from the French.

Strategies for securing legitimacy sometimes backfired, however. Mr. Raynaud recounted a terrible faux pas committed by one of the wealthiest Maltese women in his area. She was the daughter of a brothel owner, and had been widowed after her husband's death in World War I. As Raynaud explained, she lived in "a magnificent building, right in the center of Philippeville. A three-story building with archways. There were pillars and marble statues inside. It was quite elegant." He then outlined her predicament:

> She was upset because the army had occupied some of her property. She got in touch with me to find out how she could see the regional prefect of Constantine. At that moment I was working there, so . . . I arranged for her to meet him. She came to complain that she needed money, that her husband [was a casualty of the war] and all, and she arrived at the meeting absolutely covered in furs, rings, and bracelets. *Voilà* the Maltese personality. It's a bit bizarre. There were some who were more socially adept. But she didn't have natural class, you see, she wasn't raised properly, and thus she thought she could make up for it with jewelry and furs.

Mr. Raynaud explained that it was preposterous to claim poverty dressed in such a manner, and he wasn't surprised when her plea fell on deaf ears.

In the process of severing ties to Malta, the language, too, was quickly lost. For most of the elderly people I met from Algeria, this occurred as early as in their parents' generation. This language shift was often a strategic choice. Mr. Mifsud and his wife were members of the second generation born in Algeria. He told me emphatically that in his family there was never any question of speaking Maltese. Even his parents refused to speak it:

> And why? Because the Maltese, among others, wanted so *much* to integrate that they wanted to speak *good* French. And anyhow, my wife will tell you; at her house, when they wanted to speak Corsican or Italian, they said, "No, we speak French! Here it is France!" So that they wouldn't be viewed as foreigners, they wanted to speak good French . . . they spoke French out of preference, they tried to integrate.

While their grandparents or great-grandparents focused almost exclusively on economic advances, never stopping for schooling, and thus could barely communicate in French, the next generation ceased speaking Maltese altogether, and even the most minimal terms and phrases were lost, a pattern typical of that generation. So few Maltese of Algeria learned the language that the elderly individuals who did speak it were sometimes viewed with suspicion, as we saw in the case of François' cousin from Tunis. Knowledge of their Maltese identity, let alone linguistic or other cultural attributes that might mark them as "non-French," was carefully denied by the following generation so that, over time, such cultural knowledge was lost forever. At the same time, many of the men who grew up in rural areas or who farmed spoke Arabic, like Mr. Sultana. When I asked Michel about his fluency in this language, he replied simply, "Of course I speak it. I was born there, lived there, and if you wanted to go to the market, or talk with people, you just picked it up."

MULTIVOCALITY IN
COLONIST NARRATIVES

Some scholars have already noted that oral history and social memory research is dialogical in nature in that it is created out of a conversation between interviewee and interviewer (Roche and Taranger 1995, 24–25; Portelli 1997, 3). We can move past the wider interview setting now to consider how the concept of dialogism applies to the structure and composition of these conversations.[1] The Russian philosopher and linguist Mikhail Bakhtin argued that because each individual utterance is responding to preceding utterances, speech becomes polyphonic. No matter how monological it seems at first glance, each utterance will be in some ways a response to what has already been said, and thus will be filled with other voices or discourses, the "half-concealed . . . words of others" (Bakhtin 1986, 91, 93). He also highlighted the ongoing struggle between centripetal and centrifugal forces that are always at work in any given language and society. Centripetal forces, such as state language policies and the fixing of language in print, work at unifying the "verbal-ideological world" (Bakhtin 1981, 270). At the same time, centrifugal forces, such as the development of particular ways of speaking associated with different occupational, ethnic, and regional subgroups, encourage heterogeneity, stratifying language into multiple linguistic codes, each representing distinct points of view on the world. In any given historical moment, each generation at each social level has its own language, as does each age group, profession, and so forth: "these different world views may be juxtaposed to one another, mutually supplement one another, contradict one another, and be interrelated dialogically" (Bakhtin 1981, 291), leading to a phenomenon known as multivocality. We can communicate with each other because we are able to identify and understand these multiple perspectives or "voices" that are necessarily present in any speech setting and, according to Bakhtin, even in the speech of any one individual.

It follows that everyday discourse about the past, like discourse on any other subject, will contain multiple perspectives and voices. Such narratives may in fact provide examples of multivocality *par excellence.* Not only will members of each society share a multitude of stories and perspectives on the past that should be identifiable due to their distinctive style, composition, thematic content, and ideological flavor, but also other voices may be even more prevalent here than in other kinds of discourse as the speakers touch on previous themes and prior points of view. Such distinctions will be evident in the two principal "voices" I identify in the Maltese-origin *pied-noir* narratives about intermarriage.

STORIES OF INTERMARRIAGE: WHEN MEMORIES COLLIDE

I. Everyone intermarried. There were no more Maltese. After my father, everyone married people of different backgrounds. In Algiers, people intermarried, and there wasn't a Maltese "colony."

II. [Later in the same interview]: In Algiers, people didn't like the Maltese at all, to such an extent that I had a friend, of French origins, his name was Crétois . . . every day I went to fetch him, we went to school together, and [one day] his mother said, "Are you Maltese, you?" and I said, "Why do you ask me that?" And she said, "Because if you are Maltese, I don't want to you play with Georges anymore." So I said, "No, I'm not Maltese"—I lied— "I'm Corsican," and he was my best friend! The Maltese had a reputation, I don't know why, but I know there was a bad stereotype of the Maltese in Algeria.

Mr. Camilleri

Intermarriage is sometimes viewed as a litmus test of social integration and features prominently, along with the schools and the military, in the official narrative of the great assimilating forces of colonial Algeria (Baroli 1967, 254). Historians have claimed that, at least after World War I, members of the different European ethnicities stopped their former practice of marrying primarily members of their own group and intermarriage became common (Ageron 1991, 55). The "melting together," then, occurred through the actual mixing of genes. Intermarriage thus serves both as proof that colonist distinctions were no longer significant socially, and as a process that facilitated the further blurring of ethnic boundaries.

Like these historical texts, the elderly *pieds-noirs* also claimed that "everyone" intermarried, citing as examples marriages in their own families. This was quite a pervasive theme in my interviews with colonists of all backgrounds, who often contrasted this marriage pattern with the nearly complete absence of intermarriage across religious lines (i.e., between the European Christian settlers and either Algerian/French Jews or Muslims). But, while intermarriage between naturalized French of different European origins was often cited in such stories, I met only two couples, the Pisanis and the Galeas (out of over thirty), that represented a union between French-origin and Maltese-origin families, the two ethnic groups at the opposing poles of the settler hierarchy. In each of their interviews, the couples first asserted the dominant view that intermarriage was common and of no notable consequence. But, over the course of these taped conversations, the spouses of Maltese origin (in one case, the husband; in the other, the wife) eventually contradicted this assessment, presenting a different argument and using, as illustration, accounts of their own marriages.

These discussions are rife with contradictions, and the passages highlight the multivocality that characterizes stories of assimilation among this population. Two voices are clearly identifiable. The first voice, which we may refer to as the "official" or "melting pot" voice, illustrated by the first part of the quotation from Mr. Camilleri at the beginning of this section ("Everyone intermarried. There were no more Maltese"), represents the hegemonic viewpoint, asserting that colonist assimilation was complete since all colonists of different origins ultimately "melted" together. When addressed with this voice, the past appears remote. This is illustrated especially well in tape transcripts by the speakers' use of third-person pronouns when discussing their own past ("they all melted together"). It also involves an absence of descriptive detail and of actors' agency. These features suggest that this voice does not necessarily reflect the individuals' own experiences, but instead may be based on a generic model of history learned in school or other venues and spread more widely through various media and subsequent conversations.

The "contrasting" voice offers a different perspective on the same past, in which assimilation emerges as a difficult process. Narratives in this voice are typically accompanied by more detail, often involving anecdotes of specific events or persons and sometimes including reported speech, as we see in the second part of the quotation ("His mother said, 'Are you Maltese, you?'"). Here, stories tend to be told with first-person pronouns. Individuals are depicted as having to make choices, albeit difficult ones, and thus as having agency. This voice is also saturated with ethnic- and class-based terminology used to identify different segments of the colonial population, and stories of class bias feature prominently. When analyzed in this way, contradictory statements no longer appear confused, but reflect speakers' accommodation of two very different and distinct ways of interpreting a complex and undeniably ambivalent colonial past.

Michel Pisani is part Maltese, part French; his wife, Rose, is of "pure" Maltese ancestry. Michel first claims that where he grew up, in eastern Algeria, there were many Maltese-French marriages:

MICHEL: And families of more modest means, well . . . they married each other. But in our region, there were many . . . marriages be tween French and Maltese, hein? Between French men and Maltese women and Maltese women and French men [*sic*] . . . yes.

AUTHOR: And this wasn't badly viewed?

MICHEL: No, no, no, no. Where we lived, no.

Author: Oh. Not at Souk-Ahras.

MICHEL: The Maltese— [pause]

AUTHOR: And at Constantine, was it . . .

MICHEL: At Constantine, yes.

AUTHOR: . . . more segregated, perhaps?

MICHEL: Yes, yes, yes. In Constantine . . . But, well, we can't really say that . . . classify that . . . The French in particular considered the others like . . . second-class [people], second-class French, second rate. But even between Italians and Maltese, what's her name? . . . Anne-Marie. Her mother didn't want [her to marry him] because he was Maltese. Huh? She liked a guy and her mother . . .

ROSE: [*interrupting*] But even Michel, when he said to his mother, "I know a girl," she said, "What is she?" She asked you what nation . . . what background, whatever. He said, "*Maltaise.*" She wasn't happy about it. Why? Because I wasn't . . . um. Well. We were French, yes, but of origin . . . uh . . . um . . .

MICHEL: But not of origin . . . French origins [*d'origine française*].

ROSE: *French origins.* I was of Maltese origins, huh, and my mother-in-law, she was not pleased.

In this conversation, Michel first asserts that in his small village, mixed Maltese-French marriages were common. His parents, in fact, were an example of an early mixed marriage: his father, a first-generation Maltese immigrant born in Algeria, married the Algeria-born daughter of a French family after having served four years in World War I. Apparently his decoration for his war service after being gassed in Europe convinced the woman's father to permit his daughter to marry the man despite his stigmatized ethnicity. However, even though Michel's mother was ultimately quite happy with her husband, she was displeased when her son decided to follow her example and marry a Maltese-origin woman. Michel had somehow "forgotten" this part of his own history when he was making positive generalizations about the prevalence of French-Maltese marriages. He then thought of a case in which intermarriage was frowned upon. At that point his wife could listen no more; she finally interrupted to discuss with emotion the ill-will her mother-in-law had harbored against her due to her Maltese heritage.

We should note the persistence in this narrative of the use of national origins to identify colonists, despite the fact that the people discussed were French citizens. Moreover, when discussing her own experiences, Rose found it difficult to describe herself any way other than as "Maltese," and had to rely on her husband's assistance to present the more correct usage, "*d'origine maltaise*," a usage she may have felt compelled to follow since she was being taped. Finally, we see a shift from a distant, third-person narrative in the official voice ("they married each other") to the recounting of first-hand experience that directly contradicts it in a first-person voice, complete with reported speech.

In the next example, Mrs. Galea is of French origins while her husband had four Maltese grandparents. When I stayed with them in their tiny apartment in northern France one cold winter weekend, we discussed at length the colonial past. Here, the couple also first presented to me the optimistic official "melting pot" narrative, this time in a fast-paced, coconstructed narrative (the first five lines). However, when prompted by one of my questions, Mr. Galea began to talk about the discrimination and hatred he felt from the French:

MR. GALEA: But in Algeria, it was a mixture of races . . . a mixing/brewing . . .

MRS. GALEA: Yes, it happened very fast . . .

MR. GALEA: . . . the mixing together of all the French of for— foreign origins . . .

MRS. GALEA: . . . and, they all went to the same school . . .

MR. GALEA: . . . married each other, mixed together, and spoke French. Because, like I was telling you before, my grandfather, who was born in 1870, never spoke Maltese.

AUTHOR: Did you realize, back then, that you were of Maltese origin?

MR. GALEA: Yes, yes, yes.

AUTHOR: But it wasn't very important?

MR. GALEA: It wasn't important . . . [*hesitating*]

MRS. GALEA: But, it was . . .

MR. GALEA: . . . but for me, I was always affected because the French of the metropole, the "French French," were always a superior class in Algeria. And contemptuous. And contemptuous. Contemptuous, *hein*?

AUTHOR: Yes.

MRS. GALEA: Yes. So it was a bit shameful to marry an Italian, or to marry a Maltese . . .

MR. GALEA: I remember your mother's contempt for the Maltese. My mother-in-law hated the Maltese.

MRS. GALEA: Yes.

The speakers here begin their narratives in the official voice and outline the process of assimilation, including intermarriage, in positive terms. Note too that both Mr. and Mrs. Galea first use impersonal third-person pronouns as would a French history text, even when referring to their own past ("they went to the same school, married each other"). But when I ask Mr. Galea directly about his own experiences, his narrative begins to shift. He first discusses the contempt he felt from the French, which he states has always affected him (*ça m'a toujours marqué*); these memories have left their mark. He then illustrates this point with the example of his own experiences with his mother-in-law's anti-Maltese sentiment. While at some level he may still believe in a vision of Algeria as a melting pot, he could not ignore his own personal memories of the discrimination he had felt from "the French."

Intermarriage between Catholic colonists was widely considered by my informants as the final "proof" that the different European populations in Algeria had blended together. However, as these two cases indicate, people who were actually involved in mixed marriages, at least those between naturalized Maltese and "pure" French, confronted personally the lingering animosity felt by many in Algeria against the Maltese. After they had talked about intermarriage in positive terms, their personal memories surfaced, awkwardly contradicting and calling into question the larger narrative they had been trying to construct. The excerpts nicely illustrate distinct voices, the close correspondence between form and content, and the shifts between them. Ideological orientation and pronoun use each index a distinct voice and a particular point of view on the past.

An advantage of exploring social memory with a discourse-centered approach such as this is that we can refer to the rich literature in linguistic anthropology and sociolinguistics on heteroglossic speech communities to better understand which factors might motivate speakers to choose among an array of voices at different times. Shifting voices becomes meaningful, and attention to "codeswitching" can yield particularly fruitful insights (Hill 1985). Social settings or speech events may influence which voice a speaker uses.[2] In the case of the discourse of Maltese-origin former settlers, the official voice, which presented the settlers of Algeria as a unified whole, was most widely used in large gatherings of relative strangers, while the contrasting voice emerged in more intimate settings with only a few people present, and never in mixed French and non-French company. One might argue that the official voice, then, represents the "public transcript," which is presented in the open interaction between subordinates and dominant groups, while the contrasting voice represents a "hidden transcript," whose place is "off-stage," away from direct observation by those in power (Scott 1990). That this example is more complex becomes clear when we pay closer attention to situational codeswitching. Gumperz writes that when a speech style is regularly associated with a certain class of activities, "it comes to signify or connote them, so that its very use can signal the enactment of the activities even in the absence of other clear contextual clues" (1982, 98). Mr. Mifsud's shifts between the official and contrasting voices in the first passage may be examples of this type of codeswitching. He commenced in the contrasting voice by referring to his comrades as "Spanish," but then corrected himself. This may have been due to the influence of the thematic content of his story: when discussing military service, an experience undoubtedly permeated with associations to official discourse, Mr. Mifsud caught himself and replaced the alternate voice with the official voice midsentence. When we explore his narrative as an example of multi-vocality, the shifts in language use, ideological perspective, and, ultimately, the way the past is represented all become meaningful.

AUTHORITATIVE UTTERANCES, MULTIVOCALITY, AND CONVERSATIONAL DISSONANCE

The question remains as to why the official "melting pot" representation of the colonial past would be so widely reproduced, especially if it did not entirely encompass the speakers' life experiences. One possibility we should explore is the degree to which settlers' long residence in France has influenced their ways of discussing the past. Since the 1970s, the questions of immigration and its impacts on French society have been increasingly important topics of public concern. Debates among social scientists and politicians have centered on the question of whether or not France is, or should be, multicultural, and the processes by which assimilation has occurred in the past (Blum 2002; Brubaker 1992; Hargreaves 1995; Hargreaves and McKinney 1997; Noiriel 1996; Schnapper 1998; Silverman 1992; Weber 1976; Weil 1991). In these debates, the melting pot metaphor sometimes appears as shorthand for a society of immigrants. The metaphor even appears in titles of works on French immigration history (Noiriel 1996), and has become so widely used that the phrase "melting pot" sometimes appears in texts in English without quotation marks (Green 1991, 78).

It is difficult to know the degree to which the elderly colonists have followed and been influenced by these debates. It should be noted that such discussions are often scholarly in tone, and certainly focus on contemporary France, sometimes in comparison to the United States, not colonial Algeria. The former settlers did sometimes discuss contemporary French immigration with me, however. Unlike common French parlance, in which *immigré* (immigrant) and *étranger* (foreigner) are often conflated and used as code words or euphemisms for "Arab" or "North African" (Silverman 1992, 3), the speech of the *pieds-noirs* was more direct, specifying the ethnicity of the specific immigrant group being discussed (*les Arabes,* or *les Italiens*), paralleling colonial usage. They sometimes drew connections between these debates and their own past. More than once in the middle of a discussion of their family's migration history to Algeria, individuals turned to me and exclaimed, "*C'est nous, les immigrés!*" (*We* are the immigrants!). In fact, due to their double migration, many *pieds-noirs* saw themselves as more "immigrant" than any other group in contemporary French society.

It is unlikely that discussions of immigrant assimilation in France were primary in shaping how the settlers discussed their own past with me, if only because similar debates wracked colonial Algeria, where the melting pot metaphor was employed in ways similar to that which I observed in *pied-noir* discourse. We should then ask how this particular representation of the past became so widespread and enduring in colonial times. Bakhtin's writings are again illuminating. He emphasized a distinction between "primary" and "secondary" speech genres. The former, he argued, are based in "unmediated speech communion," while the latter are more complex forms that are primarily written. He focused in particular on the incorporation of primary genres into secondary ones, as in the incorporation of oral sources into written texts such as novels (1986, 62). While fragmentary on this point, his work suggests that the reverse occurs as well:

> In each epoch, in each social circle, in each small world of family, friends, acquaintances, and comrades in which a human being grows and lives, there are always authoritative utterances that set the tone—artistic, scientific, and journalistic works on which one relies, to which one refers, which are cited, imitated and followed. (Bakhtin 1986, 88)

The melting pot metaphor can be viewed as representing one such author-itative utterance, a dominant perspective on colonist assimilation that gained wide circulation in colonial Algeria at the time of the naturalization laws. Because it presents a model for the past, it can also be viewed as a *selective tradition,* which according to Raymond Williams is the most overt expression of the dominant hegemony's pressures and limits (1977, 115–16). It is a version of the colonial past, as I have argued, that is intentionally selective. Moreover, it is the version that best served the cultural, political, and economic interests of the dominant French faction of colonial society, by glossing over the socioeconomic realities of the decidedly subordinate "second-class" colonists and by uniting, at least symbolically, all settler fac-tions. This was an important step in the elites' ongoing effort to consolidate this greatly outnumbered population in the face of nearly constant resis-tance by the colonized. The French state, via school texts and other materi-als, was not the only source of these "authoritative utterances," for novelists and essayists in the *Algérianiste* movement promoted the melting pot no-tion in their writings as well (Bertrand 1920; Randau 1911). This represen-tation has continued to play a similar role since decolonization by encour-aging the French public to welcome the one million *pieds-noirs,* with their great diversity of backgrounds, and to accept them as thoroughly "melted," as all French, and thus as their own.[3] Selective traditions are vulnerable, however, for, as Williams writes, "the real record is effectively recoverable" (1977, 116). In this case it is recoverable from peoples' memories. The offi-cial version of the past does not represent colonial Algeria as all colonists experienced it, and thus it is supplemented by contrasting views that are rooted in individuals' lived experiences. Because the narrative of the past that the elderly Maltese settlers had learned from others does not corre-spond with what they had experienced in their own lives, a "conversational dissonance" develops.

Conversational dissonance does not merely reflect different points of views or encapsulate voices, but can also serve as impetus for changing them. The way that social memory's multivocality can encourage change is especially apparent in a longer narrative of Mr. Mifsud's. The contrasting voice, when placed alongside the official hegemonic voice, begins to trans-form into a forcefully articulated, oppositional stance in the course of a sin-gle conversation.

Mr. Mifsud was troubled by his ambivalent Franco-Maltese identity, and raised this topic, without my prompting, each time we spoke. During one of our first interviews, he explained his rather tardy discovery of Malta:

> You see, over there (*là-bas,* i.e., in Algeria), we were blended together. All mixed together. But, well, the Maltese weren't very well thought of, so we wanted to blend in. Soon people didn't even know they were from Malta.

Sure, I had friends with "those" names [i.e., obviously Maltese names], but there was no way to know for sure. At school, we wanted to be at least at the same level as the *Français de souche* [French stock], the *vrais Français* [real French], you know, those with names like "Jean Ballard" and so forth. So we ate Provençal food. We didn't really have much of an identity.

Mifsud elaborated on his ambivalent identity several months later during another taped interview. Again he applied the melting pot metaphor when he referred to assimilation of the different immigrant groups in Algeria, using the verb *fondre* (to melt). However, in this case, he described this process as one that was *actively* pursued by the naturalized French to avoid discrimination. In the following passage, he first tried to explain why it was so important for people to hide their immigrant origins in Algeria. He began this discussion using an impersonal third-person voice, but toward the end of the passage, he revealed that this was also his experience as well. When referring to the fate of the different immigrant groups in Algeria, he altered the metaphor to construct a different vision of the same past. I distinguish the different voices here in the following manner: the first set of italics signifies the *official voice,* standard font highlights a transitional variation on that voice, and the second set of italics indicates an altered *contrasting voice.*

> *In Algeria, people . . . melted together, really, uh . . . like I was telling you, people who were . . .* the children of immigrants didn't want to call too much attention to the fact that they were immigrants' kids. To be French, to receive all of the advantages, and then, and then . . . Well, no, especially because immigrants in general are people of a lower social class. It's not the rich who, who leave their country. It wasn't the rich Italians, Spanish, or Maltese who left their countries, it was those who were really from a pretty lower class who left because they didn't have any work, anything to eat. And they didn't want people to be able to know that they were from that class of society . . . that wasn't, well, rich, who came there because otherwise they would starve. Thus, it was a bit to save face, if you will, to retain their dignity, out of pride, not wanting to be recognized as one of those people. *So they tried to melt in, to melt together, to blend in, and me, during my entire youth, there was never a question of my being Maltese! And furthermore, I had a lot of education! I had civil and military training . . . and it was never a question of being Maltese. I was Mifsud, French, Mifsud, French! I never would have said, "I'm of Maltese origins." Now, though, I say it . . . But in my youth, I never would have said it, never. I was French.*

Mr. Mifsud first outlines the melting together of the diverse colonists, beginning in the official voice (note for instance the impersonal third-person statement, "people melted together"). Once we move into the transitional passages, we find that his narrative remains for a time impersonal, told with third-person pronouns, but the content begins to change. He reminds me of a previous conversation we had and continues to explain to me why it was so important for people to hide their immigrant origins in Algeria. His story then shifts to the difficulties experienced by the lower classes, a subject usually evaded in the dominant melting pot perspective. In the third section, he resurrects the melting pot metaphor, extracting it from the fabric of the official narrative, and uses it to tell another story altogether. Here, those who assimilate are not passively shaped by an invisible hand but are active participants. Mifsud describes their conscious effort to erase all vestiges of cultural difference, willingly throwing themselves headlong into the smelter. By the end of this passage, he finally reveals that he is speaking from personal experience in a detailed and passionate conclusion, employing first-person pronouns ("I was Mifsud, French, Mifsud, French!"). It appears from this excerpt that through talking with me and actively noting the contrasts between the official version of colonial Algeria and his own quite distinct memories, the cognitive dissonance that resulted from the multivocality of his own storytelling, he has begun to interpret his past differently, and the conflicting voices are evolving into a powerful counter-narrative.

As Mr. Mifsud's passage attests, assimilation is often a conscious process sought out by individuals of immigrant origin themselves. Members of the first generation born in the new country may be especially vulnerable to the attractions of the dominant identity. People in this category, which for Noiriel includes children who have been socialized in the culture of origin by immigrant parents but who are also exposed to dominant norms of the host society through engagement with its various institutions, often serve as the family's representative to the outside world. When they discover at school or on the street that their origins are considered inferior, they may begin to distance themselves from the country of origin, leading to denial of their background or even self-hatred. Noiriel (1996) cites many examples of Italian- and Polish-origin French men and women who wrote about their subjection to anti-Italian "witch hunts" or the cruelty of teachers in the 1920s and 1930s in metropolitan France, and their growing dislike of their own heritage. It is important to note that the analagous generation of Maltese in Algeria would have been the generation of most of my interviewees' parents, or perhaps even their grandparents. This helps explain the loss by the time the interviewees entered the world of cultural knowledge about Malta.

The settlers' testimonies reveal another key "assimilating tool" of colonial Algeria to add to the more obvious institutions of the French schools, army, and legal system; as in France, anti-foreigner discrimination and prejudices were also involved. People were not motivated only by their attraction to the new culture, as Mr. Grech outlined in his vivid description of growing up in the "cult of France." While some talked about being drawn to the positive aspects of France, they also wanted to avoid at all costs being singled out as Maltese, and tried the best they could to blend in, consciously suppressed all awareness and manifestations of their former culture, and were active participants in this process. As Mr. Mifsud explained, "they didn't want people to be able to think they were from that class of society."

Stories told by the elderly *pieds-noirs* of Maltese origin indicate a continued concern with Frenchness in the colony that lasted long after the naturalization laws and the *peril étranger* of the late nineteenth century. The foreign-origin colonists, particularly those from southern Europe, remained a subaltern colonist mass, holding occupations that defined them as members of a lower status, which in turn barred them from further upward mobility. Neighborhood, language, dress, and occupation were all signs that other settlers could read, allowing them to place one another into the relevant categories in the settler hierarchy. The foreign-origin colonists experienced some upward mobility, certainly, compared to their forebears, and many reached a comfortable standard of living. But to the "pure" French, those of Maltese descent remained a step below them. Even those "Maltese" who had obtained great wealth were held apart due to the enduring nature of early stereotypes. It was hard for many non-Maltese to see this population as truly "white," truly "French," and truly "European." Populations viewed as "not quite European," such as the Maltese or Algerian Jews, who wished to enter the middle or upper classes and who adopted the cultural practices of the ruling French elite were sometimes criticized by the dominant elite for "putting on airs," just as was the case in British Guyana (see Williams 1991, 192–94). Stories told by French-origin settlers about the ignorance and gauche dress of the Maltese *nouveaux riches* indicate the extent to which wealthy Maltese-origin settlers were scrutinized and ultimately found lacking. This lasting subaltern status is perhaps most clearly summarized in the derogatory label applied to working-class whites, *petits blancs* (little whites).

Living in a world rife with contradictions, in a place defined as both France and not France, a "democracy" that was anything but democratic for the vast majority of the population, a "melting pot" where opportunities awaited naturalized Europeans, regardless of origin, but where only those from France would ever be considered "truly" French, the Maltese internalized contradictory perspectives in their development of a sense of self and their place in the world. The internalization of the dominant faction's view of them compelled many of the Maltese to wipe away all signs of their suspect background as thoroughly as possible. At the same time, they did not forget the stories confided to them by their relatives who had suffered discrimination at the hands of other French. Deborah Reed-Danahay has noted the coexistence of a French and regional identity in her work in Lavaille in the Auvergne, France. While the Maltese in the colony were managing diverse identities, as did the Auvergnat (1996, 207), they worked hard at suppressing one identity most of the time.

The Maltese *pieds-noirs* who form social clubs such as the *Amicale France-Malte* share a collective memory, but not one based on Malta and the stories of relatives who once lived there. Rather, theirs is a story of discrimination and assimilation in the colony, a collective memory rich in multivocality and in contradictions, as we might expect from a people in a liminal social position. This collective memory partly resolves the enigma of the Maltese clubs, the puzzling tendency among settlers of this background to organize along ethnic lines. However, additional dimensions to this enigma become clear when we follow the settlers to France after the French-Algerian War, consider the identity politics they faced, and, finally, reflect on what it is about Malta itself that fascinates them so.

SIX

*The French-Algerian War
and Its Aftermath*

The French-Algerian War is the great break dividing the lives of the settlers in half: the times before the war, which tend to be remembered tinged with a gilded nostalgia, and the years since, which are discussed with considerably less enthusiasm. Life in Algeria, followed by life in France. "It's as if we went from life in color, to life in black and white," one woman explained to me. The war represents a major turning point for the settlers and set the stage for their experience in contemporary France. To fully understand the meaning of the Franco-Maltese social clubs, we must return to this major trauma, which has set the course of the club members' lives in the aftermath of colonialism. This period continues to shape the settlers' orientations toward Algeria, the past, and contemporary France and the French, and even dictates the very structure of everyday conversation.[1]

THE FRENCH-ALGERIAN WAR,
1954–1962

While in hindsight one could argue that the end of French Algeria was inevitable, such a position was not widely shared in France, even in the 1950s. Most French in the metropole as well as those in Algeria were taken by surprise by the November 1, 1954, proclamation from Cairo of the principal objectives of the *Front de libération nationale* (FLN), which coincided with attacks on French civilians by the associated *Armée de libération nationale,* for many the starting point of the war of independence.[2] Perhaps even more surprising is the fact that French officials did not predict the mass migration from Algeria of nearly a million settlers at the end of the long war. Settlers, officials in Algeria and the metropole, and the general French public all were utterly unprepared for this sudden mass movement, further compounding the disruption it caused. Algeria declared its

independence from France on July 5, 1962. The seven and a half years between these two dates included periods of calm and optimism, which were
punctuated by coordinated attacks by Algerian organizations on European
civilians in cities and rural regions, counter-terrorist attacks in Muslim
quarters, all-out assaults by the French army, and violent internecine feuds
within each faction involved.

The conflict exhibited many features of a civil war, and yet war was
never officially declared. It remained officially the "operations of the maintenance of order" (*opérations de maintien de l'ordre*) until 1999.[3] Algeria
since the Third Republic had comprised three French departments. As
some *pieds-noirs* asked rhetorically, "How could France declare war on itself?" The conflict remained the "war without a name" (Talbott 1980; Rotman and Tavernier 1992), and French officials labeled those they were
fighting "outlaws," "rebels," or "terrorists," but "systematically and deliberately denied them the status of warriors or combatants" (Alexander, Evans,
and Keiger 2002, 3). Groups who together, however awkwardly, had
formed a common society began to pull apart and battle each other while,
at least on the surface, still behaving as parts of a whole: they lived in the
same small villages, traversed the same city streets, and patronized the same
shops. Algerians continued to work on the farms or in the factories of the
very people they were hoping to overthrow. Settlers continued to employ
office managers and family servants who, in some cases, warned them about
imminent attacks, but who, in other cases, were active participants. Further
complicating this period for those living through it was the fact that the
sides of the dispute were not as clearly drawn as it might seem. The label
Français d'Algérie, "French from Algeria," theoretically encompassed people
of any ethnic origin. Draft laws required young men to serve, regardless of
origin, and thus naturalized Muslim Algerians and Muslim career officers in
French military service at the time of the war served on the side of the
French.[4] In addition, thousands of Algerians volunteered to assist the French
in various services (and were sometimes referred to generally as *harkis*).[5]
Rural security units (*groupes mobiles de protection rurale,* or GMPR, later
groupes mobiles de sécurité, GMS) included thousands of Europeans who
did the same tasks as the Arab and Berber men in these units (Hamoumou
2004, 322–23). Finally, substantial numbers of settlers, including members
of communist parties and leftist Christian organizations, broke ranks with
their fellow settlers and supported the Algerian independence movement,
sometimes quite secretly.

The French army began large operations in the Aurés Mountains less
than three months after the November 1 attacks, and the number of troops
stationed in Algeria steadily increased as national service conscripts were

sent to the colony. While the army attempted to destroy armed bands in rural mountainous regions, French political leaders considered a range of ineffective political reforms (Ageron 1991, 109). The suicidal operation of the FLN in the department of Constantine in August 1955, in which some seventy European civilians were killed and hundreds wounded, led to horrific French reprisals[6] and an increased polarization of the society between the indigenous populations and the settlers, or in the settler vocabulary of the time, between the *indigènes, Musulmans,* or *Arabes* and the *Européens* or *Algériens.* As the French army increased its presence in Algeria, the ALN began to organize an urban guerrilla offensive in Algiers. In January, the infamous General Jacques Massu and eight thousand paratroopers were brought in to stop the attacks in the capital city. They succeeded, but only after ten months and having resorted to the systematic use of torture, thus bringing to the war a new level of brutality and heightened international attention.

The war destabilized the polities involved as well. Conflict over French policy in Algeria and the growing war expenses exasperated an already fragile political climate in the metropole, and government after government collapsed: President Mollet's government fell on May 21, 1957; another, formed in June, collapsed in September of the same year. A third, established November 6 by Félix Gaillard, fell on April 15, 1958. Strict government censorship throughout the war led to bitter conflict between French intellectuals and the state.[7] In Algeria, massive demonstrations following the April collapse culminated in the seizure of power by a "Committee of Public Safety" formed on May 13 by military officers and settlers, who occupied the administrative headquarters of the colony. The war came very close to being fought in France proper, and the nation was on the brink of civil war. Military officers were planning parachute drops in Paris, and managed to take Corsica on May 24, 1958, without any resistance. On May 27, with complete disregard for the constitution, General de Gaulle announced his plans to form a new government. The prime minister resigned, and President Coty, after considering the alternatives of a military coup or a government formed by de Gaulle, invited de Gaulle to become the last prime minister of the Fourth Republic. De Gaulle was granted emergency powers for six months starting June 1, 1958. He traveled to Algeria immediately to calm the settlers, reassuring them that he had "heard" them, which to the settlers meant that he understood their determination to maintain the status quo in Algeria. But, within a year, he began to pursue a different policy, referring in his speeches to Algerian self-determination. The settlers viewed Gaulle's policy shift as a betrayal, and responded with an uprising in January 1960. In early 1961, generals of the French

army created the *Organisation de l'armée secrète* (OAS) and nearly succeeded in their planned coup. They took Algiers and Oran in April 1961.
After failing to secure the rest of the country, they transformed themselves
into an underground organization. As such, OAS members carried out as-
sassinations of French and Muslim leaders and terrorist attacks in both
France and Algeria.

The last years of the war were times of increasing violence and chaos
in both France and the metropole. The French government handled mass
demonstrations in both places with increasing violence and repression.[8] *Attentats* (bombings) in both the colony and the metropole increased in
1962: in France, there were 107 *attentats* between January 15 and February 11 alone, while in Algeria, in only the month of January, there were
over eight hundred *attentats* that killed 555 and wounded nearly a thousand, and during the first two weeks in February, there were 507 (Stora
1993, 74).

French officials signed a cease-fire agreement with the leaders of the
provisional Algerian government, the *Gouvernement provisoire de la République algérienne,* in Evian, France, on March 18, 1962. The conditions
agreed upon corresponded only partly to the subsequent events, as the
signing parties were guilty of "a measure of self-delusion if not substantial
hypocrisy" (Clayton 1994, 173). The French government accepted an independent Algeria, but planned to further link the new nation to France
economically; Algerian leaders agreed to some economic stipulations, but
planned to ignore them following independence. The accords guaranteed
settlers special protection in Algiers and Oran, full civil rights, propor-
tional political representation, dual nationality for three years with an option for Algerian nationality or the status of resident alien, and the maintenance of property rights; they were also guaranteed that there would be
no expropriation of property without compensation (Clayton 1994, 173;
see also Stora 1993, 77). Most of these were later revealed to be empty
promises.

The Evian accords did not lead to a return to order; in fact, violence
only escalated. Desperate to prevent the end of French Algeria, the OAS
began an all-out offensive, taking control of an entire quarter of Algiers,
Bab-el-Oued. When French soldiers fired on a massive OAS-organized
demonstration on March 26, killing nearly fifty people, the OAS responded with a scorched-earth policy, killing dozens of Algerians a day in
Oran the following month. They attacked property, the municipal library,
the town hall, and four public schools in Oran, and blew up the main library of Algiers (Stora 1993, 79). These activities in turn encouraged further FLN reprisals. The French army, bound by the accords to maintain a
policy of nonintervention, remained a spectator during these final months

of bloodshed (Clayton 1994, 174). Settlers began leaving the country daily by the thousands in the days leading up to and immediately following Algerian independence on July 5, 1962.[9]

EVASION THROUGH EUPHEMISM:
LES ÉVÉNEMENTS

It might be expected that the experiences of the war years would be an important topic of conversation. For the elderly former settlers I interviewed, the war spanned nearly eight years of their adult lives. Those who were seventy-five in 1996, for example, were thirty-three at the start of the war and forty-one by its end. Most had already married and were starting families, and the men were launching their careers. The end of the war marked their great rupture with their home country, and their flight to and permanent exile in France. And yet, after months of meeting with *pieds-noirs,* I had learned few personal details from this period and even today know little about how the war influenced their life choices or their everyday routines, unlike scholars interviewing people in France who had resisted the war (Evans 1997).

The politics of naming the conflict are both fascinating and revealing.[10] When elderly former settlers wanted to refer to these eight years of conflict, they used the strikingly simple expression *les événements,* the events. The use of this euphemism, instead of the more standard usage over the past decades, the *guerre d'Algérie* (Algerian War), is indicative of a specific attitude toward this period. This time, fraught with such conflicting perspectives and emotional weight, was better left undefined. *La guerre d'Algérie* was difficult for many of the people I interviewed. Some argued that it wasn't a "real" war, fought in the usual way; if it had been such a war, surely the French would have won, given their overwhelming military superiority, they felt. These events also could not be called the "Algerian war of independence," a formulation that carries an implicit understanding of the war as a stage in the inevitable process of decolonization. They avoided taking such a position, necessarily calling into question their presence in Algeria over the generations, and which would suggest that their lives were merely anachronistic remnants of a fundamentally untenable enterprise. If colonialism were so untenable and morally reprehensible, they argued, why were some obvious settler colonies, like the United States, able to persist, and even garner international respectability? Instead of participating in these or other debates, and to elude the pain of this period of time, they emptied the war years of affect and of meaning and referred to them simply as a neutral stretch of time, those "things" that happened, the "events."

EVASION THROUGH OMISSION
AND COLLAPSING TIME

Speakers used several strategies to avoid discussing the war directly. Some simply skipped over the war years. They outlined details of their life in Algeria, circumventing the years of the war, and proceeded to describe their settlement in France. A second and more common strategy of silencing is one I call "collapsing time." Autobiographical accounts were detailed before and after this great gulf, while the war years were collapsed into a single phrase, such as *après les événements* ("after the events"). Following long discussions of their education and early careers in the late thirties to early fifties in Algeria, speakers effectively avoided the eight years of the war by starting a new section in their narrative: "*Après les événements*, we arrived first in Marseilles where I found work as . . ." The years of the war were reduced to a reference point, a point of no duration that sorted the speakers' lives into two streams, the time that occurred before the war, and the time that followed.

One interlocutor did not use this simple phrase, but achieved the same effect with the two sentences in his narrative devoted to the war. I had met Mr. Messerchmitt at the end of my first stay in France. He decided to outline his life history for me on the telephone when it became clear that I would not have time to travel to Lyons to interview him in person. During our two-hour conversation, he discussed his family's immigration history. He told me in detail about his grandparents and their reasons for migrating to Algeria from Alsace and Malta, and talked about what life was like for them in the early years of the colony. He then began discussing his own professional trajectory. At first he worked in the military as a pilot. "Then," he stated, "during the events, I didn't work as a pilot, but worked for the army as a radar specialist. France left Algeria in 1962. The army left so I did too." He continued to describe his military career in France, and, after he retired from the military, his years working for France Telecom. He then shifted to his memories of World War II. He felt that I should really try to interview him in person one day because, as he said, he can remember well "how people lived during the war." He talked about the arrival of the Allied forces in November 1942, the long lines of trucks passing his street, and his first encounter with Americans, who threw rations to children following the convoys. As I filled page after page of notes, he provided additional fine detail, describing the type of coffee the Americans brought, detailing differences between the American and British soldiers, and describing one Christmas when his family had hosted American soldiers.

There are several interesting aspects to Messerchmitt's narrative. First, the phrase *la guerre* ("the war") signified only World War II. Once he had introduced World War II into his monologue by recalling the Allied debarkation, he consistently referred to this time as *pendant la guerre* (during the war). Apparently he felt there was little chance that I could become confused and mistake this war for the more recent French-Algerian War. "The war," in his view, could only be World War II. Secondly, while he provided a wealth of detail about life during World War II, his discussion of the French-Algerian War is notable for its lack of detail or personal memories of any kind. Finally, this latter conflict, which spanned a much longer period of his life (almost eight years as opposed to three for World War II), entered into his narrative only as a bridge to a new phase, and he himself featured as a passive subject of history. He stated that he was working for the military, and when France left Algeria, he left too, implying that since he was in the military and the military was leaving, he had no choice but to follow.

SELF-CENSORSHIP AND
RESCUING OTHERS

If speakers were not careful, conversations traversing the "safe" territory of family stories, of life during the early periods of the colony, could move toward the war years. When a story was told of a specific relative, other stories about the same individual could follow. The stubbornness of Uncle Giuseppe, illustrated in a story that took place in 1943, might remind other family members present of a similar incident that occurred in 1960. It may have been partly for this reason that so many people I interviewed initially outlined their family history in a scientific, rote manner. Such a structured discourse style may have granted speakers a sense of control over this potentially difficult material, helping them to manage memories that may have been linked by subject and thus threatened to disregard the ban on the eight forbidden years. This may also explain why I learned so much more about my interlocutors' grandparents than about any other family members. Parents, and especially siblings, were more likely to have been war casualties, and male siblings at least would have served in local militias or army units. An effort to circumvent this period may have underlain their decision to avoid mentioning these people.

Narratives about a particular relative sometimes veered toward the forbidden years when speakers were not careful. On these occasions I learned that, along with trying to censor themselves, people also kept close watch on each other. Indeed, I witnessed striking "rescues" by others present who steered the speaker back to safer ground.

One of these "rescues" occurred when I was visiting a couple I knew well in their small apartment in a high-rise complex in Marseilles, where they had lived since the mid-1960s. After lunch, the Bernards were talking about how difficult life was for the first generations in Algeria. Whole families were killed by epidemics and others were ruined financially. But for the immigrants arriving from Malta, the huge expanses of land available made Algeria seem a real "Garden of Eden." Mrs. Bernard's grandparents had arrived from Malta penniless, and both husband and wife immediately set to work clearing land and digging their own wells. They died when their three children were still young, so the eldest son, Mrs. Bernard's father, Xavier, quit school to raise his sisters. He traded livestock and worked so hard at this career that he eventually became extremely wealthy. Both Mr. and Mrs. Bernard told me story after story about this unique individual: his fantastic ability to remember and later recognize every animal he ever sold and his incredible mind for figures. In the following passage, Mr. Bernard realizes that I had not yet grasped just how wealthy Xavier had become, and to illustrate his wealth, he begins to tell me a story of something that happened to Xavier during the war:

AUTHOR: Oh, so he was someone of a very . . . a rather elevated standard of living.

MR. BERNARD: *Very* high standard, *yes!* They weren't able . . . before they had cars like now, he had a carriage with two white horses . . . In the morning, the horseman was waiting for him, outside the door. After that, there were cars . . .

MRS. BERNARD: [*interrupting*] Would you like some more coffee, Andrea?

AUTHOR: [*quickly, to her*] Oh, no thanks.

MR. BERNARD: Yes. So, I remember one time, it was in 1957, he was . . .

MRS. BERNARD: [*interrupting in a very loud voice*] You *see*, Andrea, my grandparents, my grandparents on my father's side, it was really the typical Maltese custom . . . one leaves for adventure, to make money, but, watch out! To die, when they are old, they return to Malta.

I never learned what story the husband was attempting to tell me; all I know is that it happened three years into the war, in 1957. But it is clear from the recording of this conversation that I was interested. When the wife interrupted the first time to ask if I wanted some coffee, I answered her quickly and quietly, almost in a whisper, so as not to interrupt her husband's train of thought. When she interrupted the second time, her voice was loud and forceful, and she dominated the conversation for several minutes, not stopping until it had been safely shifted to a new topic. Mrs. Bernard introduced a topic that was truly "safe" in that it was far from Algeria, and yet ostensibly of great interest to me: the characteristics of the Maltese people in Malta. Thirty years ago, her sister had met a Maltese man in Algeria, married him, and had moved to Malta. For the remainder of our conversation, the couple outdid each other with hilarious stories meant to illustrate the "odd" behavior of the Maltese, despite my attempts to steer us back to Algeria.

On another occasion, a conversation that had unwittingly raised wartime memories was steered away from this period in a more overt manner. This happened when I was at a large public barbeque (*mechoui*) attended by over 350 former settlers of the Algerian city of Bône (now Annaba). I had driven Louise Marino to the dinner, a woman in her late sixties. Louise was known to many there, but had disappeared from public view for years following a difficult divorce. We were seated with a group of women in their sixties and seventies. Louise had become involved in yoga to deal with several serious health problems. During a lag in the conversation over the course of the all-day event, I mentioned Louise's rather unusual "hobby" to the other women. They were intrigued and began asking questions. Louise obviously enjoyed this discussion, and asked the women, "Would you like to hear about the time I almost had a heart attack in China?" "Yes, yes, tell us!" they responded, and they settled in to listen to her story.

Louise explained that when she and her husband left Algeria, she was sick, mentally ill. She had lost ten people in her family during the *événements,* including her favorite brother. She couldn't believe it, couldn't accept it, and needed to blame something or someone. Somebody had to be responsible, and she decided that it had to be General de Gaulle. It was because of him that that they were forced to leave, and in the way they did. She became obsessed. To set the world right, she thought, she would have to kill him, and she began to consider ways she could do this. Because her husband was an important figure in the French military, she fantasized that at a military awards dinner she would approach de Gaulle with her husband to shake his hand, and would instead attack him right there and then. This obsession developed to such a point that her husband became quite worried and tried to convince her to put the past behind her. But the obsession continued, until she had a memorable dream one night. In this dream, she was approaching de Gaulle to kill him when she suddenly saw two large tears rolling down his face. She knew instantly that he was sorry, that he hadn't meant for things to turn out the way they did. But, she told us, she wasn't sleeping; she was in fact hallucinating! She felt that he had come into her very room to tell her this, she exclaimed. There he was, de Gaulle, right in front of her! At that point, seeing the tears in his eyes, something shifted for her, she said; the spell was broken and she no longer felt obsessed.

So, her life went on. Several years later, she was on a trip to China with a study group. One day they went on an excursion to visit the Great Wall. She remembered that it was extremely hot, she hadn't had enough to drink, and was exhausted and dehydrated. She looked up, and right there, right in front of her on the Great Wall, was General de Gaulle! She was in complete shock, and felt she would have a heart attack right there and then. What was *he* doing there? The group listening to this story was transfixed—they knew very well that de Gaulle had been long dead by that time (he died in 1970). "What was it?" they asked, "a vision?"

She finally came to her senses. It turned out that, through a cultural exchange program, the French had sent a life-sized wax replica of de Gaulle to China. There it stood, on the Great Wall. That was what she had seen.

The women found this story very entertaining, and it was followed by much laughter. But Louise's story also had conjured up the *événements* in everyone's minds. One woman began talking about de Gaulle, and admitted to the others that she too hated the man and all he had done to them. Another woman offered a somewhat wider perspective. "Yes, we were at a bad point in history. Maybe we were going to have to leave anyhow, maybe it was the end of a kind of era, but we shouldn't have left in *that* way. Not in *that* way. That is what is so shameful. Maybe we should have left in 1958, even. When I think of all the young men killed between '58 and '62, and for nothing!"

The other women were nodding. There was a slight pause; they had reached an open point in the conversation. Would they begin talking about the war in earnest, the impact of history on their lives, the inevitability of decolonization, or what actions could have made a difference?

A dynamic woman in her early sixties spoke up, taking control, and completely breaking the mood. "Let's not talk about all that!" she said, and then, turning to Louise, she added, "Tell us more about China!" Louise obliged, and the conversation diverged from Algeria. Over the next hour or so, Louise talked about her trip and the strange foods she ate there. The French-Algerian War was all but forgotten.

During the vast majority of my interviews and during the conversations that I observed, *pieds-noirs* either avoided the war outright or used it only as a way of marking time. When people wandered into this silenced territory, others served as "rescuers," steering the conversation to a new topic, often quite energetically and forcefully. However, on two occasions I witnessed dramatic examples of what could happen when speakers were not "rescued" and instead fell into the dreaded abyss. These occurred in more formal settings, when codes of politeness prevented spouses and friends from intervening. Helpless, we all had to wait and watch while the two men in question completely lost their bearings.

FALLING INTO THE ABYSS

The first time I saw somebody lose control was at the annual meeting of an *association* managing a private library on Algerian history. The public meeting was held in a large auditorium of the Aix municipal library complex.

The board of directors was seated on a stage in front of over two hundred association members. The president stood up, a tall, older, thinner, and impeccably dressed version of Paul Newman, with graying hair, blue eyes, and the tanned and wrinkled face of someone who spends his free time on a yacht. When I had been introduced to him before the start of the meeting, he had been extremely welcoming to me, and exuded confidence and warmth; a very skillful politician, I thought at the time. He began to make the mandatory initial presentations, introducing the other board members and outlining the status of the library's collection. He then turned to the organization's finances. Additional funding was needed for the upcoming year, he explained, to pay for the computerization of the library's collection and to give the librarian a small raise. He outlined which kinds of funds might be obtained over the next year from nearby municipalities. If he was unable to raise the money needed from public sources, however, he told us he would do whatever was necessary to keep the library operational. He would turn to private funds, if necessary, and would not hesitate to use his own money. "We have to think about our children," he added. "The next generation is important, and they need this collection." He went on to tell us that his children were so important to him that he had taken five years off from his career to raise them. He began to raise his voice. "Our children are important, and I know from *experience* that they *need* this library, they *need* a place where they can learn the *truth* about their parents' past." He continued, becoming more and more agitated: "What I mean is, *we* know what happened, *we* were there, *we* were at the barricades, on the 26th of March, we were there in '62, and before, even, we held out to the very end. We *know* what it means to hold out, to keep on going. *We* know, *we* were there when—" and he was off, tracing with great emotion the pivotal episodes of the war.

The president pulled himself out of this mental pathway only with great difficulty. He wrenched himself back to the present time and space and paused for a moment, looking out at the somewhat shocked and uncomfortable audience with a blank stunned stare. Finally, his politician side took over, and he moved back to his presentation, wrapping up his financial discussion and moving on to questions from the audience.

I did not know the president well, but his leadership position in this very elite and well-funded organization suggests that he is widely respected by its members. Judging from the audience's reaction, it seemed that such a lapse had rarely if ever occurred before. How did this happen? One of the goals of this *association* is to provide a repository of resources to develop and sustain an alternate reading of colonial Algerian history, including the war. Consequently, the president may have wished to mobilize association members by reminding them of the uniqueness of their perspective due to their direct experiences. And yet his war memories were too emotionally charged for him to manage this rhetorical strategy effectively. Once he had tapped into his own memories of that time, he lost control of his own discourse.

I witnessed another outburst at a large multifamily dinner party. This occurred over the winter holidays. Two families I knew well, the Pisanis and the Bernards, had their children visiting. Marianne Vella, daughter of Michel and Rose Pisani and a dynamic mother of two in her mid-forties, had come down from Paris, and Jean-Pierre Bernard had come home for a few weeks from Brazzaville, where he worked for a French company. I had been looking forward to the dinner, for it presented a rare opportunity for me to observe interactions among second-generation *pieds-noirs* and their parents.

During dinner, we were first locked into a long discussion about African religion and African *marabouts,* with all contributing to the best of their knowledge. Then Jean-Pierre's parents entertained us with engaging stories of their latest trip to Africa to visit their son. But the conversation returned to religion, in this case Islam, and whether or not there was any possibility for solidarity between Christians and Muslims. Mr. Bernard felt that the argument presented by others at the table, that Christians and Muslims were inherently incompatible, was simplistic and wrong, and embarked on a story to illustrate his point. He told us about a time in Algeria when he came across two "Arabs" fighting on the beach. One man's abdomen was sliced right through and his intestines were spilled out all around him. The point of his story was to tell us that while the other "Arab" (i.e., Muslim) wanted to finish off the wounded man, he (i.e., a Christian) insisted on calling for help and ultimately saved the Muslim man's life. However, in telling the story, Mr. Bernard lost track of his main point, and continued to elaborate on just how voluminous human intestines are, and how, when no longer contained by our skin, they really spill out: "You can't imagine how they could possibly fit back in," he explained. "It's amazing, you can still be alive, festooned by your own guts splayed all around you—in the case of the poor Arab, just spread out, all covered in sand." Perhaps my expression of amazement encouraged him, for he continued in this vein, moving on to stories of the French conscripts he saw during the war with a whole array of injuries—legs blown off, huge holes in their bodies—and how remarkable it was that doctors still managed to put them back together. As these graphic stories followed one after the other, I noticed that Mrs. Bernard and her son had their heads bowed, suggesting some embarrassment at their relative's loss of control in this public and somewhat formal setting. Everyone was clearly relieved when Rose Pisani returned from the kitchen to announce with conviction that it was time for dessert.

PRIVATE STORIES

On a few occasions, people did address the war years with me privately. This occurred quite rarely, and in the process, some interesting gender differences emerged that may stem from a tacit agreement by male veterans that war experiences in general should not be shared publicly. The men I met rarely discussed the war, aside from the occasions already mentioned in which they related their memories in an uncontrolled fashion. However, on a few occasions, a few men were able to consider the "events" in a particular narrative style. In the following excerpt from a taped conversation, Mr. Frendo outlines which family members had served in the French army:

> My father was in the war [*la guerre,* i.e., World War II] in Tunisia, uh, I had an uncle who, who was part of the liberation, who left from Libya with General de Gaulle . . . Hmm, who else? The other was a prisoner in Germany in 1940, he was captured in France and stayed a prisoner for three years in Germany . . . Marius was too young, he didn't serve. Oh yes, after, their kids, uh, me, I was a parachutist in the *guerre d'Algérie,* I had a cousin . . . who was a parachutist as well, who was killed at the Tunisian border, who died in combat, uh . . . my brother was in the marines, my other brother was in the Spahis, in other words he ran around the, the mountains chasing the rebels. And after that, the girls, who else?

Mr. Frendo back-tracked at this point to a discussion of World War I and then moved on to other topics entirely. While listening to him that afternoon, I realized for the first time that many of my interviewees probably had lost family members during the French-Algerian War, perhaps even in active duty. One technique of silencing the past is to overwhelm a narrative with many minor details, a process Trouillot has termed banalization (Trouillot 1995). I felt that Mr. Frendo had achieved such a silencing here. Despite the potential import of these revelations, he recited this material to me without elaboration or emotion, as if presenting facts from a book, and never strayed from a highly structured narrative style. He never again discussed this period, these people, or what these losses may have meant to him or to his family. While he did address the war years here, the whole period and these terrible losses were contained, and thus silenced, through this disciplined narration.

Some of the Maltese-origin women I met, on the other hand, addressed these years directly, with the goal, it seemed, of communicating to me the emotionally charged nature of this period. One might assume that, since women did not serve in the French-Algerian War, they would remain especially mute on this subject. This war was different from other wars,

however, and was closer to a civil war in that it took place at home and resulted in the permanent ripping asunder of the former colonial social fabric. It was not always conducted through the "usual" means, but involved
individual and guerilla actions that were by nature difficult to predict.
Everyone everywhere was a potential victim, and most people would have
witnessed some kind of atrocity. Furthermore, women did serve in a
sense—in hospitals, as nurses.

The narratives I heard emerged organically in conversation as examples
used to illustrate some larger point already under discussion. As others have
found in their research on women's memories, these narratives were highly
personal and often involved as protagonists the women themselves, their
children, or other close family members (Roche and Taranger 1995).
While the events they described were often gruesome or wrenching, the
women I observed seemed to have mastered the material in such a way that
they did not lose their train of thought or larger point. The first time I saw
this was when I was visiting the Galeas in northern France. We had first
met on the *Amicale France-Malte* trip to Malta. They lived in Burgundy,
and it was midwinter: because of the subzero temperatures, we spent much
of our time together inside the Maltese/Alsatian couple's tiny apartment,
talking about Algeria and the Maltese experience there. Pierre Galea had
worked for the national rail company, and was a staunch union supporter.
Although he had not attended high school, he loved to rummage through
his many books, and had filled a scrapbook with articles, letters, and po-
etry. His wife, Chantal, a petite woman with rosy cheeks, cropped brown
hair, and a marvelous smile, had considerably more education than her
husband and had worked as a schoolteacher, first in Algeria and then in
France. They were both strong supporters of the Christian left in Algeria
and now in France. The husband spoke at length about the time he spent
in the French Army in World War II and his difficulty feeling comfortable
with other *pieds-noirs*. However, the French-Algerian War did not surface
during our conversations. After her husband went off to church that Sunday morning, Chantal made a point of trying to explain to me some of the
pain and confusion of this period of time.

Like many other inhabitants of small villages in the province of Constantine, she and her brother had had close Algerian friends.[11] During the
early years of the war, unknown revolutionaries burned the homes of some
French residents of her village as well as those of Algerians who had refused
to join them. Chantal was pregnant at the time, she remembered, and
hence staying at her mother's home. Her mother's house was spared. She
felt that this was because her mother, a nurse and midwife, had always been
friendly with the Muslim women in the neighboring *douar*, the indigenous
town associated with the village, giving the children shots and helping the
women deliver babies.

The reaction of the French to this incident was extreme. The army rounded up all of the men in the *douar* and killed them. They lined up the bodies, and the French settlers went over to look at them to reassure themselves that the suspects had been captured. Chantal was horrified. Two days later, the wives of these men came into town. Their husbands had been massacred and they had no food; they were crying and in a pitiable state. Her mother went out to the bakery, bought quantities of bread, and gave it to the women, risking her own safety and reputation. "How could she not do so?" Chantal asked. But this event traumatized others in her immediate family as well, notably her younger brother. Like all other male settlers, he had been drafted into the local militia at the start of the war. Right after the attack, when the local Muslim men had been gathered, his lieutenant told his militia unit, "OK, now kill them." Her brother refused; he couldn't carry out the orders. "These are my friends!" he said. "I grew up with these guys my whole life. If you want them dead, you do it! Don't ask me to kill my own friends!" He threw down his rifle and ran home horrified, where he became violently ill.

Chantal told me this story in part to explain the difficult position she and her husband found themselves in, and why they could no longer defend the French position in Algeria and instead decided to aid the cause of the revolutionaries. This decision had lasting repercussions, and she and her husband had to flee Algeria before the end of the war to save themselves from potential attacks by fellow settlers. While they still retained their relationships with other members of the Christian left in France, their position during the war had put them at permanent odds with much of the *pied-noir* community. Through this narrative, Chantal was able to vividly represent the horror of the time, the escalation of violence, and the adoption by both sides of increasingly extreme measures, and especially the heartwrenching separation of childhood friends as they were forced to choose sides. Her stories were told through the experiences of immediate family members, her mother and brother, and she connected them to her subsequent decision to take a stand. I felt that she wanted me to understand why she and her husband had adopted difficult political positions that had left them alienated from other *pieds-noirs*. Interestingly, she waited until her husband was away before she embarked on this topic. Perhaps this was an indication that her husband was unable or unwilling to discuss this period.

The other woman who outlined the war in detail was Louise Marino, the yoga instructor discussed previously who had had the vision of de Gaulle. The war first came up in a taped conversation when we were alone, sitting at her kitchen table drinking tea. Since her divorce, she had inhabited a tiny apartment on the seventh floor of a high-rise complex that was crammed with her belongings; chests were stacked atop chests, creating a tiny hallway and dividing the space into two small rooms. She was trying to explain to me her feelings of disconnectedness from France. Even her children were only partially integrated, she said, and—thinking particularly of her eldest daughter, who was four when they emigrated to France—she embarked on a narrative to explain why.

Soon after settling in France, she was watching her children when her daughter, quietly putting together a puzzle with a picture of Bambi, started shouting, "Mama, Mama, come see, come see!" She went over to her daughter, who showed her mother her puzzle, saying, "Look, look, it's like that man!" She continued with her story:

> But this puzzle was Bambi, and in Bambi, there is no man. So she showed me, she put one piece down, she picked up another, saying, "Yes, Mama, it's like that man." "*What* man? There isn't any man there." "Yes, yes, *là-bas* [back there]." "Where back there?" "You know, back there, in Bône. In Algeria. The man, in Algeria. Yes. When there was the bomb, Mama, you put the head, the foot, the leg . . ." Yes. So, you see the memories of my five-year-old daughter. She had watched one morning, at the end of Mass, on a busy street, where there were just as many Arabs as French, and we never knew, we never figured out who had placed the bomb . . . And I, I went down right away to help. Of course, we helped the wounded, and evacuated them, there were ambulances and so forth. And then after that, because there were seven dead and thirty-five wounded, the seven dead were torn to shreds, practically, by the bomb, because they were so close to it. So, obviously, on the electric lines, against the posts, against the windows, there were pieces of human flesh, and we had to put them back together to identify the dead. So, inevitably, we had to put a foot, a leg, OK. And the little girl. *Voilà.* When I bought her a puzzle, look what it brought to mind!

A second story about the war surfaced an hour into our conversation, when she touched on the great tragedy that struck her family: on Christmas Day, 1956, someone threw a grenade into her grandfather's home during a large family gathering, wounding many and killing her brother. The death of her brother in her arms was an incident she had recounted to me before, and I knew that the memory was still very difficult for her. She told me how, after the explosion, a neighbor took her brother to the hospital. She worked as a nurse during the war years so she jumped in a car, covered in blood, with her husband and uncle following behind. The surgeon knew her and tried to prevent her from going into the morgue, but she insisted. While there she encountered the nun who ran her nursing unit, and whom she had just described to me as remarkably naïve. She continued,

> I get there, and suddenly, if it isn't the nun who was cleaning up my brother, it was the nun who I was telling you about before . . . When she saw my brother, she didn't know him as my brother. She said, "My God, isn't this

sad." She had been crying, saying, "God, only a child." You see, it was the beginning of the terrorist activity, it was 1956. We . . . there weren't yet lots and lots of deaths . . . but she didn't know who he was. And when she saw me . . . like that, she suddenly looked at me—I'll always remember this— she looked at my brother, she touches his cheek, and comes over to me, grabs me, and starts crying. Then she says to me, this nun, "Louise, God doesn't exist any more." The nun said to me, "God doesn't exist any more."

Louise explained that the "kids" who threw the grenade hadn't targeted her family specifically. Because it was Christmas, there were twenty-seven people gathered in the house, and the people who threw the grenade were probably teenagers given a grenade already discharged. She told me what it was like to have such memories:

> It's true that these are things we can't forget. And even, we don't really think about them during the day, but sometimes at night I wake up with a start, and, even now, I relive scenes like that one. So, I try to go back to sleep telling myself, "It's over."

When I told her toward the end of our interview that I was amazed at how well she has mastered this past, she disagreed with me. "No, I don't think that I have mastered it, but at least I have tried to *manage* it as much as possible." She told me that it was good for her to talk about these times; that the process of telling helps "exorcise" the pain.

THE WAR WITH NO NAME

Both men and women were constrained in group settings by a prior but widely recognized social convention, and avoided the war in all conversations that I witnessed, regardless of group composition or social setting. The settlers actively silenced each other when conversations began to stray into this period of time, and from what I observed, men and women played the roles of silencer and silencee equally. In private interviews, however, some people did bring up the war years, and here the men and women I met addressed them in very different ways. Men's narratives tended to be highly structured and almost void of emotion or connection to their own lives or experiences. If these narratives had been the only information I had about their relationship to this period of time, I might have concluded that the war held little place in the speakers' corpus of memories and personal identities. However, the very active everyday silencing, coupled with the occasions I witnessed of people losing control while discussing this period in formal settings together, suggested instead that this period was still extremely emotionally charged for some. Its silencing indicated not an absence of memory but an active avoidance of it, and the highly structured nature of some peoples' narratives may indicate an effort to discipline and contain memories that might otherwise take over.

The narratives of some women indicated to me a greater mastery of this period of time, for the stories emerged only as appropriate, to illustrate some larger question or theme. After completing their stories, they returned to their wider topic of concern and did not "spin out" obsessive chains of similarly horrifying tales, despite the fact that they had witnessed horrors as well. These narratives seemed designed to try to convey to me how it felt to live through these various experiences. They were remarkably detailed in reporting the thoughts, feelings, and statements of others and sometimes even entire conversations that had transpired in the past.

Why did some women talk about these horrors while most men did not? A somewhat simplistic answer could be that, in this particular generation of settlers, men were more socialized to control emotion than women. The fact that at the time I was a relatively youngish woman may have inhibited them further. In addition, we must consider the politics of telling such stories. The darker secrets about this war, in particular the use by the French of torture, and the fact that those in active duty were sometimes killing, torturing, or spying on life-long neighbors, may have made stories about this period difficult to tell, if not forbidden. I said at the outset of this book that in many ways I did not want to know what my interlocutors had done during the war, and perhaps we were coconspirators, then, knowing that once discussed and out in the open, the war memories might render research among this population difficult at best. Others who have interviewed former French conscripts have found a similar silencing of the entire period of time, even among members of *associations* of war veterans (Pascaud 1986). What seemed to unite most of the men Pascaud met was their absolute lack of interest in discussing their war experiences. The subject, they claimed, was "taboo" (1986, 328).

The war has been silenced not only by elderly settlers and war veterans, however. The changing contours of this silencing on a national scale are the focus of Benjamin Stora's work *Le gangrène et l'oubli* (1992). Stora points out that the war was silenced even while it was underway. The French government never issued a declaration of war; the logic at the time was that since Algeria was officially a part of France, such a declaration would be absurd and at the same time a tacit acceptance of the idea of a "France-less" Algeria. While many war veterans, political figures, *pieds-noirs,* and Algerian revolutionaries have since published their own accounts of the war, until recently these have remained isolated from public discourse.[12] Remarkably, the war was only officially identified as a war in 1999. There are still no national commemorative sites, and the key dates of the war are not fixed in national calendars as are those of the world wars.

Perhaps, as some war veterans stated to Pascaud (1986), this war *was* different. Not only was it a colonial war of independence and thus an odd form of civil war, but in addition, for those involved in the French side, it was embarrassing on several levels: France lost; the country was defending colonialism, viewed then and certainly since as an unconscionable way of life; and the methods used to fight this war were sometimes unspeakable and shameful. For these reasons, this particular war has not been, and indeed cannot be, validated by a patriotic nationalist master narrative. From the vantage points of the French state and the settlers, in contrast with the Algerian perspective (see Cooke and Woollacott 1993), it is a story better left unsaid.

The unspeakable nature of the French-Algerian War represents a real dilemma for the former settlers of Algeria. The war represents the major turning point in their lives, yet its narration has been silenced both privately and on a national level. Repression of this sort, as Stora suggests, inhibits healing (1992). Most *pieds-noirs* cannot mend themselves through its telling, and remain unable to connect the pieces of their lives across this great rift. Collective repression of the war years may thus be implicated in the intense nostalgia many *pieds-noirs* feel so strongly. It is time to consider this nostalgia further because not only is it tied to the drama of the war's conclusion, but it also nourishes and underlies the Maltese-origin settlers' interest in Malta.

SEVEN

Diaspora, Rejection, and Nostalgérie

During an interview in her tiny high-rise apartment overlooking the Aixois treetops, Louise Marino struggled to describe the time of her family's departure from Algeria to France, and tried to account for her confusion. "France is our *patrie* [fatherland, nation], but it isn't our *pays* [homeland, country]," she explained. "The most beautiful country in the world is the one in which you are born." She elaborated, "You see, I am not completely integrated, a part of France . . . to the extent that I don't feel *chez moi* [at home]. When I go to California, it's as if, as if . . . I were in France." She admitted that California is certainly unlike France: the languages spoken and the food are cases in point, "But, as far as nature is concerned, I feel better in California than in France!" She seemed to have surprised herself with this declaration, and tried to explain:

> You see, in France, nothing reminds me of my country [*pays*]. I can go from the north to the south . . . and I don't find the . . . plains, the, the mountains, the . . . the same landscapes [*paysages*], the same smells . . . the same colors, like *chez nous*. So, I get the feeling that I'm always *en voyage* in France. I'm floating . . .

It was surprising for me to hear Louise talking about her life in France in this way. Louise is the woman who discussed with honesty her obsession with de Gaulle, and who, unlike most, was quite open about her difficulties working through her war memories. Over tea, lunch, or apéritifs, she told captivating stories of not only life back in Souk-Ahras, the small town in eastern Algeria where she spent her childhood, but also her years in France studying Oriental religions. Despite her apparently successful adaptation to her new home, it all seemed temporary to her. Louise's feeling of being a tourist in France, of floating, was echoed by many other former settlers that I met and underscores the feeling of exile, of a rupture from their "home," that is such an integral part of the *pied-noir* experience in the post-Algerian period. And yet, due to their lifelong understanding of themselves—and indeed of Algeria—as unquestionably French, this sense of loss is accompanied, for many of my informants, by ambivalence, and even surprise at their own reactions. Some, like Louise, explain this ambivalence as stemming from the fact that, for them, *patrie* and *pays* are not the same place.

To understand this population and the degree to which they remain separate from wider French society, we first must take seriously their claim of being a people in exile. The unique nature of this "exile" experience, and the difficulties many former settlers have faced in France since their arrival in 1962, stem from the abrupt nature of their mass migration at the end of the French-Algerian War, and the many gaps that appeared between *patrie* and *pays,* giving rise to the formation of *pied-noir* associations, such as those created by the Maltese.

EXODUS AND EXILE

Despite the escalating violence during the final years of the French-Algerian War, and the continued departures of thousands of French from the nearby protectorates of Morocco and Tunisia, government officials in France had not planned for a mass settler flight from Algeria. Although legislation was already in place in December 1961 (*Relative à l'accueil et à la réinstallation des Français d'outre-mer,* enacted December 26) that made the reintegration of former colonists an overriding national priority, de Gaulle had estimated that of the 1,075,000 French in Algeria, only one to two hundred thousand would migrate to France at the conclusion of the war (Frémeaux 1996, 21). In fact, during the last months of the war, an effort was made to prevent a mass departure of settlers. As the violence of the war increased in the spring of 1962, French officials requested that trans-Mediterranean ferry companies reduce their crossings between France and Algeria to sixteen per week, and then to seven in March, and to three by April 1962 (Jordi 2003). Probably reflecting this reduction in ferry service, only approximately sixty-eight thousand settlers left Algeria between January and April 1962. On May 16, however, in response to the ever-increasing demand, the companies decided to increase their services without waiting for government approval, and emigration increased dramatically: over half a million people crossed the Mediterranean from May through August 1962 (Jordi 1993, 66).[1]

This mass flight was characterized by chaos on both sides of the Mediterranean. Many settlers were leaving out of fear of reprisals. Others, exhausted by over seven years of war, could tolerate the uncertainty no longer. The departures were rushed. Even those who realized that they would probably never return could bring only two trunks with them on the ferries (Clayton 1994, 174). Most migrants abandoned their homes, their boats, their cars, and the majority of their belongings. One woman described to me the chaos of this period: people handing the keys to their automobiles and apartments to strangers as they made their way to the ferry station, abandoned vehicles strewn along the roads leading to the ports, many of them burning shells. There was no room for these cars on the ferries, she explained, and bitter emigrants who were determined to prevent their later use by Algerians simply set them on fire before boarding the ships. Abandoned pets roamed the streets, and freed birds clung to their cages in panic until they finally died of starvation or were caught by roving cats.

Conditions upon debarkation in France were certainly an improvement on the chaos they had left, but local French authorities were utterly unprepared for the hundreds of thousands of postcolonial refugees. Official government spokespeople even attempted to convince the French public (and perhaps themselves) that this movement was not out of the ordinary, and sometimes referred to the refugees as *vacanciers,* people in France for their summer vacations (Jordi 1995, 69). The city of Marseilles, which served as a transit point for over 60 percent of the migrants, experienced tremendous disruption (see Jordi 2003).

This experience marked both colonists and metropolitans alike. Migrants, who had to live for months with their entire families crowded into makeshift housing in barns and garages, felt that they had been completely abandoned by the French government and even today retain extremely negative memories of their reception (Jordi 1993, 89–92). This was true of Louise Marino, who spent weeks moving from one hotel room to another with her family, including a young daughter stricken with polio, as I discuss below. Metropolitan French who had lost sons and friends fighting in Algeria already blamed the colonists for their losses, and were further disturbed by the sudden swamping of local services and the priority awarded to these newcomers in employment, housing, and loans.

THE POLITICS OF LABELS

The arrival in France of hundreds of thousands of former settlers posed a problem of terminology, and French officials and the public struggled to find a suitable means of identifying the colonial refugees. *Colon* (colonist) has a narrow meaning in French and is applied exclusively to people actively involved in "colonizing" the land, which by the end of French Algeria was a very small percentage of the settlers.[2] Interestingly, the terms used in colonial settings and presented in Memmi's *Portrait du colonisateur* (published in English as *The Colonizer and the Colonized,* 1977)—*colonisateur, colonial,* and *colonialiste*[3]—were not employed to indicate the French returning from the overseas empire. Instead, the first colonists arriving from Indochina were referred to simply as *Français d'outre-mer* (overseas French). This neutral term makes no explicit connection to a colonial context, suggesting a distancing through language and a subtle denial of French participation in imperialism. Ironically, French officials who wanted to distinguish the migrants according to their former positions in the colony soon discovered that the term was too vague to serve this purpose, for, in a strictly legal sense, it applied to both the French from France and the naturalized members of the indigenous populations, i.e., both French "colonists" and the "colonized." As a result, we find a temporary proliferation of compound terms. In official missives regarding the settlers of Algeria, for example, de Gaulle refers to them alternately as *la communauté de souche française d'Algérie* (the community of French origin or descent of Algeria), *les Algériens de souche française* (Algerians of French origin) and *les Algériens de souche européenne* (Algerians of European descent), among other formulations (Bénichou 1992, 203).

As government bureaucracies continued to coordinate the settlement and integration of the increasing numbers of *Français d'outre-mer,* a new term was applied to the migrants, one with a precise legal definition in France, which quickly entered common parlance: *rapatriés* (repatriates). A *rapatrié* is a "person returned to his homeland or country."[4] France, like most other nations, had a repatriation policy prior to this period, coordinated until World War II by the Ministry of Foreign Affairs, and after 1939 by two separate institutions responsible for the reception of French who for political reasons were required to leave a foreign state (Dubois 1994, 98). As the immigration of former French colonists increased following the loss of Indochina, a *Centre d'orientation pour les Français rapatriés* (Orientation center for repatriated French) was created in early 1957 and transferred to the Ministry of the Interior in 1958, reflecting a growing sense that the problems associated with these migrants were more internal than external matters. Yet the linguistic continuity remained. As both the numbers of migrants and the problems associated with their integration proliferated, a secretariat of state for repatriates was created in September 1961 and provided funding to assist in their resettlement (Dubois 1994, 99).

As a result, all "returning" French, despite their diverse ethnicities and regardless of their colony of origin, were labeled by French state officials *rapatriés* and the migrations *rapatriements,* or repatriations, terms that are still used today. The politics of this terminology are revealing. The identification of this mass migration phenomenon in official French discourse as a "repatriation" (a bringing home) is nothing short of euphemistic language that downplays the disastrousness of this debacle, which marked the collapse of the French Empire. The use of a term already in existence also creates a false sense of continuity with previous repatriations, such as the return of French prisoners of war from Germany at the end of World War II, and masks the novelty of the current situation. It is revealing, moreover, that the government chose *rapatrié* and not another term, such as *exilé* or *réfugié*.[5] These latter appellations may have been avoided because they suggest a situation out of control. Perhaps most significantly, the label "repatriate" emphasizes the refugees' unquestioned belonging to the French nation-state, and may have been a strategic choice to prevent or minimize any metropolitan backlash to their arrival.

The "repatriates" from Algeria differed from those arriving from other colonies in many significant ways, and for this reason many refused to accept the "repatriate" label. Many had had family in Algeria since the 1830s or 1840s, and had viewed Algeria as their home for generations. More importantly, they had truly believed the legal fiction that Algeria was France and imagined themselves to be moving from one part of France to another. The fact that Algeria was France's premier settler colony and had been incorporated into the French state led to a unique sense of geography and identity. A travel agent of Maltese origins told me, "Don't forget that Algeria was a department of France, we were in France, it was like in France. In Tunisia, on the other hand, we were foreigners." According to François Xuereb, growing up in Tunisia also led to very different attitudes toward decolonization and independence:

> If you want, the relationship between the French, or the French authorities, and the Arabs was the same in Tunisia as Algeria and Morocco, it was the same. The only difference is that in Tunisia and Morocco, us Europeans, or French—it's the same thing—we *knew* that it wasn't French territory. We knew this. We knew that it had a French administration, but that it wasn't French *land*. We were conscious of this fact. And this is why at the moment they got their independence [in Tunisia], there weren't so many clashes. There were a few small conflicts, but not many. While in Algeria, the French of Algeria, who for the immense majority weren't originally French—they were Spanish, Italian, Maltese, Greek—the immense majority of the French were persuaded, they were absolutely *persuaded* that Algeria was a French territory . . . [In Tunisia], there were a few small conflicts, some insignificant encounters, there weren't even fifty deaths, huh? . . . While in Algeria there were thousands of deaths. Thousands and thousands of deaths. Why? Because the French who settled there, not only did they believe that the land belonged to them, but also that that land was French. Yes, the land belonged to them, but was the land *France?* No. They confused their homeland with another country.

François presents another way to understand Louise Marino's confusion, discussed at the beginning of this chapter, regarding the distinction between fatherland (*patrie*) and country (*pays*). The French living in Tunisia understood that these were distinct places, and, moreover, they knew that they were foreigners living in a borrowed territory. The French in Algeria, however, had been convinced that Algeria belonged to France, was in essence France, and their conflation of the two places led to an especially traumatic rupture at independence.

The settlers from Algeria rejected the "repatriate" label on other grounds as well. Because they felt that the French had treated them as foreigners when they arrived, this migration to them was no return "home." As one woman exclaimed, "We haven't been repatriated; we are the *déracinés* [the uprooted]!" But there were few good alternate labels. In the colony, the settlers had referred to themselves as *Algériens* or *Tunisiens,* autonyms that occasionally slip into contemporary discourse, especially when people are comparing different groups of "repatriates." Some prefer the official usage of the time of the French-Algerian War, the *Français d'Algérie*. However, since their arrival in France, many settlers have claimed the once derogatory appellation *pied-noir* for themselves.

Not only do they claim a distinct autonym, but most repatriates from North Africa told me that the *pieds-noirs are* different from the rest: culturally, in outlook, and in their perspective on France and on the past. I learned the most about these contrasts from people in the Franco-Maltese social club. Those from Algeria often say that the repatriates from Tunisia are not real *pieds-noirs.* For them, what distinguishes the *pieds-noirs* is the traumatic circumstance of their migration. Mr. Grech, the man of "pure" Maltese heritage who had led a club in Paris for years, explained, "There wasn't the drama in Tunisia like in Algeria. The colonists who grew up there can return without any problems. Going back is easier for them— they aren't marked by the events, they go on trips, they see old school friends, there isn't this wound." The "wounded" Algerian *pieds-noirs,* on the other hand, have avoided returning out of fear of reprisals, and are stuck with their memories frozen in time and isolated from their source.

PIED-NOIR INTEGRATION
AND ITS LEGACY

The government agencies that were designed to accommodate repatriations numbering only in the tens of thousands annually were overwhelmed by the arrival of hundreds of thousands of *pieds-noirs* from Algeria in just a few months. An acute housing shortage developed and the state enacted emergency measures in the summer of 1962 to requisition unoccupied properties. Families were housed in collective dormitories at military bases, in hospitals, and in old factories, and others lived for months crowded into tiny hotel rooms, wine cellars, and even haylofts (Dubois 1994, 101; Zytnicki 1998, 508). Employment was another major concern. Having already worked at reintegrating the French arriving from the other colonies, the government now needed to find positions for the more than three hundred thousand men and women arriving from Algeria who had been actively employed.

The plight of the Sultanas illustrates well the human side of this migration and integration into a whole new economy. Victor and his wife Paulette had lived in the outskirts of Bône (now Annaba), where they were dairy farmers who sold vegetables at market as well. Victor's father had come from Malta as a laborer, as we have seen. Unlike many of the other people I knew, such as Mr. Mifsud, who had worked for a national utility company, Mr. Galea, who worked at the train yards, and Louise Marino, whose husband was in the military, the Sultanas were self-employed and thus had no position guaranteed in France. Moreover, most of their equity was in land, which they would have to sell at a greatly reduced rate at the war's end. They had no idea where to turn. They explained to me their predicament, and how they became, in essence, yet another charity case for the *Petites soeurs des pauvres* (an order of nuns). "I used to provide them with milk, and I brought up free vegetables every morning. Every single morning," Victor told me. "Today there would be one crate full, tomorrow two, the next day three, and sometimes even four or five. I brought them vegetables after the market, what didn't sell. So I was known. But I never would have thought to ask them for work, and they wouldn't have thought of it either." According to Victor, toward the end of the war, the nuns asked a mutual acquaintance if he would work for them in France as a driver, but he declined; as a police officer, he had a career awaiting him there. He mentioned this one day to the Sultanas while eating lunch at their house. Victor said that the choice was easy:

> Well, we had five children. So I said, "Me, I have five kids, I've never been to France, What am I going to do?" And the children were very young—the youngest wasn't even two years old. So, he said to me, all of a sudden: "Do you want to go back with the *Petites soeurs des pauvres?* When he said that, I said, "What? Work as driver for the *Petites soeurs?*" But, then, thinking about it, I thought, "Why not?" But then, even the sisters said, "This isn't the kind of job for you." They thought I was some kind of millionaire or something. Well, I wasn't a millionaire, we lived well, that's all. So I said, "Just keep me on for a while, and you don't even have to pay me."

The sisters needed him to leave right away, so he departed alone, hoping to secure lodging for his family. But the monthly price of most apartments

Figure 7. *Néflier* in a *pied-noir* garden. Photograph by the author.

had already risen to a sum roughly equivalent to his prospective salary from the religious order. He was getting anxious, as his wife was back in Algeria managing a household of five children in a rapidly deteriorating political situation. The nuns finally allotted him an abandoned building at their headquarters in Aix. They cleaned it out and installed electricity and a WC. Victor sent for his family. His wife, Paulette, reminisced about this time: "I came over with my brother. We were so full of hope of buying another farm. When my brother saw the place, he warned me. He said, 'Paulette, if you become part of this whole enterprise, you'll never leave. You'll never leave.' And he was right, wasn't he?"

The family never did purchase a farm, but after thirty years in France, Victor retired from his chauffeur position and the family was able to purchase a home in the outskirts of Aix, where they now live. His love of the land is still evident in his remarkable vegetable garden and the exotic Mediterranean trees that adorn his yard. He seemed to me to be trying to turn this little piece of France into Algeria, for not only did he grow an abundance of tomatoes and other standard crops, but he also showed me one day an abundance of black beets that he said were usually grown in North Africa; fava beans, which he prefers to grow himself; a *néflier,* a fruit tree often found on the other side of the Mediterranean and which adorns the gardens of many *pieds-noirs* (see fig. 7); and a prickly pear cactus that a friend had brought back from Malta that he keeps potted so that he can bring it indoors in the winter. When I visited them in the summer months, he was invariably outside working in the yard, where he also has an unusual collection of domesticated fowl and pigeons.

The professional reintegration of the colonial refugees was further complicated by the fact that most *pieds-noirs* from Algeria had lived primarily in
urban areas in the colony (Lefeuvre 2004, 274–75) and resettled in economically depressed regions in the southern part of France, where demands
for employment exceeded opportunities by the thousands. The converse
was true in many northern departments, and the French government began
a concerted effort to encourage the *pieds-noirs* to move north that involved
the development of seventy thousand industrial positions for Algerian
"repatriates." In the end, however, only four hundred such contracts were
signed (Baillet 1975). Not only was the geographic redistribution a failure,
but *pieds-noirs* who had originally settled in northern departments began
to move southward.

This internal *pied-noir* migration was not motivated by economic con-
siderations. In his 1975 study, Baillet found that the *pieds-noirs* from Algeria living in the Midi were under-employed; *pied-noir* households in Marseilles and Avignon earned 37 to 54 percent less than metropolitans in the
same cities, and they lived primarily in small high-rise apartments. In contrast, the *pieds-noirs* who had settled in northern departments or Paris easily found the positions they were seeking, and had achieved what Baillet
describes as "complete" economic integration. Despite these differences in
socioeconomic status, even those *pieds-noirs* who were settled in the north
began to move south. Baillet interprets this migration as a result of their
difficulties forging new social relationships with the metropolitan population, and of their desire to be closer to relatives and former friends. By the
1970s, more than half of all *pieds-noirs* in the country were living in the
eight departments of the Midi, and the city of Marseilles was receiving
three thousand *pieds-noirs* per year from the central, eastern, and northern
regions (Baillet 1975; Hunt 1992). According to statistics from 1990,
pieds-noirs are still highly concentrated in departments bordering the Mediterranean, as well as in Paris, Lyons, Bordeaux, and Corsica (Dubois 1994,
108).

French journals periodically publish special issues on the *pied-noir*
legacy in France that highlight prominent individuals in French society,
such as politicians, musicians, artists, and writers, who grew up in Algeria,[6]
with titles such as "The Unstoppable Ascent of the *Pieds Noirs*." The underlying message in these articles is that this population has not only integrated into French society, but in many cases has excelled. But whether
these exceptional individuals are representative of the rest of the *pied-noir*
population is a question that remains neglected. Moreover, professional
success does not preclude difficulties with social and emotional integration.
Despite the fact that it is now forty years since the final wave of decolonization migrations, remarkably little research has been conducted on its

long-term effects. Estimates of the total numbers of both *rapatriés* in general and the Algerian subset in particular are based on various methods of extrapolation, for only the census of 1968 included a category for *rapatriés*. Since 1968, French censuses have not provided a separate *rapatrié* category, a policy interpreted by some to indicate that they are now considered integrated into metropolitan society (Jordi 1993, 108). The reality, I believe, is subtler. In France, official state statistics rarely if ever indicate ethnic, national, or religious origins, and, consequently, an analysis of how ethnic groups compare nationally in terms of employment levels, schooling, or salaries is achieved only with great difficulty. This official government policy of nondifferentiation originated in the Revolutionary period and was compounded with a renewed conviction following World War II and the deportation of French Jews that the state should ensure the safety of its citizens by refraining from compiling data that could be later used to discriminate against them.[7] This policy also could be interpreted as an attempt by the government to mask difference and to present French society as far more unified than it actually is, an important feature of state formation (Corrigan and Sayer 1985). Many *pieds-noirs* subscribe to such a view and are frustrated by their inability to secure concrete proof of their numerical significance or of the proportions of *pied-noir* economic or social successes and failures in comparison to wider French society.[8] In response to their invisibility in the official state imagination, *pied-noir* organizations go to great lengths to estimate the size of the *pied-noir* populations in the various cities and nationwide.

The "repatriates" have officially "dissolved" into wider French society statistically, and their social and economic integration is difficult to elucidate. There is some evidence suggesting high degrees of intermarriage with wider French society in the second generation (Alba and Silberman 2002). Psychiatrists have published papers on the high rate of *pied-noir* suicides and writers such as Jordi refer to pervasive psychological problems associated with the trauma of the war and the permanent loss of their homeland (1993, 186–87). However, few systematic studies of these problems have been completed. Even the relationship between *pied-noir* integration and the *Trente glorieuses,* the three decades of rapid economic growth in France following World War II, is unclear. Some argue that, following their first difficult years in France, settlers' economic integration was successful because they benefited from the rapid economic growth that characterized the period from 1958 to 1973. However, an alternative view suggests that we look more closely at the impact of the settlers on the *Trente glorieuses* period itself. The arrival of one and a half million people in immediate need of housing, clothing, transportation, and all other basic goods and services must have fostered at least localized economic growth (Baillet

1975, 311). Lees believes that the economic growth, at least along the Mediterranean, was directly linked to the economic expansion caused by the postcolonial migrations. Not only was housing required to accommodate the migrants, but buildings were also needed for schools, hospitals, social service centers, and new administrative offices. Commerce, transportation, and public and private social services were also stimulated by the sudden increase in the population. Demand fueled inflation, and apartment prices increased 90 percent in some regions between 1958 and 1964. Although most settlers arrived with little capital of their own, the sudden flow of money in the form of subsistence allowances, indemnities, and the special low-interest loans that were granted to them allowed them to embark on consumption in a way France had not seen before (Lees 1996).

EXILE AND *NOSTALGÉRIE*

The abrupt rupture with Algeria and the inability of most *pieds-noirs* to return there even briefly have allowed an elaboration of, and, for some, even an indulgence in a nostalgia for Algeria. The intensity of *pied-noir* nostalgia may stem from features specific to this migration. The exodus from Algeria was the culmination of over seven years of trauma and, given the strange, liminal character of the war years, it would have been difficult for participants, many of whom had lost spouses, parents, or siblings, to go through a normal grieving process. In most cases, *pieds-noirs* realized that this migration represented a final rupture with their birthplace only after several years of being in France, and, therefore, few were able to prepare themselves emotionally for this transition. Because many did not know that they would not be coming back, and because there was so little space on the ferries that were the most popular means of emigration, most material possessions were left behind. Depending on individual family circumstances, some managed to bring away family photos or small heirlooms, but much else stayed in Algeria.

This loss of possessions held great symbolic meaning for some of the people I interviewed, but I did not truly understand its import until one day during a meeting with Mr. Grech. I was admiring his impressive collection of rare books on North African history, many of which I had been searching for in libraries in France. "Yes," he told me, with obvious pride, "it is a unique collection." I asked if he had been a collector his whole life, and he looked surprised. "Oh no!" he said, "I am not a collector— These are mine. I still have them because I was working for the army during the war and was allowed to ship them to France." I had not seen many books, paintings, or family photos in other *pied-noir* apartments or homes, and now I wondered if this reflected not the families' different priorities or in-

comes, as I had assumed, but instead the precipitous nature of their departure. The abandonment of most material belongings, which, during their
years in "exile" in France, might have allowed them to reconnect at least
symbolically to the lost place and their past lives there, would have had
long-lasting repercussions. Some of these lost items, such as tools, dishes,
furniture, and clothing, would have been passed down through the generations and would have represented a material embodiment of the family
past.

Connection to the family past was lost not only indirectly in this way,
but literally as well: the remains of their dead were necessarily left behind
in Algerian cemeteries. This separation caused particular pain to *pieds-noirs*
during the annual Toussaint holiday (All Saint's Day) on November 1,
when people in France typically visit and beautify their loved ones' graves.
One woman I spoke with broke down when she described her first Toussaint in France. She and her husband were civil servants in Algeria and were
transferred to new jobs in dark and gloomy Lille in the north of France.
The holiday took them by surprise and they had no idea what to do that
day. They had no gravesites to visit and driving around the countryside
would have been unbearable, for they would have seen all the other families
gathering at their cemeteries. So they stayed home, all day. "That was the
worst day," she told me, in tears. "It was on that day that I first realized that
we were never going back."

LIFE ON TWO LEVELS

To deal with such loss, some people have put considerable energy into moving forward, like Louise Marino, who has learned and now teaches yoga.
Others started new businesses in France and some returned to agriculture.
For many *pieds-noirs* I encountered, however, the tug of *nostalgérie* was
quasi-permanent. They lived a double life, residing in France but living
emotionally in Algeria as well. Evidence of living simultaneously in both
worlds appeared with surprising frequency in the form of unconscious verbal slips or errors. The first of these slips involves a confusion of verb tense.
Individuals sometimes talked to me about Algeria in the present tense for
some time before realizing it. When their children were also present, they
immediately, and sometimes harshly, corrected their parents, suggesting
that slips of this kind were recurrent. One day I visited Joseph Zammit, the
elderly widower of Maltese origins who sang in Arabic during our trip to
Malta. We were in his tiny apartment in Aix overlooking a highway under-
pass (see fig. 8) and, at one point, he got up to show me a book of reproductions of old postcards of his hometown, Philippeville. Turning to an
image of the coastline, he pointed out to me, "Look, there is the lighthouse

Figure 8. Zammit's building, southern France. Photograph by the author.

you can see from my house. There, that's *my* house—that is where I live, right there. OK, now this, this is another view of my house. This is what you see from my living room window, and that, there, is the main street in the center of town." We continued to look as he turned the pages. "There, again, that's where I live, I mean, where I lived—" He caught himself only after several minutes, and seemed slightly embarrassed. This was the most animated he had been that day, and his wistful return to old photographs of his beloved house and former home town made a very poignant impression on me.

Another slip indicating the entangling of two consciousnesses occurred when individuals responded inappropriately to simple questions, leading to awkward confusions in everyday conversation. Slips of this nature not only indicate that people are mixing the present with the past, but also reveal the dominance for some of an Algeria-based consciousness. I experienced this at a large outdoor picnic held annually at a regional park a good hour's drive from my apartment in the outskirts of Arles. This reunion of *pieds-noirs* who were former residents of the department of Constantine usually attracts thousands of people from throughout southeastern France. This year, however, it had been raining across the region for nearly a week. It was still raining hard on the day of the event, and the meeting location had been changed to a covered area in a village parking lot. It was very cold that day. I was talking with a group of elderly women, most of whom were wearing thin summer dresses, and we huddled together near their small barbecue to keep warm. One woman asked her husband to get a blanket for her from the car and turned to tell us how cold she was. Her friend spoke up. "Thank goodness I wore pants!" she said, and then, turning to me, explained, "When we left, the sun was shining!" This surprised me, and I realized that she must have driven quite far to the reunion because clouds were still blanketing most of southwestern France. "Oh really," I asked, "where did you come from?" "Bône," she responded, "like Michèle," gesturing to a woman in our group. This reference to Algeria was immediate (and used the old, colonial name of the town), and I was caught off guard, unsure what she meant. Is it possible that there is a town called Bône in France? I wondered.

A similar slip occurred at a formal dinner dance uniting former residents of Souk-Ahras. I was talking with Pauline, a woman in her seventies who was seated at my table. Her friends, sitting across from us, had driven up for the evening from Marseilles, and they were complaining about how late the meal was and about the impending long drive home. I asked Pauline, "Did you come from Marseilles as well?" "Oh no!" she exclaimed, rather startled. "No, I was repatriated from Algeria! I arrived in Marseilles only recently, thirty-three years ago!" I was somewhat at a loss for words, wondering how it was that she had misunderstood me so completely, particularly given the conversation immediately preceding my question. I was also struck by the fact that she knew without a moment's hesitation exactly how many years she had been in Marseilles. I asked if she had been back to Algeria. "No, it's impossible," she told me. She sighed. "It is hard, very, very, very, hard. I think about my old house all of the time. It was terrible to leave, just terrible."

In these two cases, I had made a minor mistake in French by asking the women where they were from, and not where they were coming from. However, given the wider conversational context and my overt foreigner status, my meaning should have been apparent. Instead of interpreting my question within the context of the ongoing conversation, however, the individuals responded literally, referring immediately and inappropriately to Algeria, as if Algeria, and not the weather or the long drive to Marseilles, were the current topic of discussion. It is clear that Algeria occupies a central place in the imaginations of these individuals, and represents not some distant past but a time and space of considerable immediacy.

NOSTALGIA AND
METROPOLITAN *ACCUEIL*

A longing for a lost place and time can also be a reflection of the difficulties one is experiencing in one's present setting. I did not need to spend much time with *pieds-noirs* to learn that their nostalgia for Algeria is nourished regularly by their hardships in France and with other French. One afternoon while I was visiting the Mifsuds, Mrs. Mifsud returned from the store in an unusually agitated state. "Those people!" the spry seventy-five-year-old woman spat under her breath. She proceeded to unpack a few things. "I couldn't get the apéritifs," she told her husband, on the brink of tears, "I'm sorry." She retreated to the kitchen where she prepared an alternative snack and, when she emerged, she explained what had happened. She had been waiting in line at a local shop while the saleswoman chatted with a friend. After some time had passed, Mrs. Mifsud had had to interrupt her for assistance. Then the cake she was trying to purchase had had no price attached, so she was ordered back to the aisle to find another box, only to lose her place in line. The cashier rang up her groceries slowly—deliberately, Mrs. Mifsud felt—and then further insulted the elderly woman by hurling her purchases down the chute. When the cashier announced, "You owe me X francs," Mrs. Mifsud had had enough. "No, *I* do not owe *you* anything!" she retorted, and left the store, leaving all her items on the counter. "I just couldn't take it any more!" she explained, "Constantly being mistreated like that!" Mr. Mifsud responded with stories of his own from their first years in France, attempting, it seemed to me, to explain why such a minor incident would infuriate his wife. One story led to another, and I heard in this way a whole litany of frustrations, an experience that was repeated in subsequent conversations with other *pieds-noirs*. The pain of rejection and of having their membership in the wider collectivity regularly challenged were themes generated by these stories. After having exploited their repertoire of anecdotes of this nature, people often contrasted them with stories of life *là-bas,* in Algeria. This narrative sequence implied that their feelings of rejection were not an indication of their own mental imbalance or paranoia, for they could remember a time and place when they felt very differently. They had once belonged somewhere. Algeria in these instances became the reference point against which their troubles in France were judged.

A nostalgic yearning to return to a better time or place can be viewed as representing a disappointment with the present circumstances, a "disenchantment with and disengagement from the here-and-now" (Nosco 1990, 4). *Pied-noir* nostalgia implies a disenchantment with France, which some articulate quite overtly and consciously. Many repatriates were arriving in their *patrie,* their fatherland, for the first time, and the discrepancy between what they had imagined France to be and the France they encountered was great. Even greater was the gulf between the "France" they did know (i.e., Algeria) and the metropole. A difficulty connecting with the new geography was mentioned frequently, and may help explain Louise's feeling of being a perpetual tourist, of never finding her "place" in France. Some confess that they still have a hard time finding France beautiful, and disappointments with the French landscape or the weather lead many to think about how beautiful it was back "home." On the way home from a tour with members of the Maltese association, I sat on the bus next to an older white-haired woman with clear brown eyes. We discussed the countryside as we passed rugged white cliffs dotted with shaggy green bushes of wild rosemary, thyme, and other herbs. I told her how much I enjoyed the lovely Provençal scenery. My companion suddenly said in a markedly lower voice than before, "When we arrived from Algeria, I couldn't believe it. There, the mountains are green. So much larger than these here, and so much richer in vegetation. Here, it is just rocks. I just couldn't believe it." Many also retain vivid memories of their first encounter with Northern European winters. Some describe this feeling of not quite belonging as a floating, drifting feeling, or as having lost their bearings. "We are the shifting sands," a woman explained when I first met her at a large gathering, "we don't belong anywhere anymore." But the greatest disappointments involve the reception of the *pieds-noirs,* their *accueil* by people of France, the *métropolitains.*

Accueil is a rich word in French that carries multiple meanings, including "reception," "welcome," "accommodation," and "greeting." When using this term in connection to the French, *pieds-noirs* are referring to how they were "treated" by the French, but also seem to be implying that they had not received the welcome they expected. I heard many tales of outright cruelty: people purposefully blocking in their cars, graffiti calling for their expulsion from France, the theft of their belongings from military warehouses, hotel managers one after another refusing to admit them. Some French took advantage of their desperate circumstances and ignorance by selling them poor farmland at exorbitant prices or cars with hidden flaws. People told long sagas of their first (miserable) year in France. Louise Martino, for instance, spoke for over an hour about her family's repatriation. Because her husband held an important position in the French army, the family was required to leave for France under military orders near the end of the war. They quickly packed the crates provided for repatriating military personnel and departed separately, at night. Upon finally arriving in France with their four children, one of whom was stricken with polio, Louise found no shelter awaiting them and had to seek out accommodations herself. Hotel owners, already overwhelmed by the sudden strain on their services, turned her away regularly until Louise began to leave her children behind, bringing the rest of the family only after she had registered. Yet when hotel managers saw the large family, they invariably told her that they had made a mistake, that she could stay only one night because the hotel was booked solid after that. She carried out the same charade daily at other hotels until one day she finally broke down. She had had enough, and she stormed into the local headquarters of the French army with her toddlers and caused a scene, demanding to see the general in charge and shouting at him that he would have to take her children because she did not have the courage to kill them herself. She sobbed while telling me that she had actually threatened to kill her own children. Only after this desperate act did her family receive temporary shelter. But their troubles were not yet over. When they finally settled into an apartment of their own several months later, she and her husband reported to the military center where their goods were stored, only to find that all of their wooden crates were empty. They had been robbed of all of their belongings. After pursuing their case, she was informed that theft had been widespread in the military warehouses and was offered no further compensation or, it appears, even apology.

HOSPITALITY

The difficulties of the first years are not always foremost in everyone's mind, and many former settlers have worked at integrating into their new work environments, schools, neighborhoods, and even the local political scene. In the process they encounter yet another source of alienation and disorientation. The French were also not what they had expected. I heard two main complaints: a lack of hospitality and a certain provincialism. These complaints parallel those encountered by researchers working with Greek refugees from Asia Minor (Herzfeld 1991; Hirschon 1989). Mrs. Perez, a woman in her eighties whom I met in her ground-floor apartment in an old building in central Aix, talked about what she perceived as the French hostility to neighbors: "The French are not a warm people, not like people from *là-bas*. Take this building, for example," she said, pointing to the apartments above. "There are four apartments up there. We have lived in this building for thirty-two years and I have never been invited inside anybody's apartment. Never. That is how the French are!" Such a lack of hospitality would have been unthinkable in Algeria. I asked Mrs. Perez if she thought the French might be afraid of people they did not know, of *étrangers* or foreigners. She took some time to answer my question, considering it carefully. "No, I don't think that's it, because from what I can tell, they are that way with each other too." She told me a story of a metropolitan woman she knew, Thérèse, who had moved into a new home in a very chic, renovated quarter of Aix-en-Provence. When Thérèse moved in, she sent the four or five neighbors sharing the courtyard an invitation to a house-warming party in her apartment. "That is the right thing to do," Mrs. Perez explained. "When you move in, you want your neighbors to feel at ease about the new person. So Thérèse made up invitation cards for the neighbors. A few called to say that they were busy and the rest did not even have the courtesy to respond!" Thérèse told her that she had sat there all afternoon in her newly decorated apartment, with apéritifs ready, in vain. "She told me it was the most painful day of her life."[9]

That people would behave so coldly toward others living in the same apartment complex was shocking to many former settlers, who had internalized quite different hospitality traditions. As Herzfeld has noted, hospitality does not always mark acceptance of an outsider so much as the moral superiority of the host (1991, 81). One woman told me that, upon arriving in France, she was surprised to find that the *pieds-noirs* had better manners than the French. "If you stopped by somebody's house in Algeria, you were invited inside for coffee at least," she said. After years of feeling purposefully slighted socially, however, many people I met had begun to view these disappointments as reflecting less a malicious and willful stance on the part of the French, and more as representative of what they saw as peculiarly provincial metropolitan norms. *Pieds-noirs* spent considerable time trying to understand what they viewed as the marked lack of hospitality of the "French" and their coldness to outsiders, and I was often asked for my own opinion on this apparently puzzling behavior. Such judgments may be part of the process of constructing a moral boundary between "the French" and *pieds-noirs,* a process that in all probability was being carried out simultaneously in the other direction by the metropolitan French.

THE HOSTILITY OF BUREAUCRATS

While former settlers might be able to forgive cultural differences they viewed as being based on divergent traditions of hospitality, they found their treatment at the hands of local and state bureaucrats particularly galling, for these officials often challenged their Frenchness, the very core of their identity. Once in France, *pieds-noirs* and other repatriates were required to file various forms to "regularize" their status vis-à-vis the French state's administrations. Many told me of their trials with bureaucrats who either refused to accept their Algeria- or Tunisia-derived paperwork and forms or denied their requests for services, stating outright that since the people concerned were born in Africa, they were not French. The treasurer of the Franco-Maltese association, Mr. Calleja, of Maltese heritage, had grown up in Tunisia. When he first arrived in 1961, his cousin told him to get his *carte d'identité* (identity card) first, because it would facilitate his later encounters with other French bureaucracies. Calleja only had a certificate of French citizenship obtained from the French embassy in Tunisia. When he went to the proper agency, he was asked by the French official there for his *livret de famille,* the state-prepared booklet listing births, deaths, and marriages. Calleja did not have one, for these were not mandatory in Tunisia. Mr. Calleja

Figure 9. World War I medals displayed in a *pied-noir* home. Photograph by the author.

was informed that, in this case, he could not obtain a card. Calleja then presented his paperwork documenting his completion of thirty months of military service in the French army during World War II. The functionary still refused to give him a card, and suggested that, since he was born in Tunisia, it was doubtful that he was really French. "Wasn't really French!" Calleja exclaimed to me later. "My God, why would I waste thirty months of my life in the French army if I wasn't French?"

The calling into question of their French nationality was remembered by former settlers with special moral outrage. After having served in World War II for three years and sometimes even longer,[10] and having lost family members in World War I and II and sometimes even the Franco-Prussian War, many interviewees felt not only that their French nationality was unquestionable, but that their war sacrifices in World War II in particular gave them a moral edge over many French of the metropole.[11] Through their participation in World War II, during which they felt that they were instrumental in saving France from the Germans and the Vichy regime, they had demonstrated themselves to be the true French patriots. Some even argued that during that war they had saved France from herself. This military service, along with that of their ancestors during previous Europe-centric wars, was cited by many former settlers as having guaranteed their membership in the national community, and it is prominently displayed in the form of framed war medals in family homes (see fig. 9). In a conversation with a Spanish-origin couple, Mr. Costa began outlining his family's service record: "Me, my grandfather served in the war of 1870. My father served in 1914–1918. Me and my brother, we did the war of '39–'45. All the brothers of my mother did the war of '14–'18 and '39–'45. Some never came back. And, even still!" His wife added, "But then, when they asked for the *carte d'identité,* we had to go back to the generation of our grandparents to prove that we were French!"

Mr. Costa was further irritated by another, related form of discrimination he felt had set "repatriates" apart. This had to do with the numeric codes used by the social security administration to indicate the department where an individual was born. For the French of North Africa, the number granted was 99, the same number given to foreigners living in France. According to Costa, the logic was clear: "For us, the French of North Africa, it's 99. Like who else? Like all the foreigners living in France. *Voilà.* 99, for all the foreigners in France: Italians, Arabs, blacks . . . thus they consider us foreigners as well." These early encounters between *pieds-noirs* and French bureaucrats may indicate a simultaneous love of the *patrie* and hatred of the state and its representatives similar to that identified by Wylie (1957, 206–39). Yet they also reveal two different visions of how the French nation should be delimited, two different imagined communities. The French of Algeria had been taught and had wholly embraced the official ideology that they were living in France. For many French of France, by contrast, the nation was delimited by the Hexagon, the metropole; people born elsewhere, such as in North Africa, were outsiders.

THE *PIED-NOIR:* A "SEPARATE BREED"

While I didn't feel comfortable revealing this to my *pied-noir* interlocutors, I often felt that their tales of metropolitan animosity were not far-fetched and the incidents reported may have been willful, as they had suspected. During my years in France, I have noticed that when I explain my project to non-*pied-noir* "metropolitan" friends and associates, their reaction is usually one of surprise and distaste. A woman in her forties told me, "Oh, *them,* I really *really* hate those people!" Some people visibly shuddered the first time I mentioned the word *pied-noir.* When I asked why *pieds-noirs* were so disliked, one friend described them as too loud and obnoxious, as flashy dressers, or as having no artistic sense or taste. Others considered them to be *gros colons,* rich colonists with vast estates, or extreme racists.[12]

University students in particular highlighted alleged *pied-noir* racism and right-wing tendencies.

Interestingly, there is a racialized quality to some metropolitan anti-*pied-noir* sentiment as well. Most of my research was conducted in a *pied-noir*-dominated environment, and thus I rarely observed conversations between *pieds-noirs* and metropolitan French. When I did observe such a conversation, it often revealed remarkable gaps in understanding and considerable awkwardness. The following interaction occurred while I was taping a conversation with the Mifsuds. As was often the case, their daughter, Catherine, was visiting that day with her friend, Juliette, a forty-year-old French woman. We had been discussing the term *pied-noir*. Mr. Mifsud was telling me that he felt the French sometimes used it in an insulting manner. At this point, Juliette joined in:

JULIETTE:	Yes, it is pejorative.
MRS. MIFSUD:	No, not at all.
MR. MIFSUD:	There are even associations, associations of . . . *rapatriés*, that use an image of a black foot. OK, I don't like that, but they use the black-foot symbol to identify themselves.
JULIETTE:	However, whenever the French use the term *pied-noir*, one senses . . . a certain animosity.

Here, there is an obvious disparity between two views of the label *pied-noir*. From Juliette's perspective, it is derogatory. However, Mrs. Mifsud disagrees, as does her husband, and they outline how often it is used by members of the community themselves. The elderly couple then continued to explain how they believe the French view them:

MRS. MIFSUD:	There are people who even wonder if we are French. They don't know if we are Arabs, if we are Jews.
MR. MIFSUD:	They wonder about us!
MRS. MIFSUD:	Some haven't learned anything at all! I lived in Paris in 1950, and I had a concierge who asked me one day, "Do you eat pork? Do you wear a veil? Do you go to church?"

Juliette listened to the family continue with their stories about the amazing ignorance of the French regarding the *pieds-noirs* until she could no longer remain mute, and she tried to explain this French behavior by outlining what she had learned about *pieds-noirs* from the media as a child:

JULIETTE:	I remember, I was a little girl, and they made us believe that the *pieds-noirs* were massacring the Arabs. I saw that, I lived through that. I didn't understand it all very well, I was only eight or nine years old, but we watched the TV screen, and they told us, "The *pieds-noirs* are really savages."

As the conversation proceeded, she finally blurted out, "But the *pied-noir* was considered a completely different breed, according to the French. I mean, according to the French of France."[13] These statements are revealing. While anti-*pied-noir* sentiment is often associated with the war and the *pieds-noirs'* ties to colonialism, Juliette's description of the *pied-noir* as a completely different breed suggests an apolitical, racialized image. She also made an error that she undoubtedly noticed, for she corrected herself in midsentence. By contrasting *pieds-noirs* with "the French," she was suggesting that these were distinct categories, from which it could be inferred that the *pieds-noirs* were not really French, a statement she knew would be insulting to her hosts.

Metropolitan racialization of the *pied-noir* may be best demonstrated by the label itself. The term *pied-noir* became widely used during the French-Algerian War.[14] It appears to have been an "exonym," a name granted by outsiders. Such terms are often "tinged with implied inequality or negative valuation" (Proschan 1997, 91). Since their arrival in France and, over the years, the consolidation of a distinct consciousness, many repatriates from Algeria have reclaimed the term for themselves, claiming exonym as autonym. In the process, an array of explanations for its origins have emerged and can be found in *pied-noir* publications. The most widespread of these is the legend of the "black boots." According to this explanation, the first troops of the French expeditionary forces arrived in Algeria in 1830 wearing a uniform that included black lace-up boots (*bottines*). The indigenous population supposedly thought that these men had black feet, and thus began to call the French in Algeria *pieds-noirs,* or "black feet." A similar explanation imagines that the Algerians came up with this nickname after watching the early settlers making wine, which stained their feet dark purple. These legends are interesting primarily for the paternalistic attitude toward the Algerians that they reveal. It is preposterous to imagine that at that time indigenous Algerians had not seen Western shoes; there had been regular contact between Algeria and peoples from across the Mediterranean for centuries. Furthermore, these "explanations" are not backed by any linguistic evidence. If the term had been developed by Algerians in the 1830s, it certainly would have first appeared in Arabic, Berber, or some other local idiom. Not only was the expression developed in French, but it was first used in Algeria only in the late 1950s, over a century after the initial French military operations there.

Mr. Mifsud was well aware of this problem and outlined his concerns. He explained that, having grown up in the suburbs of Algiers, he was a real *pataouète* speaker: he grew up in the neighborhoods playing with little kids from Naples and local Algerians, he said. He was thus *truly* integrated, he told me, and yet throughout this time he had never heard the word *pied-noir.* He remembers vividly the first time he heard the term used:

In '54 . . . '57 . . . maybe '57, there was a professional meeting . . . I was a member of the General Confederation of Senior Managers . . . and at a meeting of metropolitan managers in Oran, an engineer was talking about the *pieds-noirs*. I said to my colleague next to me, I said, "Who are these *pieds-noirs*, and he said, "Well, it's us!" "Oh, it's us, the *pieds-noirs*?" It was a word I had *never* heard before, *never*. It's a word that came from France. And afterward we learned why they called us [that] . . . it seems, the legend is that the first French who came to Algeria wore black shoes, or boots, and the Arabs said, "They have black feet." But what surprised me is that my whole family—my parents were born there, I was born there, and we never heard this name. Never, never. We never heard this word *pied-noir*. We only heard it first during the *événements*.

When I pointed out that it almost seemed as if the "black boot" legend had been invented much later, Mr. Mifsud agreed, and thought it odd that it was invented a full century after the fact.

While *pied-noir* legends of the origins of the term tend to attribute it to Algerians, I heard an entirely different explanation from French-Algerians living in France. According to a retired professional French-Algerian soccer player, Saïd, the origin was obvious and had clear racist undertones. The label was created by the metropolitan French who wanted to distinguish themselves from the French from the African colonies. They referred to them as *pieds-noirs* as a warning to other French: these imposters might look "white" on the surface, but if you looked carefully at the bottom of their feet, you would see that they are really "black," "tainted" from their long stay in Africa.

That the *pieds-noirs* are viewed by metropolitan French as a distinct race was supported by other narratives about their encounters with the French. Sensing the pervasive anti-*pied-noir* sentiment that surrounded them, many *pieds-noirs* told me that they did not tell their new colleagues where they were from. Some confessed to me that they were still hiding this information from their neighbors. When Chantal Galea finally told a colleague at the school where she taught that she was born in Algeria, the colleague was shocked, and exclaimed, "But you aren't black!" "And this was an educated woman, somebody working in the national school system," Chantal explained to me, struck by her colleague's ignorance.

Further evidence suggests that a view of the *pied-noir* as a distinct "African" people has roots that precede the French-Algerian War.[15] Some people told me about metropolitan anti-settler discrimination that they experienced as early as the 1930s. Families of French origin with means sometimes traveled to France for vacations and to visit relatives. One family I became close to, the Flournoys, were quite proud of their "pure" French heritage, and were greatly wounded by metropolitan misconceptions and discrimination. In one instance, Mr. Flournoy's uncle, Jacques, was sent from Algeria to France for his military service, where he fell in love with a French woman. They wanted to marry, but the woman's parents refused to permit the marriage because they believed that Jacques was really an "Arab." ("He was somewhat dark," Mrs. Flournoy explained.) She was finally allowed to marry him several years later, but, after the wedding, the couple had tremendous difficulty finding an apartment. Every time the husband was asked where he was born and answered, "Algeria," the response was inevitably, "Well, then, you're not French!" and the application was rejected. Fed up with this treatment, Jacques finally found a place to live after he began telling potential landlords that he was from Marseilles. Suzanne Flournoy herself encountered metropolitan suspicion when she visited this family later on in the 1930s. She brought gifts from North Africa that she had purchased at the *souks,* including a vase. One day she picked some flowers and put them in the vase while her hostess was out shopping. The next day, she noticed that the vase was gone, and found it hidden in the kitchen cupboards. She assumed that her relative had put it there without thinking while cleaning, so she took the vase out and put it back on top of the radio in the center of the room. Later that day the vase was again hidden. This went on for a few days, and she became intrigued. Suzanne Flournoy continued with her story:

> So, one day Odile said to me, "No, Suzanne, don't keep taking out the vase. Because, when we leave, I am sure that everyone is looking in the windows." And then she showed me. We went up to the attic, and there was a huge trunk, and inside was linen from Algeria, bibs, slippers, things like that. She said to me, "Look," and she took them out. They were all new. Completely new. She said, "I never put them on the kids." So, the whole family had been sending presents, and to be original, we didn't send French things, we sent Arab baby clothes, things like that. She said to me, "Look. I have never dressed the kids like that . . . Everyone was already saying that Marcel [her son] was an Arab—just think if I had dressed him like one!"

Even after having been settled in France for years and having begun to raise a family, Odile and her Algeria-born yet "pure" French husband found themselves the subjects of their neighbors' curiosity and suspicion regarding their ancestry, race, and Frenchness. As a result, Odile felt compelled to deny any family connection to Algeria by hiding the many gifts she received over the years from her husband's relatives.

But Suzanne Flournoy's story was not over. She told me that, during her visit, a neighborhood woman dropped by regularly. She later learned that this was unusual:

Whenever we were there, every day a neighbor stopped by: "Oh, Mrs. Ponty, I don't have any more coffee—can you lend me some, I will go buy some and return it." Another time, it was another woman, for sugar, you see? And one day, Odile said, out of the blue, "Suzanne, they never visit me, never! This is just to get a look at you, to see if you aren't an Arab, to see if you aren't black!"

Clearly, metropolitan French sometimes conflated birthplace, nationality, and race, and these early anecdotes provide a yet untapped resource from which to better understand the shifting relationship between race and culture in the French imagined community.

RACE, CULTURE, AND NATION

In his work on Antillean ethnic activists in Paris, David Beriss asserts that explicit racial ideologies "lack legitimacy in France," and there is little social scientific literature akin to that found in the U.S. and Britain regarding race or "race relations." French state statistics distinguish only between nationals and foreigners, and unlike in the U.S. and Britain, for instance, official documents do not take note of ethnic origins or "race." It is culture, not race, which is fetishized in France. Cultures are viewed as essentialist, and organized in a hierarchical fashion, with non-European cultures seen as less worthy and unsophisticated. Balibar has described this phenomenon as "racism without races." It results in a negative stereotyping of people who have inherited an "inferior" non-European culture, who are viewed as unable to develop more sophisticated attributes (Beriss 2004, 42). Beriss explains that Antilleans may experience animosity, but understand it not as racism per se, but as an "unjust invocation of cultural difference" (2004, 42): what incenses the Antilleans is being confused with less acculturated, non-French, immigrants.

This is not the place to trace the periodization of this culturalist classification of peoples; some argue that this is a "new" racism, while others argue persuasively that this "racism without races" has its roots in the very model of the nation upon which France was founded (for a review, see Silverman 1992, 20–30). What is important to consider is that a kind of racialization based on essentialist cultural differences does occur. Moreover, the colonial past continues to play a key role in determining the evolving hierarchical framework of nationals and non-nationals.

The legacy of colonialism persists in "postcolonial" France not only in the perpetuation of legal and ideological structures, but in more subtle ways as well. After the 1960s, a consensus developed across the political spectrum that France was experiencing a shift in forms of immigration. A dichotomy emerged distinguishing "old" from "new" immigrants, the "assimilable" and the "unassimilable," which corresponded roughly with immigrants from within Europe (Poland, Italy, Portugal) and those from the colonies. As Silverman and Noiriel argue, the myth of the easily assimilated European migrant was developed retrospectively. Previously racialized immigrants, such as Italians and Poles, were reimagined as closer culturally to the French, while the peoples of the Maghreb were distanced. This shift located France's contemporary problems not in failures of government, crises in capitalism, or poorly designed social programs, but in the presence of more culturally different non-European others (Silverman 1992, 84). These changes in the perception of the assimilation experience and of immigrant cultural distance developed with two key changes in the postwar geopolitical context: Europeanization and the loss of Empire (Silverman 1992, 105). Balibar emphasizes decolonization in particular. With decolonization, the line between the metropole and colonies was blurred, leading to profound anxieties. Prewar immigrants were viewed as closer culturally because they had not been colonized, while the postwar immigrants were imagined to be culturally distant because they had been (Balibar 1984). A cultural essentialist "racism" associated with decolonization emerged with the threat posed by the collapse of us/them, here/there, and the fear of a loss of cultural difference in its wake. As Silverman explains,

> In the new "mixed" context of post-colonialism it is precisely the prospect of non-differentiation and *equality* which is of deep worry: that is, the problem of accepting as equals those who were previously inferiors . . . It is the moment when those previously defined ethnically/religiously *and* as inferiors (in the colonial context) come to resemble "the French" culturally and socially . . . that they pose a problem and must be differentiated (especially culturally). (1992, 144–45)

What is especially interesting is the fact that this "new" racism affects the invisible colonial migrants, such as the *pieds-noirs,* as well as those more phenotypically or religiously marked. *Pieds-noirs* often find that in interactions with the metropolitan French, they are first assumed to be "real French," bearers of a common cultural heritage. Over the course of their encounters with metropolitan French, however, such characteristics as their distinct dialect, dress, or African birthplace distance them in essential ways in the minds of many French. They are suddenly viewed as members of a distinct race, "*une race à part.*" They are, after all, *pieds-noirs.*

A blurring between race and essentialist notions of cultural difference is evident here. Anti-*pied-noir* sentiment is sometimes articulated in such a way as to reveal an underlying racialization; in other instances, cultural differences are highlighted. Some metropolitans I met linked this cultural difference, with an emphasis on their suspect political behavior, to the colonial context. Their former position of outrageous privilege made them a different breed politically, some feel, and explains their alignment with the extreme right and racist groups in France. Many academics in particular explained their animosity to *pieds-noirs* in these terms. Others described the *pied-noir* difference in more class-based terms, reflecting a hostility toward the *nouveaux riches*. Some attributed the most salient aspects of this cultural difference to their lengthy stay in North Africa and their assimilation over the years to North African cultures. A retired couple who ran the laundromat I used in Aix talked with me one day about how life there took a dramatic turn for the worse following the arrival of the *pieds-noirs*. According to this couple, the area was "swamped" by the *Français d'Algérie*. "They came here with their bad manners," the wife explained. "You see, they had adopted bad habits over there in Africa, and now are like Arabs (*comme des Arabes*), and this exasperates us. Since their arrival, things have really gone downhill." Statements such as this were uttered periodically and are informed by French anti-Arab prejudices. Ironically, then, while some French justify their anti-*pied-noir* feelings by the widespread view that *pieds-noirs* are anti-"Arab," there is a strong French prejudice against the *pieds-noirs* based on their supposed cultural affinity to North Africans. Such statements may make use of indexicality to allow the listeners to draw their own conclusions, as when *pieds-noirs* are linked with "bad taste" or "bad manners," which index their "North African" or "less civilized" land of origin, and with "Arabs." In this way, speakers avoid appearing overtly racist.

My interactions with metropolitans and *pieds-noirs* underscore the metropolitan view of the *pied-noir* as a fundamentally different breed, as Juliette pointed out. Through these narratives I also learned how *pieds-noirs* view metropolitans. Many told me how stunned they were by the strangely provincial outlook of many French. This was not at all what they had expected of France, a place they had learned to revere in school. The settlers had grown up in a multicultural, multiethnic, and multireligious world, and enjoyed outlining to me the depth of their knowledge—whether of the specific practices of the different Muslim sects, North African Jewish customs, or terms in different languages. Having grown up in North Africa, the *pieds-noirs* also had a keen understanding of geography and of the contours and history of the French Empire. They were cosmopolitan, and they often highlighted the contrasting provincialism of the French. That the French lacked a basic knowledge of their own colonies was seen as especially surprising. The curiosity of the French metropolitans about Mrs. Flournoy when she was visiting family members, the unwillingness of landlords to rent to people born in Algeria, the questioning of the schoolteacher's physical appearance upon learning her birthplace are all palpable examples of how little the colonies featured in the daily lives of most metropolitans.

The *pied-noir* example also brings into focus conflicting conceptions of the French nation. What is often missing in discussions of French national identity today is a consideration of how locations outside of the Hexagon were implicated in or even central to evolving notions of self and other. In his study of Quebec, Richard Handler underscores how nationalism is an ideology concerned with boundedness, continuity, and homogeneity. Nations are imagined as "precisely delimited" in both space and time (1988, 6). In his exploration of salient features of Quebec nationalism, he finds that all versions "agree about the existence of a nation which is taken to be bonded, continuous, and at least minimally homogenous," but he encountered disagreement regarding its content. In the case of the French of both Algeria and France, however, we find some agreement on the content of French nationalism, but less on the nation's boundaries. Agreement on content is suggested by the many *pied-noir* statements I heard about the significance of the French language and their ancestors' military service. It is also indicated by Mr. Grech's statements about the power France, his *patrie,* held for him while growing up in Algiers, around which all else revolved, and which extended to a passionate love for the diverse regions of the beloved Hexagon. His words could have been uttered by a French man from the metropole of the same generation, such as the residents of the Vaucluse whom Wylie studied (1957, 206–208). On the other hand, the very boundaries of the imagined community are in question. Did France stop at the Mediterranean? Gaps in the two conceptions of the "national" geography, of the nation's location, probably persisted for much of colonial Algeria's history. An illuminating example of this disjunction can be seen in a misunderstanding that occurred during the 1937 Paris World's Fair. When trying to determine exhibit placement, delegates for French Algeria requested that their exhibit be placed near those of the metropolitan regions rather than in the Colonial Center, citing its status as three French departments. A member of the World Fair's Regional Commission responded curtly, "This issue can be easily dismissed, and shows some education is needed on the colonial side" (quoted in Peer 1998, 76). That most metropolitan French saw Algeria as an utterly disconnected, foreign land is suggested here, as well as by the many reminiscences I heard of times when the overseas French were treated with suspicion.

Because a nation is also bounded by the "exclusive allegiance of its members" (Handler 1988, 6), the fact that the French of Algeria were living in some place other than the nation called into question their fealty and belonging. Their different nationalisms in turn yielded quite different relationships to military service. While the French of Algeria may have felt they were defending *la patrie* in 1914 and in 1942, a reciprocal attitude was not common among metropolitans fighting in the French-Algerian War. The discrepancy between the two loyalties, and the two different nationalisms they represent, were noted by *pieds-noirs* who viewed the metropolitan attitude as a very clear rejection of themselves and of the colony. A *pied-noir* author at a public lecture I attended stated, "The kids coming over to fight in Algeria [during the French-Algerian War] didn't see themselves defending the *patrie,* but instead felt they were simply fighting for the economic interests of some rich *colons.*" For most metropolitans, Algeria was not a part of the French nation and, consequently, their military service in its defense was resented.

Negative encounters with metropolitans have left many former settlers feeling disconnected from their new home. Their common experience of exile, compounded by the difficulties they have experienced in their efforts to integrate into French society and in their relationships with metropolitan French, has encouraged them to turn to each other for moral, economic, and social support. Immediately following their exodus, they began to form hundreds of mutual aid and social clubs.[16] These organizations have helped reweave the social fabric that links *pieds-noirs* scattered across the alien landscape. We will now explore the *Amicale France-Malte* in this light.

EIGHT

Settler Ethnicity and Identity Politics in Postcolonial France

RECREATING ALGERIA IN FRANCE

The settler interest in forming *associations* is not unusual for France, where these institutions form a general template for all voluntary organizations. However, many French from North Africa told me that these activities are more important for repatriates in general and the *pieds-noirs* in particular. Lucette Buttigeig is a middle-aged nun of Maltese heritage who was born in Tunisia but who spent much of her adult life in Algeria following independence. I met her in Tunis, where she offered perhaps the most dispassionate analysis of this *pied-noir* activity. She has many siblings who migrated from Tunisia to France upon independence and who now demonstrate little interest in repatriate clubs. She finds them and their children to be well-adapted to the new culture, while, on the other hand, feels that settlers from Algeria will require two to three more generations to reach the same level of integration. François Xuereb concurred that *pieds-noirs* need such organizations more than repatriates from Tunisia:

> Well, you see, the French from Algeria, when they went to France, they were considered to be foreigners. They felt like foreigners in France. So they quickly saw the need to get together, with each other, people from their country. You see? To give each other some support. Because the French never finally accepted them . . . They said, "You are colonialists, you are this, you are that!"

These statements echo those of Louise Marino, quoted in the previous chapter, who explained this experience to me as a loss of cohesion: "Since we were repatriated, we no longer have any points of reference. Families for the most part have splintered, and everyone is dispersed. We used to live in colony [*en colonie*]! In other words, we were all banded together." A man who grew up in Algeria had a more powerful way of explaining this same fact: "Nowadays people walk past each other on the street, and they don't even know that they are related, that they are cousins."

Many settler clubs represent an overt attempt to recreate the social "points of reference" they lost in the diaspora. For some, connecting with an entirely new social matrix was just too hard, and many people still think in terms of their colony-based sociogeographical coordinates. This can explain why people today are still classified by location as well as ethnicity. "Rose the Maltese" might not identify a woman as clearly as "Rose the Maltese from Philippeville." For *pieds-noirs* especially, organizing around colonial geographic or institutional affiliation makes sense, since French Algeria was so vast. Travel was a difficult luxury, and many people I interviewed who had lived in eastern Algeria had never even visited the capital, Algiers. Because it would be difficult to bring members to meetings from throughout France, settler clubs typically are based in a region of France as well, and unite people in that region who were originally from the same place in the colony. Examples include the *Amitiés oraniennes de la Côte d'Azur* or *Amicale des batnéens de la région parisienne* (uniting people from Oran living along the Côte d'Azur, and people from the Algerian city of Batna living near Paris). Others are organized around schools, such as the *Amicale des anciens élèves du Lycée Duveyrier de Blida* (former students of Duveyrier High School in Blida, Algeria). *Amicales* of a religious nature are often linked to a specific parish or patron saint, and thus are similarly localized, such as *L'association des amis de Notre-Dame d'Afrique* (a basilica in Annaba).

André Fischer, a man from eastern Algeria whom I met in Bouc-bel-Air, a Marseilles suburb, described his desire to reconnect with old friends from his home town. He is a heavy-set man with white hair, blue eyes, and a ruddy complexion, of German and Alsatian descent. He worked in the central train depot in Souk-Ahras, but grew up in the village of Mondovi, where Albert Camus once lived. After several years in France, he decided to try to find his former friends and neighbors. It started as his own private game as he tested himself to see just how many names he could remember of the hundreds of settlers who once lived there. He explained his method: he concentrated hard on his former village, which he recreated in his mind's eye, and then retraced the town center, shop by shop, house by house, writing down the name of every single person he could think of associated with each building. He proceeded in this way, from street to street, and finally from farm to farm in the countryside, recreating a social map of the entire village. He then rearranged the names in alphabetical order, and started looking them up in Minitel, France's electronic telephone directory. He sent out invitations to a grand gala dinner, and an *association* of the

Figure 10. Recreating French Algeria. Photograph by the author.

"children of Mondovi" was formed, which Fischer still directs with enthusiasm.

Club meetings and parties allow the former settlers to recreate in small ways the world they lost and miss so much (see fig. 10). In the context of a generalized hostility many feel from the metropolitan French, these organizations provide them with a "safe" place where they can feel accepted. It is also when meeting with other club members that many are able to express and share their nostalgic longings for Algeria. Attending *pied-noir* dinners and parties affords participants a means of returning, at least in spirit, to Algeria. During association meetings, parties, and picnics, people often talked about the beaches back home, the mountains, a special plant or type of tree. "It was a paradise," I heard repeatedly; Algeria was a *région paradisiaque*. During the dinner dances (*soirées dansantes*), the music played was that of the 1940s and 1950s. One night I was sitting in a large rented hall finishing dessert, when the dancing started simply with the peal of a trumpet. At that moment, everyone assembled stopped their conversations and shouted in unison *Oh lé!* and many couples leaped out of their seats onto the dance floor. "You should have seen us *là-bas*," one man told me coming off the dance floor with his wife, gasping for breath, "any excuse for a party! We were always singing back there!"

These gatherings featured foods of a variety of origins, such as Sardinian, Sicilian, Balearic Islands, southern Spanish, Jewish, and Algerian, that

Figure 11. At a lamb *mechoui.* Photograph by the author.

people remembered from the colony. These included grilled sardines and cumin-spiced appetizers such as the fava beans mentioned earlier. During a large reunion of *Bônois* (former residents of colonial Bône, now Annaba), one elderly woman was delighted to learn that the lamb being served was going to be roasted on site, and she brought her grandson over to see how they used to make it *là-bas* (see fig. 11). It was among other settlers that they were able to eat these foods, cooked the way they remembered, with abandon, and in doing so they returned "home."

At the annual meeting of the former residents of Souk-Ahras, the atmosphere throughout the weekend was lively and boisterous. Much of the time was spent at long meals talking with friends. There was clearly no need to go anywhere to sightsee, for the attendees were already all happily back in Algeria, talking about the "good old times there." At my table, former playmates, now in their seventies, were doubled over with laughter during much of our meals together, talking about their childhood antics: the time when Colette, the association president, was put in a baby buggy by the slightly older Jean-Claude, who proceeded to push her down a steep hill, resulting in some calamity and Colette's mother chasing Jean-Claude around the village with a hatchet. Then there was the time, during the dreaded catechism class at church with the very strict village priest, when Jean-Claude and his buddy, Marc, the one with the wooden leg from the knee down, were sneaking around upstairs trying to find pigeon eggs in the bell tower, when somehow Marc's wooden leg became unhinged and came crashing down through the rafters into the middle of the Sunday School class like a message from God, to the hilarious amusement of the children gathered below. As one man told me, "It's Algeria, Algeria . . . that I see around me, when I spend time with *pieds-noirs*."

Events held by the club of *Bônois* were so large that they were usually held at rented municipal buildings in the outskirts of Aix. In order to guide the hundreds of *pieds-noirs* trying to locate the hall, signs were regularly posted along the way, stating simply "Bône," with an arrow. In Algeria, the city "Bône" no longer exists; it is now called Annaba. However, it was not to Annaba that the elderly *pieds-noirs* were returning during these reunions, but to an imaginary city they have constructed from their nostalgia-imbued memories of colonial Bône. The demarcation of space for the "Souk-Ahrasian" reunion was even more pronounced: signs were even posted along the national highway indicating the proper exit to take, stating simply "Souk-Ahras →." As we followed the directions, more signs were posted, as if we were driving in Algeria: "Souk-Ahras, 10 km," "Souk-Ahras, 5 km," and finally, in front of the rented vacation complex where the reunion was held, a sign announced, "Souk-Ahras, O km!" The former settlers have created their own version of colonial Algeria in France.

INCLUSION AND EXCLUSION

Regional gatherings also recreate the clannish, exclusive nature of colonial society. These reunions and parties, and the clubs that organize them, tend to attract only certain segments of the former colony, the Christian settlers, and thus reproduce the fault-lines that had divided people from each other. Religion was an especially important distinction in colonial Algeria, where even Protestant settlers were kept at a distance. The settlers were perhaps most infamous for their anti-Semitism, in some ways the one ideology that united them, and the strict social segregation of Christian and Jewish communities there has been reproduced to a certain extent in France. I became painfully aware of the ramifications of this life-long segregation when, during the otherwise jovial reunion of the Souk-Ahrasians, a "stranger" and his wife entered the room. The two hundred attendees were eating dinner as the couple made their way to the association president. The conversation in the room noticeably faltered as people tried to determine who the visitors were. This was understandable—*pieds-noirs* often meet each other for the first time in thirty-five years at these reunions, and the changes wrought by the passage of time have often rendered even the closest of childhood friends unrecognizable. The town's former elementary school teacher, seated at our table, finally got up to meet the gentleman, greeting him warmly. After a good five minutes' conversation, she came back to finish her dinner. "It's Roland Lévy," she announced. This news passed down the table: *"Lévy, oh, c'est un Juif"* (It's a Jew). "Do you know him?" "Nah . . ." Nobody seemed to know this man, or if they did, they did not show it. The boisterous joking ceased, and Lévy's presence seemed to put a damper on the gathering. He and his wife appeared eager to meet others, and they stayed in the center of the room talking to the four or five individuals who came forward. Finally, after what seemed to me to be twenty-five excruciating minutes, Mr. Lévy went out into the adjacent hallway. When I followed, I found him crouched down in front of some old photos of school classes, laughing to himself. I introduced myself, and he was quite pleasant, telling me how nice it was to meet some of the "old-timers" from his home town. He and his wife left soon after that.

The Lévys' arrival seemed to cause some discomfort. Beforehand, the conversation had been consistently positive, and the good old days recounted in glowing terms. People made a special point of telling me of the comradeship of people of all backgrounds and religions. However, judging from the reaction to the Lévys, it seemed clear that relations between Christians and Jews, at least in some parts of Algeria, had been strained at best. The Lévys' presence had called into question people's nostalgic image of the colonial past. Unable to break old habits or defy the will of the group, people remained in their seats, and, in doing so, demonstrated the great gaps between the vision of the past they were indulging in and colonial-era habitus, their deep-rooted memories of former ways of acting they now found difficult to transcend in the postcolonial context.

While Jews were not automatically or officially excluded from *pied-noir* functions, I met no individuals who were openly Jewish at the settler functions I attended in Aix, although I was invited with Michel and Rose to a special couscous dinner sponsored by an association of Algerian Jews in Marseilles. The Maltese and Jewish men bonded especially well around their shared knowledge of Arabic. On several occasions, Mr. Raynaud pointed out his minority status as the lone Protestant settler. Also excluded from these functions were Algerians, although I often wondered what North African immigrants and *beurs* would think about the signs posted along the highway and announcements of *pied-noir* lectures, and wondered if they ever ventured into one of these events. Communists and other leftists were also rare participants at the events I attended. The reunions reuniting former friends and neighbors from the same village thus presented a partial and distorted version of that former community. A new "Souk-Ahras" or "Guelma" was created temporarily in these symbolic spaces, one that better matched the nostalgia-imbued memories that these reunions celebrated and generated.

THE FRANCO-MALTESE:
LOST IN FRANCE?

The Franco-Maltese clubs share many features with these other settler clubs, especially the desire to associate with others from the colony, but they differ in several key respects. They attract people from across Algeria and even include settlers from Tunisia, and thus unite settlers via precolonial ties. Their members are motivated by prior ethnic attachments to Malta, Maltese liminality in the colony, and identity politics in contemporary France.

When I asked people why they thought the Maltese associations existed, some suggested that this was due to a growing French, if not worldwide, interest in genealogy. Mr. Camilleri, a man in his early seventies from Algiers who had had a distinguished career as a geologist for a major petroleum company, met me at my apartment to discuss his family's Maltese heritage. I asked him about the origins of the associations, and he responded,

> I believe this is a general trend, it isn't only the Maltese! You take anyone, the Italians . . . there are people trying to attach themselves to something, there is a regionalism that is growing, the Bretons are searching, people living near the Nice border, they are returning to Italy to look in the archives. This is *la mode*. It's the trend these days.

Several of the elderly interviewees showed me elaborate genealogies and reports they had written on their family histories. They explained that this interest stemmed from their age. Now that they were retired they had more time for such activities. In addition, several mentioned having watched the broadcast on French television of the American program *Roots*. "Since that show, it's a trend, all over France," Mr. Camilleri told me. "After *Roots*, everyone is learning more about their past." When I asked, some claimed emphatically that this was not exclusively a *pied-noir* phenomenon. Certainly scholars of contemporary France have also noted a French fascination with the past (Greene 1999; Nora 1996; Wood 1999). One could argue that the elderly settlers who participate in the Franco-Maltese clubs have simply found a rather unusual way to comply with these national trends. However, some people who had spent considerable time tracking down their ancestors told me that they wanted to put together this information for their grandchildren because they would never know French North Africa. While the grandchildren had not displayed much interest in this past to date, their grandparents felt that they might develop such an interest in the future, after they themselves were no longer around to answer their questions. Because their pasts in Algeria had not entered into the French historical cannon, they told me, they felt a particular responsibility to their deceased ancestors to fill in the blanks themselves so that this history might not be completely forgotten.

While claiming that "everyone" was interested in genealogy, Mr. Camilleri acknowledged that there might be a special need for it among the *pieds-noirs:*

> For ten years now I've been seriously involved in [tracing my family's genealogy]. But also, people are lost now in this society, this present society, they are lost, so they are searching for a base, they want to attach themselves to something, they are drifting. Because, coming to France—in Algeria, the whole family was united, we were all grouped together, while once we returned at independence, everyone left either for work, or to find lodging, and we split up. So, all the families splintered, and now we'd really like to find—we're looking for relatives.

Interest in Malta and family heritage sometimes fuse. One of the earliest group trips to Malta that I had heard about was organized in the 1980s by a man with little knowledge of his background or Malta, but who, like Mr. Fischer, decided one day to look on Minitel to find everyone in France with his distinctive last name, Brincat. He called them all and invited them to join him on a joint "pilgrimage" to Malta.

Yet some people insisted that the Maltese clubs were no different from any others uniting former residents of North Africa. Lucette Buttigieg, the nun from Tunis mentioned previously, cautioned me against attributing the *association* phenomenon to some underlying Maltese identity:

> I really don't think this is really nostalgia for Malta, it is more a nostalgia for Algeria . . . I think that we shouldn't confuse an identity based on one's roots, and the identity associated with the nostalgia for one's country . . . And for the *pieds-noirs* of Algeria, it's nostalgia for their country. I don't think that it is a nostalgia for their origins. You have here French *pieds-noirs* who miss—who are lost in France, French people who are lost in France.

In Lucette's view, what is of paramount importance for the Algerian settlers, those of Maltese origin included, is that they are French nationals who cannot find a place for themselves in France.

Despite assertions such as these, I found the predicament of the non-French settlers, especially those of Maltese ancestry, particularly difficult. They do not have the internal certainty, as those of French origin do, of belonging somewhere in France. Their Frenchness is questioned by metropolitan French due to their North African birthplace, but also by both metropolitans and other *pieds-noirs,* due to their non-French ancestry. This was sometimes illustrated at *pied-noir* events I attended. In his opening address at the annual meeting of *Bônois,* the club president alluded to François and Michel's Franco-Maltese club. This was not unusual, because the two *associations* shared many members in common. He started his commentary by announcing from the podium, "Many Maltese are from Bône —and many *Bônois* are *Maltese!*" This seemingly simple assertion led to uproarious laughter, and it was clear from the response that "Maltese" was a label rich in indexicality. Just what associations were conjured up in the imaginations of the individuals present I did not know, but in subsequent conversations, people elaborated. Some talked about the Maltese pityingly or patronizingly, referring to them as *les petits Maltais* (the little Maltese). They were described as the poorest of the colonists: hardworking, but also crude, stingy, and with crass or ostentatious dress and a lack of education or "class." A few men of non-Maltese origin joked about the fact that the Maltese came to Algeria with herds of goats and few women, insinuating the practice of bestiality. Repatriates with no clear family heritage in France, especially those of Maltese heritage, find themselves doubly displaced.

MALTESE DISTINCTION

It remains to be explained why repatriates of Maltese background formed *associations* while people of other important immigrant ethnicities of North Africa, such as Sicilian, Spanish, and Italian, have not. The puzzle of the ethnic basis of these organizations was difficult for many members to explain. When I asked people why they thought that there were such organizations tied to a Maltese heritage, but none organized around a Spanish or Italian ancestry, for instance, several people responded, "Oh, but there are—many of them." In taped conversations, one can hear a long pause as the speaker, and sometimes his or her spouse, struggle to recall examples of such organizations, to no avail. Occasionally, then, the *Oranais* (people from the department of Oran) were cited. A variety of *associations* unite people who lived in the western department of Algeria, Oran, or in its capital of the same name, where large numbers of Spanish settled. The *Oranais* clubs may be ethnic by default, for they serve a predominantly Spanish-origin *pied-noir* population. Yet upon further reflection, people realized that, to their knowledge, these organizations make no overt reference to a Spanish heritage. It is only the Maltese associations that do so.

Current or former Franco-Maltese club leaders had plenty to say about Maltese exceptionality. Malta's diminutive size, they felt, is key: an attachment to Spain or Italy, other countries from which many settlers had emigrated, is too vague for most people, and it is hard to feel special in such a large place. Malta, on the other hand, is small, and in this way unique. As François Xuereb exclaimed one day, "You see, Malta is so very small that there are few people in the world, even of those who live along the Mediterranean, who even know where it is." Mr. Grech, one of the first founders of the Parisian club and a prominent leader in *pied-noir* cultural organizations, concurred: "The fact of belonging to a small place . . . that is not reducible to others, that others have studied a lot, this facilitates a certain sympathy, it creates a connection." He contrasted this to the experience of those whose ancestors came from Alsace, who can find out exactly where they are from, but who can find themselves "drowned" in a much larger social context. Malta, in contrast, is *un tout* (a whole).

Mr. Sicluna is younger than the other men, and briefly led a club in the Marseilles area. We met one day in his humble apartment near the Marseilles airport where he worked. Over tea, he too told me that Malta's size helps generate real pride in Maltese heritage:

> I can tell you the motivation behind the associations—because Malta is small. Malta has always needed an identity due to its small size and small [number of] people . . . we are islanders, that is the mentality of those from the islands. Comparatively, when someone says he is Italian, everyone knows where Italy is, it's big, Italy, it is popular due to its music, language, and history. Spanish—same thing—who doesn't know Spain? But when you say that you are Maltese, there aren't many who come from there. Thus the Maltese have wanted to give some force to their identity, even if they aren't born in Malta, to spread the knowledge of their history, where the island is, and that's it, that's why there have been France-Malta associations. To show other people, because you know the Maltese are hurt when people say "Maltese?" "What is that, Malta?" "What is that, Maltese?"

Mr. Sicluna elaborated on Malta's "rich and marvelous" past, and how it has a big history for such a small place, culminating in its heroic fortitude withstanding massive German and Italian bombardments during World War II. "That is why when, say, a Spanish guy says to a Maltese, 'What is Malta?' we show that Malta exists, and that it has had a rich history." Malta is exotic, unique.

Club members also attribute the existence of these clubs to the charismatic personalities of their leaders, as we saw with Mr. Mifsud, who said that he never would have even considered his Maltese heritage a source of pride if it hadn't been for Mr. Xuereb. I can vouch for the remarkable energy levels, intelligence, and engagement with the world of each of the club organizers I met. Each man—I have only met male presidents of Maltese associations—was still actively engaged in various projects, even if not also leading clubs. One was involved in the Marseilles chamber of commerce, and regularly accompanied groups of businessmen of Maltese ancestry on week-long tours of Malta upon request. Another was involved in local politics, and, in the mid-1990s, assisted a protégé who was running for a European Union office. Mr. Grech was the director of or an active participant in multiple organizations promoting *pied-noir* cultural interests, and has written and published two memoirs of his life in Algeria and is working on a third. But similarities in individual personalities can only tell us so much. We need to understand why these men decided spontaneously and independently of each other to put their energies into the organization of clubs of this nature, and why it is that they were able to gather such a following. Interviews revealed a remarkable coincidence in their initial motivations that reflects both their alienation in contemporary France and their strong affinity to Malta.

JOURNEYS TO MALTA
AS RITES OF PASSAGE

Several of the current or former club organizers made spontaneous solo trips to Malta a few years after settling in France, independently of each other. These journeys held great significance in the travelers' life histories, and the men—of different ages and living in different parts of France— each recounted tales of their first trip to Malta without any prompting, and with considerable flourish. One of these narratives fills an entire hour-and-a-half cassette tape. The voyages were clearly rites of passage, sacred journeys that represented turning points in each man's sense of self and identity. This was not something they had done before; Malta was truly *terra incognita* for them.

In the mid-1960s, Malta had only recently achieved independence from the British, and it was extremely difficult to reach from France. The men's convoluted itineraries symbolized their determination to reach the isles. First, they took multiple trains for days across France and down to southern Italy, before boarding a boat to Sicily. They then traveled overland across what was at the time an impoverished island, sometimes by car, and then again by boat to a similarly poor Malta. In these narratives the men also tried to explain their initial motivations for undertaking such a journey. Mr. Grech began his journey narrative as follows:

> It is with the shock of 1962, when we had to leave our birthplace, our fatherland [*patrie*], but our fatherland in the French context, that we were chased
> . . . and we found ourselves without roots. This was even more so because

there was a real . . . kind of civil war between the French from Algeria and the French of the metropole. Huh? The mayor of Marseilles said about us, "We should hang them, shoot them, and throw them into the sea." Gaston Defferre. See? So, we were rejected, we had to show our identity papers, we were [treated like] suspects. And we found ourselves really . . . completely cut off from our country [*pays*], our roots. Me, I think it's this, that, personally, instinctively . . . and I questioned myself. Because I said to myself, sure, I'm French, but I'm not from here. Whether I'm in Marseilles, in Paris . . . it will never be my home. So, I said, I'm going to try to get to know Malta . . . So, what happened was a . . . story that marked me. [A long narrative of his journey followed here.] So, we get off the boat. We get off the boat, and I have my French passport. And there was a customs agent down below, an old customs agent, while in France, in '62 . . . and the old customs agent, when we show him our passports, he looks: "Grech! Maltese!" and I would have kissed him. I saw in this man my grandfather. I said, "*Finally*, I am welcomed. *Finally*, I am accepted. *Finally*, I am not in a foreign country where they chase us, where they cannot accept us." This was an, an, an . . . awakening. "Grech, Maltese!" That, I will always keep close to my heart. "Grech, Maltese!" So, there, afterward, I said, I am going to . . . and I began to research my family history.

Mr. Grech begins this narrative with his departure from Algeria and the hostile reception he experienced once in France. It was this reception that prompted him to visit Malta the first time; he says that he was seeking a place where he felt he belonged. While many *pieds-noirs* of French origin have responded to similar feelings by conducting genealogical research to locate their ancestral village(s) in France, those of foreign ancestry have no such outlet. Malta, then, as the ancestral homeland, would play a similar role. Mr. Grech was particularly struck when the customs agent in Malta recognized his last name as Maltese in origin, and also by his immediate and warm acceptance of him as an insider, a reception that contrasted so sharply with that which he had received earlier in France, his putative "fatherland." After his trip to Malta he became an active leader of the main Maltese association in Paris, and continues to travel there with settler societies.

Mr. Sicluna's first trip to Malta represented a major turning point in his life as well. Like Mr. Grech, he grew up in Algiers. He differs from most club members I met in that his father had traveled to Malta from Algeria at the age of eighteen, and had returned with stories about Valletta. Also unlike the others, Mr. Sicluna remembers developing the urge to travel to Malta while still living in the colony, at the age of fifteen. It may be significant that this was during the French-Algerian War, just after the battle for

Algiers, in 1958. He told me that he still vividly remembers finding a discarded *Paris-Match* sitting in the garbage can. While flipping through it, he suddenly saw an article about Malta: "La Valette en fête, Malte," with photos of the annual September 8 festival celebrating the Knights' victory against the Turks. He didn't know much about Malta at the time. As he explained, "It came to me with a blow to my heart. I said, 'I must, I . . .'" But he forgot about this "awakening" and migrated to France with his family in 1962, at the age of nineteen, at Algerian independence. Mr. Sicluna lived in Marseilles for several years, followed by six years in Paris working for the mass transit system, when suddenly, in 1968, he was struck with a desire to go to Malta. He recounted a remarkable story about his journey, which began when he called the British embassy for information, only to find that Malta had been independent for four years. His trip was a real odyssey, involving a journey across Italy in a railcar filled with Italian enlisted men who were returning home to Sicily. Upon reaching the island, he met a young French man of his age who, like him, was traveling to Malta. Terrific, he thought. "'But it isn't finished,' the Frenchman told me; 'I am the chauffeur of a Maltese countess married to a British man who has properties in Nice and in Spain, the Countess of Genoa.' She was below, and he was her chauffeur!" Thus began his magical first encounter with Malta, in the company of a Maltese countess and her staff. They traveled across the islands in a Studebaker Belair, and the countess took him under her wing like a son. He felt as though he were living a fairy tale: "I write a letter to my parents, because they didn't know were I was or anything, and I send it, I say, 'I am on a trip of dreams [*voyage de rêves*].' For me, it was my first time there, but it was a trip of dreams."

Like Mr. Grech, Mr. Sicluna returned to France a changed man. After he recounted his adventure to his parents, his mother told him, "You have to take me to my country so I can get to know it too." He has since taken his mother there with him ten times, by car. These trips have continued:

> After that I brought my sisters there, I brought my uncles, I brought my nephews, I brought lots of people repatriated from Algeria and Tunisia . . . even this past Sunday a group of people left, with whom I ate yesterday. You see? It continues. Because after twenty-seven years in Malta, soon twenty-eight years in September, I have made myself a place in the sun.

Trips to Malta have galvanized not only those who eventually form Maltese social clubs, such as Mr. Grech and Mr. Sicluna, but others as well. Mr. Mifsud, for instance, began to proudly proclaim his Maltese heritage only after traveling there with his local association.

INTEGRALISM, HERITAGE, AND
IDENTITY POLITICS IN FRANCE

We have seen that many of the club founders first set out to "discover" Malta after several years in France, during the tumultuous period of the late 1960s. This was in part an expression of a feeling of being rejected by the French and a desire to belong somewhere. Another dimension to these longings may stem less from a perceived rejection by the French and more from a generalized sense of unease regarding the future of France itself, an unease powerfully captured in Douglas Holmes's erudite and expansive work, *Integral Europe*. Holmes provides a thorough analysis of what he terms "integralist" aspirations, efforts to "circumvent the alienating force of modernity by means of culturally based solidarities" (2000, 4). He explores the ways these anxieties are fueling a growing political movement across Europe, perhaps best exemplified by the *Front national,* an ultra-right anti-immigration political party led by Jean-Marie Le Pen. Integralist politicians are responding to several interrelated sources of widespread concern: the demise of the socialist promise, and the failure since May '68 of the European left to offer any solutions to what now appears to be a consignment of the working classes to a new "workless class" in postindustrial Europe; "fast-capitalism," an extremely rapid new productive regime that "flattens" preexisting frameworks of meaning; and European integration, which for many undermines the salience of the one social collectivity they can still hold on to, the imagined national community. These changes have led not so much to a socioeconomic form of estrangement, according to Holmes, as to a cultural one, and people grapple with "ruptures in the experience of belonging" (2000, 5).

Integral politicians draw on a breathtaking array of political ideologies and philosophical schools, but are largely based in Counter-Enlightenment sensibilities. Holmes identifies ideas from Herder in particular that, in different forms, could have been articulated by *pieds-noirs* I knew. These include a valorization of "populism," defined here as a "belief in the value of belonging to a group or culture," and a concomitant sense of alienation when one cannot associate with others. A specific form of pluralism is central to these movements, and has been articulated quite explicitly by Le Pen and some of the overt racists Holmes interviewed in London's East End. This integralist pluralism involves a belief in the incommensurability of different cultures and societies, a sense that people are simply happiest when among their "own kind." Another concept that Holmes highlights is that of alienation, which Herder saw as the inevitable outcome of deracination, and which not only results in difficulties on the material plane, but also cuts people off from "a living center," an experience that at once degrades and dehumanizes.

Most of the former settlers I met could appreciate many of these ideas, some of which they would have encountered in the colony. While the colonial doctrine most commonly associated with Algeria is that of assimilation, the belief that Algeria could become or even had become an extension of France, the policy of association, which often implies "irreducible alterity" (Ezra 2000, 6), is more consonant with settler understandings of their interactions with others. The settlers I met presented the economic, residential, and social segregation that characterized colonial life as reflecting their enduring respect for the distinct religions, values, and cultural practices of the indigenous Algerians. At settler gatherings, people often debated the compatibility of people of different faiths, notably Islam and Christianity, in ways that could be echoed by Le Pen today (see Holmes 2000, 59–89, for extensive passages from Le Pen and *Le Penistes*). Thus, I would have to root the settler model of pluralism not only in contemporary integral politics, but also in the traditions this movement shares with colonial-era philosophies, for incommensurability was a fundamental rationale for the extreme separation of peoples during twentieth-century colonialism. What is especially interesting here is the rather seamless move some former settlers make from the colonial context to membership in the *Front national,* and the ways both integralist and settler ideas of incommensurability are consonant with the contradictions inherent in the "colonial unconscious" described by Ezra, which involves the simultaneous fascination with and preservation of cultural difference (2000, 6).

The alienation so many settlers feel also stems from the way they left their "homeland" and their inability to return since, as I have discussed in detail. This is especially the case for the former settlers of Algeria; I did not encounter alienation of this intensity among the former settlers of Tunisia I met. Yet this alienation may also reflect or be compounded by an atmosphere of generalized anxiety pervading postindustrial France. Settlers expressed to me a concern for the future that seemed to grow over the years, and which parallels that addressed by the integralists Holmes interviewed. French fears for the future are summarized succinctly by Naomi Greene, who relates these present-day anxieties to the contemporary preoccupation with the national past. This preoccupation originated in the mid-1960s when a "certain idea of France" was starting to crumble (Greene 1999, 24). The loss of this "certain idea of France" was not caused by the loss of empire alone, although that process is clearly involved, but has involved a variety of Hexagon-based processes as well. The perception, at least, is that in just a few generations tremendous changes have occurred:

A traditional and largely rural society, marked by sharp class distinctions and based on values associated with family and church, has been transformed into an increasingly urbanized and multicultural country on the leading edge of the technological revolution. (Greene 1999, 25)

This process has been referred to by some scholars as France's "second Revolution" (Mendras 1988). Generalized anxiety following the end of the long period of postwar economic growth in 1974, mass urbanization, and concerns about immigration and a multicultural France are all implicated, as is the deeper fear that France is "losing the important political, social, and cultural role it has long played in Europe and the world" and has been demoted from a great power to an average one (Greene 1999, 27). The vote on the Maastricht treaty, France's further enmeshment with the European Union, the demise of the franc, and concerns for the country's general economic health amidst growing deficits and rising unemployment were on everyone's minds over the course of my research in France.

It may be in response to these concerns that so many in France have been attracted to the version of "populism" Holmes outlines, which seems a pervasive theme in French culture today. Since the 1960s, there have been back-to-the-land movements, peasant revolts, a resurgence of interest in oral history and genealogy, and a renaissance in regionalism as people seek to reconnect with some organic community within a rapidly changing society (Joutard 1983; Lebovics 2004, 13–57; McDonald 1989). We can view the popular appeal of Nora's *Lieux de mémoire* volumes in this light as well. He may have struck a chord with French readers when he introduced his multivolume compilation with a stirring essay on the urgency of his project, which he said was due to the "acceleration of history." He asks the reader of the first volume to consider

the irrevocable break marked by the disappearance of peasant culture . . . Such a fundamental collapse of memory is but one familiar example of a movement toward democratization and mass culture on a global scale. (Nora 1989, 7)

In Nora's view, what is being lost is nothing less than the salience of the French nation: "The nation is no longer the unifying framework that defines the collective consciousness" (1986, 6). The third volume, *Les France,* carries this point further, arguing that with the erosion of the "unitary framework" of the nation-state and a decline in the state's role in commemorative activities, "sectoral identities" proliferate and increasingly demand recognition with a flood of "particularistic commemorative events housed in museums, folkloric displays . . . and a proliferating multitude of heritage associations" (Wood 1999, 29). It is outside the scope of this book to determine whether or not the nation as unifying framework is truly losing its hold on its citizens, and if so, if this process stems from a reaction against a multicultural Europe, fast-capitalism, or the European Union. What is important, however, is the fact that many perceive this to be the case, and that the elderly settlers are participating in a fundamentally "integralist" activity by seeking ways to reconnect with others they view to be like them. In their case, they regroup around both a recent home (colonial Algeria) and a more distant one (Malta) and a common heritage. Faced with anxieties for the future, they, like many others in France today, have found refuge in clubs that celebrate a more comfortable vision of past and community.

THE CHANGING VALENCE
OF MALTESENESS

Ethnicity is a fluid boundary-making principle dividing self from other that is remarkably situational in nature (Barth 1969; Eriksen 2002). People may claim membership in an array of hierarchically organized or nested social categories and thus may maintain simultaneous identifications with a wider collectivity, such as "French," and more restricted ones, such as "Provençal." These identifications may have more or less salience, and be more attractive or dangerous, depending on the situation at hand and changing identity politics. We should consider, then, what aspects of life in the postcolonial diaspora may be fostering the emergence of the Franco-Maltese clubs.

In the colony, as we have seen, a Maltese heritage was a liability, especially when settlers of this background were interacting with the French elite. The process of becoming French in Algeria involved the suppression of Malteseness. One man explained that his grandparents had purposefully cut all ties to Malta ("*ils ont coupé les ponts avec Malte*"), and actively tried to erase any distinctive cultural features to facilitate their children's integration in Algeria. Another man said that they had always tried to keep a low profile ("*on se faisait tout petit*"). In the process, they submerged as much of their ethnic identity as possible, even changing their last names. At least while they were living in Algeria, Maltese ethnic revitalization was unlikely, although of course we can never know for certain.

Malta means something very different in France, however. France has never had a very large immigrant population from Malta proper, and thus the category "Maltese" carries few if any of the associations with menial labor and lower socioeconomic strata it had in Algeria. Instead, in the Hexagon, "Malta" conjures up images of the land of the legendary Knights. From the European vantage point, the Knights were a heroic religious-military order associated with nobility and the Crusades, two foundational elements of the larger history of France. France still has long ties to Malta dating to the era of the Knights: three of the eight original *langues* (or tongues, basic administrative divisions of the Order) were French,[1] and French nobles dominated the Order. By 1798, forty-seven of the Order's seventy-seven grand masters had been French, and Frenchmen made up some three-fifths of the Order overall. In addition, the Order was very active in Europe. Starting in the twelfth century, it began to acquire hundreds of properties across Europe, often donated by wealthy entrants (Selwood 1999, 1). Southern France was home to hundreds of *commanderies,* estates that sometimes sheltered the needy and that served as home bases for the Order's brethren. This legacy remains in material form to this day as part of the French national patrimony.

The Order of the Knights of Malta has been based in Rome since 1834. Although its military functions have long since ceased, it remains a "sovereign military hospitaller order" and is a sovereign subject of international law, recognized by nearly ninety countries worldwide. It now has over ten thousand members, many more than in the seventeenth and eighteenth centuries, and many of them still trace their heritage to French nobility.[2] In France, an *association* called *Les oeuvres hôpitalières françaises de l'Ordre de Malte,* created in 1927, parallels the Order and puts its goals into practice.

France's significant Crusader legacy and the continued salience and positive valence of the Knights of Malta in France today are significant elements of the present-day postcolonial context, fostering the creation of the Franco-Maltese settler clubs. This context also helps explain why the club names never refer to a North African heritage, only to Malta and France (as in *Amicale France-Malte*). As I have shown, in contemporary France, North Africa and especially Algeria are stigmatized (one need only consider the preponderance of "Tunisian" and dearth of "Algerian" restaurants, for instance), as Malta had been in Algeria. These are not "Maltese *pied-noir*" or "Algerian-Maltese" clubs, but instead are "Franco-Maltese"; the colonial heritage of the club members is completely silenced in their official appellation. These vague club names allow club members to garner additional symbolic capital associated with the Knights, the Crusades, and nobility in the metropole while distancing themselves from North Africa.

These euphemistic club names can be misleading. While I never heard a club president outline an overt attempt to capitalize on the positive image of the Knights in France, I sometimes witnessed the confusion of French from France when they realized that the club members, while Maltese in origin, were in fact former settlers. One such misunderstanding occurred during the hectic week leading up to our trip to Malta in September. Just a few days before our planned departure, François Xuereb received a fax from the secretary of the president of Malta, saying that the president would be happy to meet with us one morning during our visit. Such a visit was not unheard of: Xuereb's group had met with the previous president the year before. Yet we could not arrive empty-handed, so Michel and François met up at the Maison to decide what to bring as a gift. Since their headquarters was based in Aix, a town made famous by the work of the local artist Cézanne, they decided that a bust of Cézanne would be appropriate. They made arrangements to meet the director of the local Musée Granet, a fine arts museum that holds several Cézanne paintings as well as the works of François-Marius Granet, a Provençal painter (1775–1849). Perhaps not entirely by coincidence, the museum is housed in an old priory of the Knights of Malta. The three of us had a chaotic, nearly death-defying trip across town, because François, already in his late seventies, was finding it difficult to see clearly and drive at the same time. We finally found a safe place to park and proceeded on the rest of our journey by bus. We arrived in a flurry of confusion. The director invited us into his plush office at the back of the museum, filled with original sepia-tone oil paintings, an antique desk, and deep-set bookshelves. He explained that he had a bust of Cézanne that we might wish to purchase. He added that he was looking forward to speaking with us since he was organizing a trip to Malta for the "friends of the museum," and could use some advice.

François and Michel were only too happy to comply, and began to outline, simultaneously, as much as they could about Malta: where to stay, whom to contact while in Malta, which hotels organized the best tours, and so forth. To my eye, the immaculately dressed museum director, with suit and silk tie, was not getting the kind of information he had hoped, and began to look impatient.

At that point they introduced me, and explained my research on the Maltese experience in North Africa. The director was suddenly puzzled. "North Africa?" he asked. "Aren't you Maltese?" "Well," François explained, "the vast majority of Maltese in France arrived here from North Africa. Only maybe one in a thousand arrived here directly from Malta."

"Oh!" exclaimed the director, surprised if not startled. "Well, I work with members of the *chevaliers de Malte*" (the Knights of Malta; members of the Order).

Michel entered into the debate, attempting to dispel any confusion: "There are plenty of Knights in Malta right now—we know quite a few of them."

"No," the director clarified, "I work with the *French* chevaliers, right here in the region, such as the Baron of Vitrolles" (patently a member of the French nobility). He seemed quite put off when he realized that the

Amicale France-Malte had no link to the Order or even to the Maltese of Malta, but instead comprised former settlers from North Africa. Despite the Order's strong presence in Malta for almost three centuries, few Maltese ever became members. The director began to treat François and Michel with considerably less warmth. We ended the conversation with as much tact as possible, but a rift had emerged. Undaunted and seemingly unaware of the director's change in attitude toward them, the club leaders purchased the bust they had desired, and we said our goodbyes. But the chill in the room when we left made me quite uncomfortable.

On another occasion I visited the headquarters of the *Oeuvres hôpitalières françaises de l'Ordre de Malte,* which is housed in an elegant building on a quiet, stately street in the sixteenth *arrondissement* of Paris, near the Bois de Bologne. I met with a woman who runs the humanitarian branch in France, who spoke at length about the difficulties of carrying out benevolent works at home. When I explained that I was working with the *Amicale France-Malte* in southern France, she distanced herself from them, stating outright that the club had nothing to do with her organization. "You see, the membership of the Order itself is closed. It used to be dominated by aristocrats, 90 percent were nobles in the past. But now that has been reduced to 60 percent, or even less: at least 50 percent of the members are now Americans!" I found her conflation of non-nobles with Americans amusing.

I asked if some of the members here in France could be former immigrants of Maltese origin, and she said no, their members were all French nationals. "Yes," I concurred, "but couldn't people who were naturalized eventually join?" I was thinking of the former settlers, all French citizens, some of whom had become quite wealthy or prominent in the colony. "Well, yes," she said, hesitating, and then added, "it would depend on an individual's particular family history." From her response it was apparent that she did not think that many Maltese immigrants were endowed with the appropriate family pedigree.

These vignettes indicate an enduring conceptual model positing a hierarchy of peoples ranked by essential qualities difficult if not impossible to transcend. We also encounter another form of fractal recursivity: the Knights of Malta (nobility) were to the Maltese (commoners) as France is to North Africa. While the Maltese may be viewed with paternalism, Malta itself carries quite a positive mystique. This interest in Malta helps explain why it is that the settlers may have found it far easier to mobilize around their ethnic heritage in France than in the colony. In Algeria, the Maltese were denigrated, while in France, the history of the Knights of Malta intersects with the early history of France itself. The North African settlers can capitalize on the special cachet associated with Malta in French society.

For the former settlers, this is a risky strategy, however, and these vignettes again illustrate a real distaste in France for *pieds-noirs* and anyone associated at some point in time with North Africa. People in the Order or otherwise highly placed in French society may find the identity claims of the members of the Franco-Maltese clubs confusing at best, and at worst may uncover their "lowly," if not downright unsavory, North African past. The stigma associated with Malta has diminished in the Hexagon, yet that associated with North Africa remains strong.

POSTCOLONIAL AMBIVALENCE

A conjunction of interwoven historical and contemporary influences can be found in the coalescence of these French-Maltese settlers around their associative activities. As we have seen, these clubs are partly nourished by a distinct, subaltern memory, one marked by ambivalence and contradictions that reflect the settlers' liminal social position in the colony, and their simultaneous attraction to and separation from the dominant colonial identity (see House 2002). At the same time, they are responding to a strong sense of longing for a former time and community, which may be more generalized in contemporary France, and perhaps around the world (see Berger, Berger, and Kellner 1973), but which we can also attribute to their departure from North Africa. This nostalgia afflicts those who were part of the especially traumatic flight from Algeria in particular. The settlers of non-French background face an added difficulty in connecting to their new home, however: as *pieds-noirs,* they are held at arm's length from French society. Continually facing suspicion and exclusion must, for some people, conjure up memories of a previous exclusion they experienced in the colony.

By reconnecting themselves to Malta, the settlers of this background have found an ingenious solution that resolves many of these competing needs and concerns. They are able to recreate community and cope with their rejection by the French, yet can do so in a way that downplays their North African origins and circumvents anti-*pied-noir* antipathy, at least for the most part. Their valorization of their Maltese heritage is not only possible but facilitated in the postcolonial setting. We should not conclude that the clubs' leaders, or their members, have planned these activities consciously or strategically. As I hope I have shown, my encounters with the club members have also revealed some "true" attachment to this place, this newly rediscovered "homeland." To complete this intellectual journey, we must travel with the club members to Malta to see what it is about this place that they find so compelling.

NINE

Place, Replaced: Malta as Algeria in the Pied-noir *Imagination*

THE TRIP TO MALTA

When I traveled with twenty members and friends of the *Amicale France-Malte* on a week-long voyage to Malta in September 1995, I looked forward to the trip with considerable anticipation. I was eager to learn what it was about Malta that proved so alluring to these elderly former settlers. Most of the people Michel and François had assembled that year had never been there before, and all but two couples were of Maltese heritage. Typical of people of this background and family history, they did not know where in Malta their families were from, nor even, in most cases, which island.

The choice of activities during our week there reflected the club members' tenuous link to the land of their ancestors. The trip was not unlike other package tours. We stayed in a large deluxe hotel that accommodates hundreds of guests, and spent our time visiting Malta's main tourist attractions: the impressive fortifications of the Knights of Malta in Valletta, the working-class neighborhoods of the Three Cities, the medieval town center of Mdina, the Neolithic ruins that dot Malta's southern portion and Gozo, impressive Baroque churches on both islands, the film set for *Popeye* (known as "Popeye village") and the painted boats of the harbor towns (see fig. 12). There was much to see: each day was packed with events. I was enlisted as driver of one of the three vehicles we had rented and struggled to keep up with François and Michel as they maneuvered around treacherous traffic circles while driving on the left-hand side of the road.

We visited several sumptuous churches, which were quite moving for the travelers—not necessarily because they remembered hearing about them, but because of their remarkably rich, Baroque, interiors. The settlers also noted the religiosity of the Maltese. While at the enormous church in

Figure 12. "Popeye village," Malta. Photograph courtesy Lucien Jullié.

Mosta, for instance (see fig. 13), the settlers were respectfully quiet as they walked by a prayer group. Once outside the church, they commented energetically on the fact that that particular prayer group consisted entirely of older men, which they found remarkable. Their distant, respectful manner inside churches marked them as tourists in my mind, people from a secular society for whom religion is a private matter, and this attitude seemed to derive from their long stay in France and, before that, French Algeria.

There were some mishaps. François once missed a meeting because his van broke down and he had to walk over a mile into town to secure a replacement vehicle. On another occasion, we somehow took different roads off a traffic circle and split into two groups, one of which went back to Valletta to window-shop while the other ended up at an artists' colony housed in former barracks of the British air force. And one day I followed Michel all day, for François's group had decided to take a break and stay close to the hotel. Through driving rain and even a major thunderstorm, Michel and I drove in tandem along a coastal route, and I started to think that he was trying to introduce me to every single road on the island so that I wouldn't get lost in the future.

In a break in the storm, we drove along winding streets that were filling with puddles tan with the muddy limestone runoff, only to find ourselves at the back of the airport. To our amazement, the chain-link fence bordering the airport runways was lined with cars, and whole Maltese families

Figure 13. Mosta church, Malta. Photograph courtesy Lucien Jullié.

were either waiting inside the cars, or standing outside the fence looking in. Some were even climbing onto their car hoods. "What do we have here?" Joseph asked, in amazement. I pulled over, and the elderly settlers in my car spent some time discussing this unusual scene. "I think they are here to watch the planes land!" Mrs. Dumont exclaimed, and they discussed this possibility seriously. "Perhaps there wasn't much to do on a day with such bad weather," Joseph's girlfriend proposed. We stayed there watching the Maltese watching the runway, incredulous. Suddenly we heard a roar overhead, and the reason for the commotion became clear: it was the day of an air show by the British Royal Air Force. The assumption that the Maltese would be so behind in their development that they would find regular passenger flights a cause for an afternoon outing revealed the degree to which some of the travelers had distanced themselves from the people of their "homeland."

Malta featured during this week as an interesting tourist destination, distinguished perhaps by the added frisson associated with the knowledge that distant relatives had once lived there. However, former settlers from North Africa travel to Malta regularly with social clubs, for which these "pilgrimages" are often the high point of the year, and others journey there on their own. As we shall see, these former settlers' fascination with Malta is informed by the politics of memory among this diaspora population, the power of place, and the often unconscious workings of sensory memory.

PLACE, DISPLACEMENT, AND HOME-LOSS

Anthropologists have begun to challenge the common, yet often covert, linkages made between a culture, a people, and a nation, as well as the polarized depictions of peoples' relationship to place in which the "local, natural and authentic" is contrasted with the global (Gupta and Ferguson 1997b, 7; Lavie and Swedenburg 1996, 1; Clifford 1992; Olwig and Hastrup 1997). Movement is not always to be celebrated, however, as people who have been forced to relocate often attest (Jansen 1998). The rich literature on diaspora is replete with the various and creative ways that peoples worldwide have coped with profound collective loss and displacement (Boyarin 1991; Kugelmass and Boyarin 1998; Naficy 1991; Valensi 1990).

The concept of "home" is a useful one for exploring such transplanted peoples, including the former settlers. The "home" concept, as Rapport and Dawson argue, allows us to "treat migrancy both physically and cognitively." Routine practices and narratives associated with "home" "do not merely tell of home but represent it: serve, perhaps, as cognitive homes in themselves" (1998, 4, 8).

Nostalgérie pervades everyday life for many *pieds-noirs*. As Casey has noted (1993), nostalgia is not only a regret for lost times, but also a longing for lost places. As with other exiles who have no hope of returning, time and place are fused in the *pied-noir* imagination. The *pieds-noirs* have been coping with profound longings for a past home, and like other displaced peoples, such as the Palestinians described by Slyomovics (1998), they discuss that homeplace, French Algeria, with deep emotion. We should not view nostalgia as limited to populations severed from their homelands: many argue that it is a condition of modernity characterized by chronic "homelessness" (Berger, Berger, and Kellner 1973, 184). Displacement may be endemic to the human condition: We are all "caught in the toils of displacement," Casey writes, and our symptoms include pervasive nostalgia—not just for lost childhood, or the places of childhood, but also for all the places that are now inaccessible or despoiled (1993, 37).

Place alienation induces a mourning process. Many anthropologists have attempted to challenge the simply conceived causal links between peoples and place, and to contemplate the complex ways in which peoples and place interrelate (Myers 1986). For this reason, Casey discusses "persons-in-places" to emphasize the fact that place alienation is a two-way process, one that has profound effects on a people's sense of self. As a result of this, a people displaced may mourn places as they mourn other people. Some may attempt to carry out a "re-placement," that is, "a re-creation of the self who inhabits (or will re-habit) the place in question" (Casey 1993, 311). It is within the context of the disorientation of home-loss and nostalgia that we will consider one possible "re-placement" implicit in the settler pilgrimages to Malta.

HERITAGE TOURISM

According to several leaders of Maltese *pied-noir* clubs, the traveling former settlers are attracted to Malta by a desire to reconnect with their family's heritage. But, in doing so, most run into an immediate obstacle: they do not know where in Malta their relatives came from. Motivated people sort through family papers, but too often they are disappointed, for nineteenth-century French functionaries preparing such documents as death, birth, and marriage certificates did not always record the town or village of origin, noting instead simply *Malte* (Malta). In my review of such records, I did not run into this problem as systematically for people from towns in Sicily, southern Italy, or Spain. A language barrier may thus be partly to blame for the lack of geographic detail regarding the Maltese immigrants. Nineteenth-century bureaucrats also may have found the Maltese place names difficult to spell, as evidenced by the wide range of orthography for these words and for Maltese surnames as well (Xerri is found spelled as "Cheri," "Xcherri," and so forth).

A second difficulty encountered by *pieds-noirs* interested in tracing their families back to Malta is the fact that there are a small number of Maltese surnames, and many individuals of this background, at least in Algeria, were given identical Christian names. Pierre, Paul, Victor, and Vincent are some of the most common Christian names found in the nineteenth-century Algerian marriage records of Maltese- and Maltese-origin males, and girls were often named Carmela, Marie, or Rose. Tracking down relatives in the French overseas records is difficult, because large colonial towns with a substantial Maltese presence, such as Philippeville or Bône, may have had dozens of people with identical names in any given year.

A Maltese priest I met in Malta knew the Maltese-origin settlers well because they often contacted him for assistance in conducting genealogical research. "This is a strange crowd," he told me. "They have a fixed idea about finding their roots, and this poses quite a problem for us. They write and ask for information about their ancestors, but don't have much information to start with, so I have a hard time helping them." While we were in Malta that week, some of the members of our group did meet with priests of local parishes, hoping to find records of an ancestor, to no avail.

Ironically, although the limited number of Maltese names often stymied peoples' efforts to find a direct link to specific people and places in Malta, it also provided an opportunity for a more immediate connection on a more superficial level. Like Mr. Grech, whose last name was recognized immediately by the customs agent as Maltese, Mr. Camilleri told me he too had felt an instant connection to Malta even before entering the country, because he and his customs agent shared both first and last names. A connection through common surnames facilitates a sense of fraternity with shopkeepers, hotel workers, and others that the settlers encounter over the course of their stay. People often find that their surname is the only tangible link they have with the Maltese people. It may be for this reason that surnames have become fetishes, and many former settlers, having failed to find family papers or birthplaces, visit instead the National Library in Valletta, where they hope to obtain photocopies of their family's coat of arms. François explained to me that one of his principal responsibilities as leader of the Franco-Maltese social club is printing out copies of these coats of arms for new members. Indeed, during my very first encounter with François and Michel, they proudly offered me a gift of my own Maltese coat of arms, which symbolized my new fictive kinship as a fellow Maltese, and represented a tacit invitation to work among them.

PLACE AS METAPHOR

While the people traveling with me in Malta that year had little luck finding concrete evidence of their ancestors, they did comment often on the familiarity of the Maltese landscape. James Fernandez (1988) has called our
attention to the ways that parts of a place can stand for the whole, such as
Andalusia for all of Spain. In particular, he highlights the uses of meton-
ymy in the development of "contrastive places" (1988, 32)—places perceived and understood as contrastive to another place. For instance, Andalusia and Asturias, two well-known regions of Spain, are often compared.
In the present example, however, we find the relationship a synechdochal
one, in which the very features found in Algeria, such as the prickly pear
cactus and the spoken language, not only symbolize that place, but also
allow people to symbolically transform one place into another. Metaphor
thus serves in the development of a different argument here, one in which
two places are not contrasted, but *conflated.* This conflation is not necessarily a conscious process; sensory memory and collective forgetting work together to make Malta, more than any other place, the outlet for Maltese
pied-noir longing for Algeria.

Maurice Halbwachs underscored the importance of landmarks in the
development of a society's collective memory, highlighting the dynamic
role of sacred sites in the development of the Christian faith (1941).
Knowledge of place may have significance beyond its use as a mnemonic
device in the consolidation of collective memories. As Edward Casey has
suggested, knowledge of place is not subsequent to perception but is an in-
gredient in perception itself: "To live is to live locally, and to know is first of
all to know the places one is in" (1996, 18). Knowledge of place is an embodied cultural knowledge, for we learn of place by means of the body.
This point is underscored in Steven Feld's work on sound and acoustemology (1990; 1996). He suggests that when we talk of a "sense of place," we
should look more closely at all of the ways that a place is sensed. While
much of the work to date on senses of place has been dominated by a European visualism, Feld suggests that we move beyond this tendency and toward a "multisensory" conceptualization of place. His work underscores
the importance of the acoustic dimension, which involves sound, hearing,
and the voice, in sensing places (1996).

A multisensory understanding of a place need not be limited to knowledge of the natural world. As Casey has written, "perceiving bodies are
knowing bodies, and inseparable from what they know is culture as it im-
bues and shapes particular places." Casey thus calls our attention to the importance of our knowledge of a place through cultural habitus: "Culture

Figure 14. *"On dirait Maroc."* Photograph courtesy Lucien Jullié.

pervades the way that places are perceived . . . as well as how we act in their midst" (1996, 34). What is often overlooked in cursory explorations of *pied-noir* nostalgia is a longing for cultural as well as natural attributes of the colony.

Mr. Dumont, who had spent his youth in Morocco, was one of the passengers in my car throughout our week-long vacation in Malta. He was fascinated by the landscape. On a rough back road through a rural stretch of the island, he suddenly asked me to stop the car. Along the way, he had been repeating to himself, "*On dirait Maroc . . . Oh, on dirait Maroc*" (One could say it was Morocco). He leaped out of the car with his camera to take photos and finally returned, beaming, and announced to his wife that he would show these pictures to his friends and tell them that they had just been to North Africa (see fig. 14). People commented regularly on the similarity between the native flora of Malta and those of North Africa. We spent a good hour in a parking lot in the blazing sun one afternoon inspecting some greenery growing up the side of an old Crusader wall several yards away from us. One of the *pieds-noirs* thought it might be a caper plant. Another man, originally from Tunisia, insisted that capers only grow as bushes. The discussion became heated, until finally the club secretary consulted the amused parking attendant sitting nearby and determined, to the satisfaction of the Algeria-born contingent, that these were, in fact, capers.

Figure 15. Inspecting Maltese flora. Photograph by the author.

The plant these elderly *pieds-noirs* most associated with North Africa and their past lives there was the prickly pear cactus (*figuier de Barbarie*, lit. North African or Barbary fig). A woman in her eighties, also traveling in my car, kept pointing out abundant stands of these hardy cacti, crying out at one point, "Wow, this is really the area of the Barbary figs!" We all looked over to where she was pointing to find them growing wild, like weeds. From time to time, the passengers in my car would ask me to slow down when the stand we were passing was particularly well kept or had abundant or especially ripe fruit, so that they could take photographs or simply admire them.

These features of the natural landscape conjured up Algeria. Conversations wandered from commentaries on cacti, the olive and fig trees, orange groves and grape vines, or the local fare to reflections on their similarities with North African varieties of flora and fauna and then to North Africa more generally (see fig. 15). While eating at a seafood restaurant, I overheard Carmel Schembri and Joseph Zammit discussing their respective homes: "It was a paradise, a real paradise, we had everything there!" Over the course of their meal, they retraced the shoreline, describing it in detail from Carmel Schembri's beloved western Tunisia to Zammit's hometown, Philippeville (Skikda), in Algeria. "Did you ever go fishing at La Caroube?" I heard one of them ask.

This reveling in nostalgia for the North African landscape culminated on the last day of the trip. While waiting for the ferry to take us back from

Gozo to Malta, we parked on a hill overlooking the bay. It was cold and damp, and the sun was setting. But just next to the parked vans along the side of the road was one of the most abundant stands of Barbary figs we had seen. It was just too much. Giggling like children, the elderly settlers in the van ahead of me began making a commotion, taking photographs of each other and rummaging through their bags. It was time for a Barbary fig feast! The secretary of the organization had come prepared with special pairs of thick leather gloves and began picking off dozens of fruits. Men had brought pocket knives for the occasion and began cutting away the spines. Everyone began gorging themselves on the delicious ripe fruits, taking photos of their friends with the red juices dripping down their chins. One rather tense, brittle woman began to talk with enthusiasm for the first time on the trip. "Oh, this is just like my youth!" she kept exclaiming. "You know, it has been thirty-three years since I've eaten these," she told me. "Thirty-three years. How they remind me of the good old days!"

LANGUAGE AND
CULTURAL HABITUS

If it were only the landscape of colonial Algeria that Malta replaced, the elderly *pieds-noirs* could easily travel elsewhere. In fact, Malta is notable today for its lack of natural features, particularly following the building craze of the past few decades, which has covered much of the archipelago (especially the main island of Malta) with massive concrete high-rise hotels. There is, in fact, very little "nature" left there at all. Other Mediterranean islands could perhaps better serve as a suitable proxy, such as Sardinia or Corsica. But there are additional aspects of this particular place that I believe make it an irresistible site for a pilgrimage back in time and space to colonial Algeria. Most notable among these is the Maltese language, which I would argue indexes Arabic and Algerians.

A sense of loss or longing for Algeria was never communicated to me directly by *pieds-noirs*. Due to the damages they or their associates inflicted on Algerians even before the war, as well as their strong emotions associated with the war years, *pieds-noirs* may never be able to acknowledge even to themselves this particular loss. It is also for this reason that most have never returned to Algeria: many fear retribution. However, non-*pieds-noirs* in France have remarked on this quality of their exile. At the reunion of the Souk-Ahrasians, I had been talking for the previous three hours with a boisterous group of gentlemen of Maltese origin at whose table I had been seated. After they got up to visit another table, Hélène, a woman from northern France in her late sixties now married to one of the men, moved closer to tell me something important. She whispered, "There is something you must know, Andrea. They are just drenched in Arab culture. Drenched. They miss that culture, that world, terribly." Hélène's assertions of an underlying "Arab" quality to *pied-noir* culture was repeated more than once by other metropolitan French during the course of my fieldwork, as we have seen.

There are oblique clues to this longing and this sense of loss. I did not find much evidence of the Orientalism that was observed by Lavie in the homes of left-wing Israelis (1996, 71–72) and that others have observed in other instances of imperialist nostalgia (Rosaldo 1989, 69). *Pied-noir* homes are modest, often one- or two-bedroom apartments in hastily constructed concrete high-rises in newer parts of French towns. Some people had brought back hammered bronze serving platters from the colony, but rugs, sofa fabrics, and wall decorations were invariably purchased in France and featured French themes. Prints of Cézanne's many paintings of Mount St. Victoire, for instance, were common in homes I visited in southern France.

Cuisine was different. Tastes and smells associated with a prior place and time can become important symbols of immigrant identity, childhood, and home (Diner 2001; Dinh 1997). As Diner explains, "Because food is so tightly woven around childhood, family, and sensuality, it serves and a mnemonic, an agent to memory" (2001, 8). I was served couscous in a wide variety of preparations at approximately one-third of the meals I ate as a guest in *pied-noir* homes, and it became clear that it was not served only on my account. This was what people ate *là-bas*. Some dishes we ate in Malta were similar to those eaten in Algeria. This was especially the case with the *pastizzis* (or, as the *pieds-noirs* called them, *caldis*), the cheese-filled pastries available in abundance at our hotel's breakfast buffet, and which, to my amazement, the elderly settler women hoarded in their purses for us to eat later for lunch. I wasn't sure if it was the *caldis* alone that were so appealing, or if it was the whole *caldi*-eating experience that was particularly reminiscent of the "good old days." Judging from their children's horrified reactions when they were told of this aspect of their trip ("Why, that's theft, Mother!"), it seemed a practice not particularly "French."

In Malta, language was an even more important vehicle for nostalgic yearnings for a lost North African cultural world. In Algeria, Maltese men, especially, were more likely than other settlers to speak Arabic (and some spoke some Berber). This may have been due to their humbler socioeconomic status: many, such as Mr. Sultana and Mr. Bernard, had been involved in smaller farming enterprises and thus hired and worked directly with Arab and Berber labor. They were also more likely to have grown up in rural village settings, and many people I knew, such as Michel Pisani, had parents who had been small shopkeepers—bakers, hardware store owners, and so forth—who had served, at least in part, an Arabic-speaking clientele.

Conversations among *pieds-noirs* often turned to the question of Arabic and Berber terms, and it seemed clear from the undercurrent of competition present at these occasions that people valued the extent of their linguistic knowledge. Mr. Bernard came back from doing errands in downtown Marseilles to report with glee about a conversation he had started in Arabic, for no apparent reason, with a North African vendor. He seemed quite proud of the fact that the vendor finally asked him where he was from, after incorrectly guessing that he was Lebanese. Arabic was also used regularly among *pied-noir* men of a variety of origins for greetings, serving an in-group, gate-keeping function. At bingo games, older men amused themselves to no end (and succeeded in exasperating their female fellow players, who often did not share their language skills) by shouting out the numbers not in French but in Arabic. This practice served to bond people together at a couscous dinner sponsored by an Algerian Jewish social club that I attended with several Maltese-origin families. Fluency in Arabic was clearly one of the points of convergence among the men present.

The Maltese language's similarity to North African Arabic becomes a central piece of this Maltese pilgrimage puzzle. It is noteworthy, moreover, that this is not how the language is viewed by the elderly *pieds-noirs*. We have seen that the Phoenician-origin language ideology is widespread among French settlers of Maltese origin. By the time I first traveled to Malta, I was well versed in this ideology myself, so I was struck by the language's similarity to the Arabic I knew. A former capital city is called Mdina, Arabic for "town," and others had names identical to places I had visited in Morocco or Tunisia, such as Rabat (Arabic for "suburbs"). In fact, many of Malta's place-names of Arabic origin are descriptive or anthroponymic (Wettinger 2000, xiv–xv), and thus meaningful to Arabic speakers, including the travelers in my car. The Dumonts, for instance, were a "pure" French couple who had lived along the Moroccan-Algerian border, an area with few Maltese settlers. As a result, they were unfamiliar with Maltese but knew Arabic. Throughout the trip, I heard Mr. Dumont's running commentary on the language and its "uncanny" similarity to Arabic. He was particularly intrigued by the street signs: just like Arabic, he declared, but written in a Latin alphabet and thus easier for him to read. While I drove across the busy roads, he pointed out signs to his wife, exclaiming again and again, "Look, this is in Arabic too!" *Marsa,* he knew, meant "port," and he was bubbling with excitement when, on the third day, we skirted the coast and came across the towns of Marsaxlokk and Marsascala. He began to use terms from his memories of Morocco to refer to elements of the Maltese landscape, calling the old Crusader fortresses we kept passing *ksars* (Arabic for "fortress" or "citadel"). "Ah," he would announce, "here's another *ksar!*"

The built environment resembled Algeria as well. Not only were many of the older buildings constructed of blocks of stone, as were many buildings in the colony, but the cars, the ambulatory vegetable peddlers, and even the music appeared as if frozen in time. The shop signs, in particular, brought up colonial memories, for as in colonial North Africa, they featured the surnames of the owners. Mr. Grech, who has accompanied over a half-dozen groups to Malta, later explained to me the reaction of people of his generation to Malta:

> Malta is a conservatory of the 1950s, the 1960s: the music one hears, "Strangers in the Night" . . . all of that, the atmosphere . . . and then there are the little details. I don't know if you saw that, in contrast to what you see elsewhere. In Malta, the stores don't have signs. Instead, there are names of the storeowners. So it's Pisani, Farugia, Buhagiar. The people with the last name Pisani, when they come, or even if that isn't their name, they say, "Hey look, I used to go to that store!" Even the non-Maltese *pieds-noirs,* when I take them to Malta, the folks from Algeria, they say, "Look, there is the name Mifsud, remember!" That establishes a link. There is a visible link.

One woman on our trip was unaware of the ethnic origins of common settler surnames and did not know that many of the shops in Algeria had been owned by Maltese. She was puzzled by what she saw and later told me in confidence that she thought it was odd that all of the stores in Malta had names just like those she had frequented in Algeria. The simple shop signs found throughout the tiny islands thus became powerful mnemonic devices conjuring up memories of Algeria.

Of all of the multiple reminders of Algeria, the acoustic "cues" were particularly pervasive, yet these cues may have been elicited covertly. This may explain why some of the travelers that year seemed to forget where they were. Joseph's Boy Scout song, described in chapter 1, makes sense when viewed in this light. He had spent the trip discussing his earliest memories: his father's return from the war, his own war service, his first job. Why that particular song at that time? Perhaps after spending time in Malta in the company of *pieds-noirs,* it made sense to resurrect the only Arabic that he still remembered. He finally had a context in which the song made sense, a context that in turn reminded him of the song. It is noteworthy that several of his companions resurrected their Arabic language skills during our trip as well. In a testament to the power of erasure in language ideologies and the tenacity of the latter, some people who had never learned Maltese took advantage of its similarity to Arabic and began employing the North African Arabic idiom they had learned in the colony to communicate with the people of Malta, such as local shopkeepers and parking attendants. All the while, they maintained that Maltese is Phoenician and not Arabic. These language practices caused real confusion among the Maltese residents. The locals would take another look at the travelers—their dress, hairstyles, and jewelry (the women often wore gold crosses)—squint, and then exclaim, often in English, "Who are you—Arabs?" In a paradoxical twist, however, it was not the Arabic-speaking former settlers who became the "Arabs" on this journey, but in many respects the Maltese. Malta was serving as a stage, allowing the former settlers to imagine themselves transported in time and space back "home" to French Algeria. Malta became Algeria, and the Maltese themselves stood in place of indigenous Algerians. It may be for this reason that friction erupted between the locals and the visiting settlers more than once on our trip, and may explain the confusion at the airport. While their contact with Maltese residents was generally restricted (again, one can't help but note parallels to the colonial context), on one occasion the elderly women traveling with us got into an argument with some Maltese women of roughly the same age who were tatting lace tablecloths at a port-side tourist spot. The settler women tried to bargain; the Maltese women refused to lower their prices and seemed insulted by the very idea. Their refusal to negotiate outraged the settlers, who later complained about the vendors' "obstinacy." While at the time I found the incident rather odd, it now seems clear that the settlers were insisting on carrying out practices with the Maltese that they remembered from their upbringing in Algeria and perhaps their encounters there with subordinate indigenous populations (or maybe even Maltese shopkeepers in the former colony).

WHY MALTA? SILENCES AND
THE POLITICS OF MEMORY

A visceral, emotional attachment to Algeria was clear whenever I asked people if they had gone back to visit. The response was inevitably quite strong. One day I had asked Mr. Sultana if he had traveled to Malta before. "Malta, no. And I've never gone to Algeria," he added. His wife and other company then took the conversation in a different direction, which he was not happy about, and he interrupted us all: "Let's return for two minutes to Algeria. So, I believe that I don't want to go to Algeria because, if it is all broken [*toute cassée*], I will be disappointed, and if it is good, I will be disappointed. Same thing. So, it doesn't interest me. Because if it is all broken, after we, we had built it all up, and it is broken . . . [that would be awful], and if it is good, like I remember, I will realize that yes, we were good there." Either outcome would be unbearable to him.

The Dumonts had never been to France until their repatriation. Since then, Mr. Dumont has become an avid photographer, and I spent much of the time in their tiny apartment in a large high-rise building near the high-way to Marseilles admiring his impressive collection of photographs. He showed me his multiple albums covering the various regions of France, an-nounced proudly, "I discovered France as an adult!" and proceeded to in-struct me, too, in the wonders of the diverse landscapes, cheeses, housing designs, and flora of the regions of France. One day he brought out an ear-lier family album that included pictures taken in Algeria. One photo of Mrs. Dumont showed her on a ferry waving to some mountains in the dis-tance. "That is my wife saying good-bye to Algeria," he told me, matter-of-factly. While his voice betrayed no special emotion, the power of the pho-tograph was stunning. I asked one day if he would ever go back to visit, and he responded, "No, never. Never, never, never, never, never! Never. I will never go back, never ever." This litany was laden with emotion and a cer-tain rigid determination. I then understood his France "fetish," for France seemed to have served as a much needed frame of reference to replace his beloved Algeria.

If the Maltese *pieds-noirs* yearn to return to Algeria but cannot for per-sonal and political reasons, why don't they travel instead to a neighboring North African country, such as Tunisia? To the former settlers, neither Tunisia nor any other North African country can serve as proxy for Algeria in the ways that Malta can. This is an expression of the politics of remem-bering and the ways that place and time are fused in *pied-noir* nostalgia. The Maltese *pieds-noirs* wish to return not only to a place, a certain com-bination of geography and the human imprint on the landscape, the sounds, smells, and sights, but also to this place in the past, this place at a prior point in time. No contemporary North African destination, not even Algeria, resembles the fused time/place that they miss.

Superficial differences are significant in this regard. Because most learned Arabic while working and living with Algerians and not in school, they cannot read it. Thus Tunisia would not do: the signage is largely in Arabic script and not in the Latin alphabet as in Malta; the all-important shop-sign cues are not there to prompt their memories of the colonial past. These countries have moved forward in time. The travelers miss a certain iteration of that place in the past—an idealized reconstruction not unlike the visions of homeland shared by exiled Iranians in the United States (Naficy 1991). In this regard, it is significant that, despite their awkward liminal social status, and unlike the Algerian Jews, the Maltese were also settlers. The colonial memories and nostalgia we are concerned with here are those of a settler population. Travel to Morocco or Tunisia would mean traveling to a land now ruled by the native population. The contrast be-tween the political context and power dynamics in these new countries and those that they remember from Algeria would be dramatic; it is very probable that they would feel like aliens in this transformed North Africa. Thus it may be the very absence of real Algerians that makes Malta so desirable a pilgrimage site. Malta serves as an idealized French Algeria, a sanitized variation on the colonial past.

PLACE, MEMORY, AND FORGETTING

Representations of the past shared by a population are strongly shaped by the needs of the present, a point made long ago by Halbwachs (1992). Because peoples and political agendas change while memories accrue, processes of forgetting are necessary for the consolidation of any collective memory, as many scholars have noted (Battaglia 1992). Indeed, remembering anything at all would be quite impossible without forgetting. As Lowenthal writes, "memories must continually be discarded and conflated; only forgetting enables us to classify and bring chaos into order" (1985, 205). It is especially important to note that forgetting, like remembering, can occur in patterned ways. Freud explored extensively the effects of emotional states such as guilt on the processes of remembering. Everyday forgetting, in his view, was a clue to deeper psychological processes at work. He outlined an array of parapraxes, which include "slips of the tongue," the forgetting of names, and other errors in everyday life (Freud 1965, 25); he interpreted these behaviors as resulting from our often unconscious yet masterful ability to steer clear of difficult emotions. We are disinclined to remember "anything which is connected with feelings of unpleasure and the reproduction of which would renew the unpleasure" (1965, 75). When memories are imbued with terrible feelings of shame, guilt, anger, or grief, the subject may protect him- or herself from them by their repression, a process that is itself often denied. It follows that when many individuals have endured a similar ordeal, this process can lead to amnesia on a collective scale. Collective forgetting can also be deliberate: as Diana Gittins writes, "silence and power work hand in hand." As a result, even whole historical eras "can become cloaked in silence." Finally, the politics of silencing are historically contingent: what is mentionable in one era may not be at another point in time (1998, 46–47).

The effect of repression and denial on the collective memory of the Maltese *pieds-noirs* is apparent when we consider which aspects of the past are discussed and highlighted and which have been "forgotten" or remain unsaid. The years of Maltese liminality feature prominently in their discussions and either have persisted as a form of "subaltern settler" oppositional memory or have resurfaced since their exile in France. These memories are powerful enough to nourish a distinct collective identity and to prompt the formation of the Franco-Maltese clubs. Algeria is also central, and they spend much of their time together reminiscing about "the good old days *là-bas.*" These conversations simultaneously reflect their pride in their French nationality and North African birthplace, an underlying ambivalence about their Maltese ancestry, and sympathy for their Maltese forebears.

Together, these discussions recreate a highly selective vision of colonial times containing interesting zones of amnesia. Algerians, violence, and repression are excluded from public discussion. Even though many individuals I spoke with cherished their Arabic language skills and enjoyed discussing in detail the warm ambience they remembered from their rich social life in Algeria, they rarely discussed individual Algerian Arabs or Berbers, a pattern also found among the North African Jews interviewed by Valensi (1990). This suggests that while the sounds of the language are essential sensory elements of that lost universe, the settlers seem to have screened its speakers from their consciousness. Given the fact that their last encounters with Algerians would have been greatly strained by the French-Algerian War, we might assume that their memories of these encounters would be entangled with strong emotions. Some Maltese *pieds-noirs* would have hired Algerian or Berber servants, nannies, or workers, and many had childhood friends of "colonized" ethnicities. Their own difficulties navigating the tension between personal relationships and group loyalties—a tension that would have become severe during the war, as we have seen it did for Mrs. Galea's brother—and feelings of abandonment, guilt, betrayal, and anger may all be at work here. The Maltese *pieds-noirs* are keen on remembering the ways in which they were subordinated by other people, but are less able to perceive the ways in which they dominated as well. While they miss their former home terribly, their vision of that world has been reconstructed as they exclude aspects associated with difficult memories unmentionable today.

RUPTURES IN MASTER NARRATIVES

The settlers' migration occurred at the time of a momentous shift in global politics, during an era of decolonization that rendered a whole former way of life not only anachronistic, but indefensible morally. It became a way of life no longer "good to think" or to narrate. A similar process was experienced more recently by residents of the former Soviet Union, East Germany, and the former Yugoslavia, which have also ceased to exist. The conflict in Yugoslavia, like that in Algeria, was in part about "the right to a home in the name of different 'we's'" (Jansen 1998, 86). Yugoslavia served as not only a physical home, but a narrative of home for the women writers that Stef Jansen reviews; it provided the cultural framework within which they positioned themselves, and served as a reservoir of discursive material for identity construction. The disintegration of Yugoslavia thus led to a major discursive break, with a resulting loss of the metaphorical homeland that was so important to so many. Not only does Yugoslavia no longer exist, but the expression of nostalgia for this entity is now ridiculed or worse, and people expressing such views are described derisively as "Yugozombies," the "living dead" of Yugoslavia who have not completely discarded the Yugoslav past. These people may even, by their very existence, pose a threat "to the new national spirit" (Jansen 1998, 96–97). In many countries, such as Croatia, a conscious effort is underway to do away with any evidence of that prior past.

Former French settlers of North Africa struggle with a similar denial of history, one that also involves a self-conscious rejection of a once-valorized former political order. The larger master narrative within which their life had meaning has been thoroughly discredited and is now untellable in the new political climate of postcolonial France. Without such a wider narrative, people find it impossible to narrate their lives without reference to places and times now imbued with shame or which no longer exist. Disorientation can set in. A former Yugoslav woman expressed this feeling as follows: "I feel robbed of my past, my childhood, my education, my memories and sentiments, as if my whole life has been wrong, one big mistake, a lie and nothing else" (Drakulić 1993, quoted in Jansen 1998, 95). Another woman writes, "I knew I had been deprived of the future, but I could bear it. But until that moment I wasn't aware that I had been deprived of the past too" (Jansen 1998, 98).

Since their arrival in France, *pieds-noirs* have been similarly afflicted. They have felt the contempt of the French; they have experienced overt discrimination, and even suspected that covert measures were being implemented against them. They told me that they felt neglected by the state, and that the real or apparent disapproval they felt from wider French society injured many of them quite deeply. National memory is one of the most prominent realms in which they felt ignored or marginalized. They found their past to be relatively unknown to most French, or understood in an especially unflattering or superficial way. I was told by many of my informants that the ethnic diversity of the settlers, their migration histories, and the various achievements of the earliest pioneers were at risk of vanishing into oblivion. I myself found only a few accounts of the ethnic heritage of the settlers, aside from some master's theses written by former settlers themselves or by their children.

At the same time, by all accounts, the French are undergoing a period of intense nostalgic fascination with the past (Greene 1999; Wood 1999). This preoccupation with the national past is perhaps best exemplified by

Pierre Nora's *Les lieux de mémoire* (1984). The many volumes published thus far include chapters on the flag, national holidays, Marianne, the Larousse dictionary, and important historical tomes and paintings. Notably absent is a serious attempt to incorporate elements of France's colonial legacy or to move beyond the boundaries of the Hexagon (Valensi 1995, 1073). The *pied-noir* perception of a national discomfort with the colonial past is not unfounded. It is no wonder that some of the more active settler clubs have been those that provide a forum for members' genealogical or historical research, and these can be seen as a veritable counterhegemonic backlash, replete with commemorative events, publications, and programs on the colonies. Settlers have written accounts of their experiences in Algeria by the hundreds, often publishing them with their own funds. Presses specializing in *pied-noir* publications have been established, such as *Africa Nostra* and *Éditions de l'Atlanthrope*. Many spouses and children of settlers have turned to this heritage for the subject of their own research, and *pieds-noirs* themselves have generated a plethora of first-hand accounts, which often have the overt goal of filling in the gaps, of "telling the truth," as many put it. These projects necessarily involve a return to the devalued past, and can be seen as valiant efforts by mostly amateur historians to connect their family-based histories into a broader historical framework. The Maltese social clubs should be considered in light of this wider movement, as *pieds-noirs* and other French from the overseas territories endeavor to create a place for themselves on the public stage, a *lieu* for their *mémoires*, and perhaps even to gain acceptance from wider French society.

Because the families from Algeria have different ethnic heritages, their strategies for coping with this discursive rift vary with ethnicity and the degree to which a prior homeland played a role in collective understandings of the past and self. I found that many settlers of French origin have worked to replace Algeria with France, a homeland they had learned to love while at school in the colony. This is the case with the Dumonts, who as adults have dived wholeheartedly into their endeavor to become thoroughly acquainted with their *patrie*.

What about the many "French" with no clear family heritage in France, however? Algerian Jews who left Algeria at independence with the other French citizens also have been coping with their break from their home—one that they inhabited for over two thousand years. In her study of North African Jewish autobiographies and oral accounts, Lucette Valensi finds that many such narratives focus on a site (a house, a neighborhood, or a town) that the narrators describe as an "enclosed place, protected and warm," where one hears one's mother tongue (1990, 92). The "home" concept is imbued with powerful affect indeed. However, Valensi found that her interviewees describe and evaluate their migration experiences differently, according to individual personalities and life trajectories. Jewish culture has been marked by a prior and enduring narrative of exile and return, and, upon leaving North Africa, many Jews returned instead to the original homeland, Israel. Valensi found that some people who made such a journey now view their departures from North Africa not as traumatic but as liberating. One man wrote that he felt free only after becoming an Israeli citizen (Valensi 1990, 96). But others had a different experience. As a woman from the extreme southern part of Algeria told Valensi, "When I left Ghardaïa for Jerusalem, I learned that the true Jerusalem was Ghardaïa" (Valensi 1990, 97).

Former French settlers of foreign origins face similar difficulties finding a way to attach themselves anew. The pilgrimage of Notre Dame de Santa Cruz, organized by the Association of the Friends of Santa Cruz of Nîmes, recreates a practice that had its origins in Oran, a city in Algeria that was dominated by settlers of Spanish origin throughout much of its colonial history. The ritual commemorates the Virgin's role in ending a cholera epidemic in Oran in 1849. This ritual persisted in colonial Algeria and was continued in France when the statue of the Virgin was brought there in 1964 (Slyomovics 1995, 343; see also Baussant 2002). However, Susan Slyomovics found that this is not a healing ritual: "the pilgrimage is a temporary substitute, or consolation for loss, at the same time as it is continually preoccupied with rupture" (1995, 347). Perhaps the fact that most of the participants are from elsewhere prevents such healing from occurring.

These experiences greatly resemble that of the Maltese *pieds-noirs*. Like Valensi's interviewee, or the pilgrims in Nîmes, for whom pilgrimage seems less about healing and more about rupture, the Maltese travel to Malta not to make a liberating journey home (it is significant that few ever decide to move there), but to undertake an ultimately unfulfilled journey back to Algeria. In these cases, as Valensi writes, there is exile but no possibility of redemption; "only mourning remains" (1990, 97).

CONFLATED PLACES AND
SILENCED MEMORIES

When I followed a group of club members on a trip to Malta, I discovered that these pilgrimages can be understood best in terms of the members' intense longing for their "other" homeland, Algeria, which is evoked in Malta through sensory memory. The conversations of my fellow travelers in Malta focused not on that country, but on their lives *là-bas* (back there), the *pied-noir* euphemism for Algeria. When Malta was evoked, they highlighted aspects of the natural and cultural landscape and their similarity to those "back home." Language is of special significance here, for Maltese is so close to the North African Arabic idiom many learned in the colony that they often used that colonial language to speak with the Maltese. For these elderly *pieds-noirs,* Malta serves, not as an ancestral homeland, but as a replacement for their "real" homeland, Algeria. When these trips are viewed in the wider context of colonial nostalgia, of the politics of memory and of forgetting, and of the sensory memory of place, we find here that one homeland, Malta, serves as a metaphor for another, Algeria. Malta has become, for these travelers, a place, replaced.

For the *pied-noir* travelers of Maltese origin who went to Malta that year, the trip was not so much a pilgrimage to the ancestral homeland as it was a symbolic journey to their *pays,* French Algeria. As I drove these elderly settlers around Knights-era fortifications, Baroque churches, and monuments, they talked almost exclusively about life *là-bas.* While Malta is a place they travel to in part because it feels welcoming to them, most have abandoned any hope of finding their ancestral families there. They travel not so much to go to Malta itself but to return to a certain version of Algeria—an Algeria without anti-Maltese discrimination, an Algeria with "pseudo"-Algerians, an Algeria that never was. In essence, trips to Malta represent pilgrimages of nostalgia.

The Malta-for-Algeria exchange was never articulated openly. Just as similarities between the Maltese and Arabic languages are denied, so too is this conflation of place. This may explain why *pied-noir* brochures and promotional materials feature Maltese tourist destinations, such as the fortresses of the Knights and Neolithic temples. Such literature notably excludes elements of the landscape that might index Algeria, unlike the brochures described by Oren Kosansky, which are designed to attract Jews from the Moroccan diaspora and purposefully feature images of the landscape to evoke a nostalgia for a lost North African homeland (2002, 359). On the surface, everyone agrees that they are traveling through Malta, but mentally they are elsewhere.

These pilgrimages and the postcolonial Franco-Maltese settler clubs illustrate the powerfully creative ways humans have coped with the grief of home-loss. This grief may be especially difficult to surmount when the departure was not by choice and when there is no hope of return. Here, the exiles have found an outlet, however temporary, and have replaced one place with another. Their two "homelands" are linked in multiple ways. The presence of characteristic flora, the landscape, the Mediterranean sky and shoreline, the climate, as well as the sounds of the local language and elements of the built environment, call forth memories of Algeria, allowing people to share in sensory memory–induced collective journeys of the imagination back home.

In an interesting contrast to many other homeland pilgrimages, the place they visit is not a classic site of memory, however. In his work on Scottish Highland heritage tourism, Joseph Basu writes that memory can be externalized in the landscape and sites of memory can become internalized through individual engagement. He interprets visits by descendants of the Scottish diaspora to the ruins of villages depopulated by the Highland Clearances as sacred journeys involving a search for the self (2001, 340–45). For the Maltese, however, the landscape is devoid of memories. Moreover, this may be the very point. Absent of memories yet reminiscent of another place and time, it serves as a receptacle for a constellation of memories uprooted from somewhere else.

This study of one of France's many migrant groups in the wake of decolonization reveals the close relationship between place and social memory. In unraveling the contours of a population's collective memory, anthropologists may wish to attend to place; at the same time, a consideration of a group's past helps us understand the power today of specific places. Attending to which places can and cannot serve as substitute sites of memory, can elucidate the underlying processes of collective memory formation, especially when the collective memory in question involves a difficult, traumatic, or devalued past—elements of which may remain unstated or unsayable, or which may be consciously and collectively avoided. This example underscores the power of nostalgia, the ways in which mourning for a place is also a mourning for a lost time, and the strong ties between nostalgia and the evocative power of sensory memory. People displaced may find alternative sites that allow them to collectively relive and return to the past when their place of memory can no longer be inhabited, or, as in the case of French Algeria, when it no longer exists.

NOTES

1. A SONG IN MALTA

1. All names of people and most names of *pied-noir* organizations are pseudonyms.

2. *Pied-noir* (or black foot; *pieds-noirs,* plural) is an appellation for the French settlers of Algeria; its origin is unknown. It may have been used in the early twentieth century (Lorcin 1995, 287n. 31), but became widespread only during the French-Algerian War and was most likely an "exonym" (Proschan 1997), a label granted the settlers by the metropolitan French. It has been claimed since by French from Algeria, including most (but not all) of the people I interviewed, and thus is used here interchangeably with "former settlers of Algeria." See chapter 7 for further discussion of this label.

3. Although the former settlers claimed the label "Algerian" for themselves, I am using it here to refer to the indigenous population at this period just before independence. This and any other work on a colonial context must grapple with the choice between value-laden terminology from the colonial setting and that which is less offensive but also less historically accurate. Anachronistic terminology is often found in the speech of former settlers. When quoting settlers using this term to denote themselves, I place it in quotation marks.

4. From 1955 to 1959, only approximately 110,000 non-Muslim French left Morocco out of a total preindependence population of 320,000. Three years after Tunisian independence in 1956, 45 percent of the non-Muslim French population remained (Frémeaux 1996, 13–15).

5. Over 80 percent of the settlers of Algeria had left for France by the end of 1962 (Frémeaux 1996, 15; see also Jordi 1993, 32–34).

6. Due to heightened publicity in France regarding torture during the French-Algerian War, there is a rapidly evolving literature on this question. Michaud and Branche 2004, Stora 1992, Sueur 2001, and Alexander, Evans, and Keiger 2002 are good introductions.

7. Ageron (1994, 160–61) estimates Algerian wartime casualties at 203,000. Stora writes that half a million people of all backgrounds, but primarily Algerians, perished in the war. The FLN claims that there were one million martyrs (Stora 1993, 91). Estimates are still debated today (Pervillé 2004).

8. On the revelation that torture had become standard French practice and the difficulty French officials and the public have had in acknowledging this fact, see Stora 1992 and Vidal-Naquet 1983. The topic has gained much public attention recently following the publication of a wartime memoir by Aussaresses (2001). See also Elgey 2001; Weill 2001.

9. The war is known by *pieds-noirs* as *les événements* (the events). In French, its most neutral appellation is *la guerre d'Algérie* (the Algerian War), a name used by French historians and social scientists but only recently accepted by the National Assembly (see Stora 1999). In English this war is sometimes referred to as the "Algerian War of Independence" (Naylor and Heggoy 1994, 20). In Algeria it is often simply the "revolution" (Stora 1992, 121).

10. In fact, the Cranberries are from Ireland.

11. The word *harki* is derived from the Arabic *haraka,* to move, and first referred to the mobile units created in 1956 to aid the French in "territorial security." It is sometimes used more generally to mean all Muslims repatriated with the French. See Hamoumou 2004. Immediately following the war, thousands of *harkis* were massacred in Algeria. Between 1962 and 1969, over forty thousand harkis and their family members migrated to France through official and unofficial channels (Font 1996, 96–97). Many were given jobs in the forest service and lived in makeshift camps in remote rural areas. Others were placed in guarded highrise apartments in urban areas.

12. Noiriel points out that these periods were all ones of acute economic crisis and change associated with the stabilization of migrant communities and thus their increased visibility in wider society (Noiriel 1996, 190).

13. Census figures reported a total of 93,068 *pieds-noirs* in the department in 1968, representing 6.3 percent of the total population (Jordi 1993, 108). Many urban areas along the Mediterranean had even larger concentrations by the end of that decade, including 11 percent in Montpellier, 10 percent in Toulon and Perpignan, and 8 percent in Marseilles, Nice, Nîmes, and Marseilles (Lees 1996, 105). *Pied-noir* organizations in this region often reported a much higher figure of 25 percent in the mid-1990s.

14. This book is based on informal conversations with hundreds of people and informal and formal interviews, as well as transcripts of audio recordings of over fifty hours of informal conversations with thirty-seven people. The people I taped were of the following ethnicities: Maltese, 57 percent; mixed and non-French origins, 19 percent; and French-origin settlers, 24 percent. The sixty-nine people with whom I conducted formal interviews were distributed similarly: Maltese, 54 percent; mixed origins, including Maltese, German, Italian, Spanish, and French, 19 percent; and French origins, 22 percent. It should be noted that these are rough categories based on individuals' self-ascription. One "Maltese" man had one Sicilian and three Maltese grandparents, and one "French" man had one Swiss and one Alsatian grandparent.

15. Historical sources include Ageron 1991, 62; Crespo and Jordi 1991, 9; Jordi 1986, 275–88. Memoirs and other journalistic accounts that use "melting pot" language include Baroli 1967; Espitallier 1987; Gignoux and Simiot 1961; Laffly 1987.

16. The decree of December 9, 1848, turned the civil territories of Algeria into three *départements,* divided into *arrondissements* (districts) and *communes,* all administered, as in France, by prefects and subprefects. See Ageron 1991, 28–29.

17. The history of Algeria has been the subject of innumerable books, reports, conferences, and articles. Even a summary of this literature now requires a whole volume. On the history of the French colonization, the works by Julien (1964) and Ageron (1979, 1968) are considered classics. Good annotated bibliographies can be found in Ruedy 1992, 258–84, and in Julien 1964, 507–88.

18. These provinces were the *dar al-Sultan,* surrounding Algiers, and the *beyliks* of Constantine in the east, Oran in the west, and Titteri in the center.

19. Whenever possible, I employ spellings for Arabic terms found in Houtsma et al. 1987 or Naylor and Heggoy 1994.

20. Pouillon (1993) and Thomson (1993) deconstruct the erroneous but commonly used term "Moor."

21. The M'zabites were Ibadi, a branch of the Kharijites, a separatist sect of Islam.

22. See Valensi 1986 for a review of various classification schemes proposed by anthropologists and historians for this ethnically diverse region.

23. On the French knowledge of the people of Algeria that predated French conquest, see Thomson 1993.

24. Grain, oil, wool, coral, livestock, and other items were exported to cities in Tunisia, to Marseilles, to Leghorn in Italy, and to other European ports. French firms such as the

Compagnie d'Afrique held profitable monopolies through treaties made with local leaders. See Julien 1964, 18; Prochaska 1990, 53.

25. This conquest began in conjunction with the Aghlabid conquest of Sicily (827–29), and occurred at least by 869. Muslims ruled the islands until 1090 C.E. (Wettinger 1986, 90).

26. Naturalization laws were enacted on June 26, 1889, and July 22, 1893.

27. This is due to French law requiring 30, 60, 100, 120, and sometimes even 150 years to pass before the release of documents, compounded by a time lag in classifying otherwise available materials.

28. Nora himself makes this point (1998, 609).

29. This contrast between memory and history was outlined in quite similar terms by Halbwachs in *The Collective Memory,* a work published posthumously in 1950, in which he argued that collective memory is an unwritten stream of continuous thought delimited by a specific social group, while history is a unitary written collection of facts, often regarding the nation, constructed by objective, impartial historians (1980, 81). The development of a universal history is a violent process, involving the severing of memories from groups, a reduction of events to comparable terms, and the introduction of universal demarcations (such as dates) into the "stream of facts."

30. For reviews of this literature, see Lowenthal 1985; also Olick and Robbins 1998.

31. This literature is too vast to enumerate here. See Marcus and Fischer 1986. Pels 1997 and Stoler and Cooper 1997 offer good reviews. On the forms of knowledge upon which colonialism was predicated, see Cohn 1996, Dirks 1992, Stocking 1991, Thomas 1994.

32. Notable exceptions include Hirschon 1989 and Dembour 2000.

33. *Pataouète* is the name sometimes given to the language spoken by settlers of Algeria that had its origins in the many languages spoken in Algeria. See Lanly 1970.

2. MALTESE SETTLER CLUBS IN FRANCE

1. The disruption of trade caused by the Order's piratical activities created lasting tension with the Republic of Venice and led the latter to refer to the Order as "corsairs parading crosses" (Mallia-Milanes 1992a).

2. A similar claim to being "aboriginal Europeans" is made in Greece (see Herzfeld 1987).

3. See Sznycer 1973 for a list of such sources.

4. Even after Count Roger the Norman conquered the islands in the late eleventh century, the terms of the peace treaty he signed allowed local Muslim rulers to continue to administer local affairs, suggesting that the Christian population of the islands at this time was relatively insignificant. It appears that a true Norman presence was not established until Roger II arrived in 1127 (Luttrell 1994, 52–53).

5. Strickland promoted the use of Maltese and English (as opposed to the then-popular Italian), and published a book linking the Maltese language to ancient Phoenician in 1921.

6. In 1842, there were approximately 960 people per square mile in Malta, a much higher population density than Barbados, which then was claimed to host the "densest population in the world" (Price 1954, 30).

7. Letter no. 14 of March 3, 1831, to Colonial Office (hereafter CO), CO 158/68, Public Record Office, Kew, United Kingdom (hereafter PRO).

8. By the end of the nineteenth century, there were only seven hundred Maltese in Gibraltar and six hundred in Marseilles. At the same time, there were thousands of Sicilians in Malta, but only some five hundred Maltese established in all of Italy (Vadala 1911, 51–54).

9. By the end of the eighteenth century, there were one to two thousand Christian slaves in the Regency of Tunis (Valensi 1967, 1278).

10. In a letter of November 19, 1938, to Laurent Ropa, E. Mallea discusses his difficulty interesting the residents of Constantine in club activities. Photocopy courtesy of Pierre Dimech.

11. In 1923, a naturalization law made it easier for the second generation born in Tunisia to gain French citizenship, and granted it automatically to the third.

3. A HIERARCHY OF SETTLERS AND THE LIMINAL MALTESE

1. August 10, 1835, M. Tanski, *capitaine à la Légion étrangère,* in *Archives du ministère de la guerre,* Algérie H226, Vincennes, France.

2. These regions include the departments of Alpes de Haute Provence, Var, Bouches du Rhône, Alpes Maritimes, Gard, Hérault, and Lozère, and parts of the Vaucluse.

3. See letter of June 15, 1844, from British consul general, Algiers, to Reade, Tunis, Foreign Office (hereafter FO) 335/88/3; July 9, 1849, letter of St. John to Reade, FO 335/97/5; CO 158/172, PRO.

4. FO 339/98, PRO.

5. Ricoux found outright errors in the official statistics of 1847 and 1851 (1880, 17–18, note). The Maltese figures are probably too low. Throughout the nineteenth century, French officials complained to the governor of Malta and British consulate officers about the Maltese who traveled to Algeria, overland from Tunisia or by sea, without passports. Because undocumented immigrants were summarily deported by French officials, we can assume that individuals in this situation would have attempted to elude the census takers, and that the numbers of Maltese are underestimated as a result. November 25, 1853, letter, French consul general (C.G.) in Tunis to British C.G., CO 158/172, PRO; July 9, 1849, letter, British C.G. in Algiers, to C.G. in Tunis, FO 335/97/5, PRO.

6. This practice was carried out without the authority of Paris and in contravention of international law (Ruedy 1967, 102).

7. In the eastern department of Constantine, approximately one-fifth of the population perished, and even the wealthier Arab and Berber families found themselves with a considerably lowered economic status at the end of the crisis in 1869 (Nouschi 1961).

8. The revolt spread and was eventually led by Muhammad al-Hajj al-Muqrani, an important Constantinois tribal leader, who was joined by the Kabyle's Rahmaniyya brotherhood.

9. Seven tribes had over three hundred thousand hectares annexed to the state domain. Hundreds of other tribes had 240,000 hectares confiscated and were charged nearly 9 million francs to regain access to the remainder. Because most tribes could not afford to pay these fees, they were forced to sell some of their land to the French state at a fixed price in order to raise enough money to purchase the rest. In this way, the state obtained an additional 10 million francs and two hundred thousand hectares.

10. Muslims sold over eight hundred thousand hectares to Europeans between 1877 and 1917 (Ageron 1991, 203).

11. Between 1880 and 1920, the indigenous population lost over 4 million hectares to the state (Ageron 1991, 203).

12. December 30, 1853, F80/1177 *Centre des archives d'outre-mer,* Aix-en-Provence, France, hereafter CAOM.

13. Cholera struck in 1849, in 1854, and again in 1867–1868; typhus and famine in 1867; and smallpox in 1871 (Nouschi 1961; Ricoux 1880, 21, 65).

14. There were 225 applications for concessions at three population centers in 1845: six from Spanish nationals and 219 from French citizens (Jordi 1986, 210).

15. Report to the minister of war from the Bureau of Colonization, January 20, 1845, IL52, *Archives du gouvernement général de l'Algérie,* CAOM (hereafter AGGA).

16. Letter to the governor-general, September 27, 1845, IL52, AGGA.

17. IL52, AGGA.

18. In the department of Oran, only 440 out of the over five thousand concessions granted by 1861 were to Spanish settlers, and most of these were the smallest plots (Jordi 1986, 239). In eastern Algeria, a minority of the immigrants from the Italian peninsula seeking concessions received them, and they too were granted small lots; in La Calle, these averaged less than one hectare (Crespo 1994, 86).

19. L 1, Rejected Applications for Concessions, 1900, AGGA. Most of the 449 rejected European applications identify lack of resources as the reason for rejection.

20. Officials lavished praise on Swiss nationals. One group was described by an administrator as "naturally honest" and "respected by everyone for their simplicity and zeal for work." F80 1391, letter of May 10, 1851, CAOM.

21. See Donato 1985, 142–48, for a full tabulation of 239 death certificates, of which these 149 list an occupation; from F80/718, CAOM.

22. Thémistocle Lestiboudois, publicist for the Academy of Sciences, is a notable example. He received six hundred hectares in April 1848 in the eastern Saf-Saf valley, without ever putting down the required deposit or complying with the title provisions. As absentee landlord, he had a manager watch over his lands and rented out two-thirds of his acreage to Algerian sharecroppers. Despite the fact that his concession was a well-known scandal, the state took no action against him. He was even named president of the *Conseil général* in Constantine when it was formed in 1858, a position that allowed him to travel to Algeria and visit his domain on state funds (Julien 1964, 377).

23. Land concessions became almost equivalent to cash donations, larger land grants prevailed, and capitalist enterprises played increasingly significant roles. The *Compagnie genevoise,* for instance, settled five hundred families on twelve thousand hectares, and for its efforts received rights to eight thousand additional hectares. The company eventually farmed the entire property with the labor of poorly paid Arab workers (Ruedy 1992, 71).

24. This practice accelerated under Napoleon, who conceded vast amounts of land to his elite supporters, including Charles de Lessups, brother of the builder of the Suez Canal, who received seven thousand acres in the Beni Salah forest (Prochaska 1990, 74).

25. Such was the case with Paulin Talabot, a prominent businessman of the Second Empire. Talabot was involved in railroad construction, exploited mines in France, and founded several banks, including the *Société générale.* He obtained several of the most profitable iron mines in the department of Constantine. When he had transportation difficulties at one of his inland mines, he convinced Napoleon's government to pay for the construction of a railroad to facilitate bringing his ore to the port of Bône (Prochaska 1990, 80–85).

26. *Communes mixtes* were areas formerly under military occupation, administered by agents assigned by the governor-general. *Communes indigènes* were remote areas in the south with little European settlement.

27. The voting rights of Muslims were further restricted in 1850 (Ageron 1991, 28).

28. Law of November 28, 1848, F80/631, *"Mendicité,"* CAOM.

29. Letters of March 22 and April 3, 1968, F80/1804, CAOM.

30. This description is based on a study of marriage records of all men married in Guelma from 1852 to 1880. 122 MiOM 2, microfilm, CAOM.

31. "Tableau de la situation de Philippeville pendant l'année 1841 et le 2ème trimestre de l'année 1842," Philippeville, October 12, 1842, handwritten report by Mr. Lapaine, the secretary of the *Commissariat civil,* serving as interim *commissaire civil,* 1L8, AGGA. When

he presented population figures for Tunisia in 1858, the French scholar J. Henry Dunant wrote that the European population, "if we include the Maltese," was a bit over twelve thousand (1858, 254).

32. Genty de Bussy described the French conquest of Algeria as "that crusade of civilization against barbarians" (1833, 6).

33. As in Guyana, the merits of each group were judged partly according to the group's potential economic contribution to the colony (see Williams 1991, 140). This helps explain the "Kabyle myth" valorizing the sedentary Kabyles over the "roaming" Arabs, for many Kabyles practiced intensive agriculture in mountain villages and were viewed as potentially more useful to French colonization efforts, while most Arabs, in contrast, relied on a largely pastoral economy involving the extensive use of land, land that was coveted by the French from the start (see Ageron 1960; Lorcin 1995, 37–40).

34. See Bahloul 1996, 85–86, for the significance of religious ascription in the colonial society.

35. This information is courtesy of André Spiteri.

36. Letter from British consul St. John, June 13, 1832, quoted in Donato 1985, 73.

37. St. John to director of the interior, December 29, 1839, FO 112/4, PRO.

38. Letter of February 17, 1838, quoted in Donato 1985, 79.

39. St. John to governor of Malta, March 24, 1839, FO 112/4, PRO.

40. Decree of February 20, 1843, letter from the minister of war, Paris, to governor-general of Algeria, F80/1666, CAOM.

41. Letter, July 26, 1845, F80/613, CAOM.

42. September 25, 1852, F80/1666, copy to prefect of Constantine, CAOM.

43. Lapaine, "Tableau de la situation de Philippeville."

44. *Commissaires civiles* were appointed by the governor-general, and carried out the functions of mayor, chief of police, and judge.

45. Lapaine, "Tableau de la situation de Philippeville."

46. In 1841 there were 1,066 Maltese, 1,950 French, 443 Italians, 179 Spanish, 443 "Moors and Arabs," and 89 Jews. Lapaine, "Tableau de la situation de Philippeville."

47. Biskris are migrants from the Ziban, an "archipelago of oases" (Clancy-Smith 1994, 11) in southern Algeria, the gateway to the Sahara. Migrants from this region formed corporations that specialized as porters, and they persisted as an identifiable social category in the city of Algiers at least into the 1930s. See Houtsma et al. 1987, 732, 1181.

48. Laws established in 1837 and 1838 provided for the maintenance of indigenous organizations in Algiers, but stipulated that the *amins* be named by the governor-general. F80/613, CAOM.

49. Commissaire Antoine Fenech was from a bourgeois family in Malta. One of his grandfathers was a medical doctor who received his degree at the Université de Montpellier in France. The family left Malta for France with the French troops at the defeat of Napoleon Bonaparte by the British, and they lived for some time in Toulon. His brother Eugène also spent time in Algeria, and has written a fascinating memoir that has been published recently (Fenech and Spiteri 2001).

50. Letters from Fenech to the director of the interior, August 14, 1841, and from the commander in chief of the militia *bataillon d'Ambly* to Fenech, August 11, 1841; F80/1439, CAOM.

51. Letter from *Colonel commandant supérieur* to governor-general of Algeria, December 18, 1841, F80/612, CAOM.

52. Correspondence of December 1841, F80/613, CAOM.

53. Letter from Fenech to the *Colonel commandant supérieur de Philippeville,* December 5, 1841, F80/613, CAOM.

54. Letter of January 16, 1842 to governor-general, F80/613, CAOM.

55. *Arrêté* of May 19, 1843, draft, F80/648, CAOM.

56. North African Jews arrived in successive migration streams, beginning perhaps as early as the ninth century B.C.E. On the history of North African Jewry, see Chouraqui 1968; Hirschberg 1981.

57. See Friedman 1988, chapter 2.

58. On linkages between the Crémieux decree and the anti-Judaic riots, see Friedman 1988, Prochaska 1990.

59. For further discussion of Algerian Jewish liminality, see Bahloul 1996, 86–90. See also Memmi 1962, 1966.

60. It should be noted that the Maltese were able to work their way more comfortably into colonizer status by identifying themselves as fellow Christians, while Algerian Jews continued to be treated by European settlers as suspect, and were even stripped of their French citizenship status in 1940 when the Vichy government revoked the Crémieux decree.

61. According to their dossier, they had been purchasing wool, grain, and livestock from local tribes for sale at inflated prices, and the army ran short of the wool needed at the hospital and for bedding. F80/612, "Expulsions," CAOM.

62. Of course this does not necessarily indicate that Maltese were not active in the rioting or in generating anti-Jewish propaganda.

63. Police report, "*Troubles anti-semitiques,*" September 24–25, 1899, 7G9, AGGA.

64. CO 158/238, 1873, PRO.

65. Letter of June 14, 1873, CO 158/238, PRO.

66. Out of 1,614 French citizens married between 1854 and 1878, only 58 married Maltese spouses. Fifty-four of these (35 French men and 19 French women) were born in Europe, while only four were born in Algeria (Ricoux 1880, 102).

4. THE ALGERIAN MELTING POT

1. This interpretation is exemplified by Nathan Glazer and Daniel Moynihan's bestseller, *Beyond the Melting Pot* (1963). In this work, the authors decry the melting pot, which they view as causing the dissolution of a group's ethnic distinctiveness. It is by attributing such a meaning to the metaphor that Glazer and Moynihan can then argue in their work that the melting pot "never happened."

2. The marginalization of Algeria's settler population in these texts is partly due to their timing. These works were published soon after Algerian independence, when the settlers' pasts were not a focus for most historians, who were inspired by the revolution and the newly independent state. Ageron and Julien concentrated instead on the political struggles over Algeria and the development and failings of colonial policy.

3. These are approximates calculated from Ageron 1979, 119.

4. *Correspondances consulaires Oran,* no. 1997, quoted in Jordi 1986, 268.

5. Foreigner naturalization in Algeria was articulated in the laws of March 22, 1849, December 5, 1849, and February 7, 1851.

6. The law also eliminated the need to receive prior formal authorization to establish residence in France, as previously required (Dalloz and Dalloz 1865, 114–18).

7. Following agreements with Britain in 1863 and Italy in 1868, their nationals were exempted from the Algerian militia obligation (Jordi 1986, 131).

8. Members of a colonization committee in September 1871 hotly debated which was a greater threat to the colony: the much larger indigenous population, whose recent insurrection had almost succeeded, or the non-French alien settler presence. One committee

member described the Spanish presence in Oran as a "permanent danger." September 7, 1871, minutes, *Comité consultatif de colonisation,* L19, AGGA.

9. "France—Report for the Year 1889 on the Commerce and Agriculture of Algeria." Foreign Office 1890. Annual Series, no. 669, Diplomatic and Consular Reports on Trade and Finance. London: Harrison and Sons. 40 MiOM, 26, CAOM.

10. Four hundred and twenty-four were of French origin, and 402 were *indigènes,* while 4,408 were naturalized French. Crespo 1994, 73.

11. For example, Ricoux 1880; Demontès 1906; and Leroy-Beaulieu 1887.

12. Six documents were required: the individual's birth certificate; the parents' marriage certificate, translated and certified by French consuls in their country of origin; the birth certificates of both parents, translated and certified; a certificate from foreign military authorities outlining the individual's military status; and a nationality certificate obtained from the individual's country, sent by that country's consul and signed by two witnesses of that nationality, stating that under no circumstances would the individual ever wish to become French. During this era, most of these documents would have been extremely difficult or costly to obtain (see Jordi 1986, 132–33).

13. The official motivation for this *Sénatus-consulte* was to facilitate assimilation of the indigenous population in accordance with the general good will expressed by the emperor toward the Algerian Muslims in his imperial letter of February 6, 1863. However, following the first declaration, "*l'indigène musulman est Français*" (the indigenous Muslim is French), the law states that, as such, "he can be admitted to serve in the army and the navy," indicating that another motivation was to enlarge the emperor's armies. A statement published with the 1865 *Sénatus-consulte* reports that many indigenous youth had already sought out the honor of fighting under the French flag, and that some seven thousand were members of the French *Armée d'Afrique* in 1854 alone (Dalloz and Dalloz 1865, 115). Indigenous troops were highly praised by Napoleon III, who viewed them as one of Algeria's most useful products (in Ageron 1968, 1057).

14. *Times* (London), December 24, 1898.

15. "Les pieds noirs: La question du jour," *Les documents de la revue des deux mondes* 18 (1961): 30.

16. The law of June 16, 1881, made primary education free, and the law of March 20, 1882, insisted on its obligatory and nonreligious character. For a succinct review of the literature on the effects of these laws on France, see Reed-Danahay 1996.

17. New taxation laws, the *Indigénat,* a demoralizing separate set of legislation governing the autochthonous society, resulted in an "irreversible" transformation of the traditional society (Colonna 1975, 23).

18. See Gosnell 2002, Lorcin 1995, and Prochaska 1996 for discussions of the *Algérianiste* school, and its vision of the Algerian melting pot that left little room for the autochthonous populations.

19. On early uses of the term *pataouète,* see Lanly 1970, 157; Prochaska 1996.

20. *Le sang des races* by Bertrand is a case in point; on the anti-Semitism of Cagayous, a newspaper serial in this movement, see Prochaska 1996.

21. Writing about the Philippeville area, Solal notes that, by the 1870s, some Maltese were systematically buying up all of the tiny plots surrounding their original properties (n.d., 242). According to documents from Peyerimhoff's assessment of the concession program in that *arrondissement,* people with Maltese surnames were purchasing their neighbors' properties, as with Joseph Spiteri, who bought properties in Dauribeau, and Joseph Teuma, who purchased the concessions of Bischoff and Mathieu, among others. See Colonisation 7L4, AGGA.

5. THE AMBIVALENCE OF ASSIMILATION

1. Olick makes a related point in a study of historical representations of commemorative practices in Germany surrounding May 8, 1945, celebrations (1999).

2. For a thorough discussion of contemporary approaches to context in linguistic anthropology, see Goodwin and Duranti 1992.

3. See for instance "L'irrésistible ascension des pieds noirs," *Le Figaro,* no. 13319 (June 27, 1987).

6. THE FRENCH-ALGERIAN WAR
AND ITS AFTERMATH

1. The many events of this period are interpreted differently even by those who took part in them, and even by those ostensibly on the same side. Any synopsis of this war would be viewed at least by some of those I interviewed as a skewed polemic, and I summarize this period with some hesitation. For an overview, see Stora 1993. An excellent new edited volume is Harbi and Stora 2004. The classic work in English remains Horne 1977.

2. When the conflict started is a matter of debate. Many of the people I interviewed had lived through the coordinated massacres in the Constantine province on the day of armistice at the end of World War II (November 8, 1945) and feel that this event and the brutal reprisals by the French army which followed should be viewed as the beginning of the confrontation. Interestingly, many Algerian nationalists also see this as the start of the uprising (Alexander, Evans, and Keiger 2002, 12).

3. For a discussion of the debates in the National Assembly culminating in the official state adoption of *la guerre d'Algérie* as the new name for the hostilities, see Stora 1999, 128–35.

4. Virtually from the time of the initial French conquest of Algiers, Algeria provided manpower for the French army. Algerian indigenous troops served in the conquest of Algeria and in most colonial and other French campaigns of the nineteenth century, including the Second Empire engagements of Crimea (1854–56), Italy (1859), and Mexico (1861–67) and in operations in Indochina (1859–63), China (1860), Senegal (1860), and the Levant (1860–61) (Clayton 1988, 62–63). With the establishment of conscription of Muslims in 1912, 81,000 from Algeria were enlisted in World War I and 176,000 in World War II (Hamoumou 2004, 319).

5. *Harki* is a term that should apply exclusively to Muslim auxiliaries, but it is often used to refer to all Muslims who actively supported France during the war, including noncombatants such as Muslim elites, elected officials, and those naturalized, who are sometimes called *Français musulmans rapatriés* (repatriated French Muslims, or FMR). See Hamoumou 2004; Evans 2002.

6. Estimates of the numbers of Algerians killed range from 1,273 to 12,000 (Stora 1992, 17).

7. There is a rich literature on this issue. See Dine 1998; Sueur 2001; Vidal-Naquet 1983.

8. During a demonstration of Algerians in Paris on October 17, 1961, nearly two hundred demonstrators were killed and thousands were wounded (Stora 1993, 64).

9. A referendum held July 1 resulted in overwhelming support for independence (5,975,581 vs. 16,534; Ageron 1991, 126). De Gaulle declared Algeria independent on July

3 while representatives of the new country declared its independence July 5, 1962 (see Naylor and Heggoy 1994, 27). July 1 is now celebrated as Independence Day.

10. Note that the appellation *la guerre d'Algérie* was not used until 1956 in the National Assembly, and first appeared in print in 1960. It was only accepted by the state as official usage in 1999. See Stora 1999, 128–35.

11. Like other *pieds-noirs,* she said not "Algerians" but "Arabs," a group she contrasted with "Europeans."

12. Stora suggests that just giving the conflict a name can be interpreted as a lifting of a collective repression (1999, 135). This name change, coupled with the opening of some war-era archives and increased public debate, has led to Harbi and Stora's optimistic title for their new edited volume, *La guerre d'Algérie, 1954–2004: La fin de l'amnésie* [The Algerian War, 1954–2004: The End of Amnesia] (2004).

7. DIASPORA, REJECTION, AND *NOSTALGÉRIE*

1. Jordi estimates that by the end of 1962, 650,000 French had migrated from Algeria to France. He notes that these figures do not include those who migrated via Italy or Spain, those who traveled through unofficial channels, such as on private boats, or those who did not sign up upon arrival at the *centres d'accueil des rapatriés.* They also do not include Muslim French, twenty-six thousand of whom migrated between May and August 1962 (Jordi 1995, 68).

2. Approximately 9 percent of the active working settler population in Algeria in 1954 were agriculturalists, compared to 26 percent in France. Most had small properties: of the European-owned lands, 6,385 *gros colons* owned 87 percent, while 8,000 small *propriétaires* owned only 1 percent. See Lefeuvre 2004, 272.

3. Memmi wrote about the *colonisateur,* the colonizer, a usurper who accepts the role of illegitimately privileged person (1967, 52). Some colonizers accept this privileged position wholeheartedly and thus go the whole distance, becoming *colonialistes,* individuals who not only colonize but who seek to legitimize the entire colonial enterprise and who actively promote colonial politics and policies (45). Finally, the *colonial* is a European living in the colony without privileges and at the same economic and social status as the colonized, a hypothetical character who, in Memmi's view, never really existed (10).

4. This is the definition given by my 1994 Larousse *Dictionnaire du français au collège,* which defines a *rapatrié* as "*Personne qui est ramenée dans sa patrie.*" The law of December 1961 specified, "Any French individual who has had to leave or is viewed as having had to leave a territory that was once French due to political events, can, if he wants, be considered a repatriate" (Zytnicki 1998, 509).

5. Ostensibly, *refugié* was inappropriate because, according to international legal definitions developed after World War II, refugees are foreigners placed in a special relationship with the receiving country in response to their persecution (Henry 1996, 150–51). The colonists, as French citizens, could not be considered refugees.

6. For instance, "25 ans après: Le pouvoir des pieds-noirs," special issue, *Le nouvel observateur,* no. 1180 (June 19–25, 1987); "On les appelait les Pieds-Noirs," *L'express,* July 16–22, 1982; "L'irrésistible ascension des Pieds Noirs," special issue, *Le Figaro,* no. 13319 (June 27, 1987).

7. These policies are hotly debated today. See Blum 2002.

8. Through a statistical analysis of census data, Alba and Silberman (2002) demonstrate that there are great gaps between second-generation Maghrebins and *pieds-noirs* from Algeria, Tunisia, or Morocco in terms of education and occupational status; interestingly, the authors do not draw contrasts between either group and French society as a whole.

9. A similar story was told to Jane Kramer by one of the *pieds-noirs* she interviewed (Kramer 1980).

10. This was the case with François Xuereb's brother, who carried out his regular military service in the Navy in 1938, only to be called up again in 1939 and discharged in 1940. He served again from November 1942 to May 1945.

11. Similar views may have been shared by Frenchmen in France. Researchers working with metropolitans have found that men who served in the French-Algerian War sometimes felt that this war helped them redeem their fathers and uncles, who had been denied the chance to express their masculinity in World War II. See Alexander, Evans, and Keiger 2002, 15–16.

12. See Jordi 1993, 188, for a summary of Marseillais anti-*pied-noir* attitudes.

13. "*Mais le pied-noir, c'était une race à part pour le Français. Enfin pour le Français de France, je dis bien.*"

14. Hureau suggests that the first use of *pied-noir* occurred in 1956 (1987, 7).

15. Stora claims that anti-Arab racism in France stems from a transfer of memories of the French-Algerian War (1999). My evidence here of an anti-*pied-noir* racism that predates the war suggests that "war transfer" can only be part of the problem.

16. The first associations were mutual aid organizations that defended *pied-noir* interests. Many of these associations lobbied the French government to accelerate the planned or promised reparations for property and savings lost in Algeria, and promoted amnesty for individuals condemned for having supported the cause of *l'Algérie française*. The original organizations of this kind were formed in Algeria. ANFANOMA (*Association nationale des Français d'Afrique du Nord, d'outre-mer et leurs amis*), for instance, was created in 1958 with the goal of promoting a French Algeria. After it shifted to a more moderate political stance in 1959, some former ANFANOMA members formed RANFRAN (*Rassemblement national des Français d'Afrique du Nord et d'outre-mer*), which declared its unambiguous support for a French Algeria. Upon arrival in France, most *pieds-noirs* joined one or the other. ANFANOMA is today the principal association defending *pied-noir* interests (Calmein 1994, 20–25).

8. SETTLER ETHNICITY AND IDENTITY POLITICS IN POSTCOLONIAL FRANCE

1. Provence, Auvergne, and France were the three "French" *langues;* the remainder were Aragon, Castile, England, Germany, and Italy.

2. Once consisting entirely of nobles, it now has a branch that is open to "good Catholics," which allows the Order to recruit members in places without a strong noble legacy. The remaining knights are documented members of noble families, a small portion of whom are also in religious orders and have taken a vow of chastity (*Ordre de Malte Hors-Série*, no. 44, "Notre histoire," n.d., Paris).

SOURCES CITED

PUBLISHED PRIMARY SOURCES

Allain, Maurice, ed. 1923. *L'Algérie: Geographie universelle*. Paris: Quillet.

Bard, Joseph. 1854. *L'Algérie en 1854*. Paris: L. Maison.

Bernard, P., and F. Redon. 1936. *L'Algérie: Histoire, colonisation, géographie, administration*. Alger: Imprimeries La Typo-Litho.

Caix de Saint-Aymour, Amédée. 1987 [1891]. "Français, Espagnols, indigènes et Italiens." In "Algérie: Histoire et nostalgie, 1830–1987," special issue, *Historia* 486:98.

Charmes, Gabriel. 1888. *La Tunisie et la Tripolitaine*. Paris: Calmann Levy.

Dalloz, Victor Alexis Désiré, and Armond Dalloz. 1865. *Jurisprudence générale: Recueil périodique et critique de jurisprudence, de législation et de doctrine*. Part 4, "Lois, décrets, avec les rapports et les discussions législatives." Paris: Bureau de la jurisprudence générale.

Dalloz, M., and Armond Dalloz. 1889. *Jurisprudence générale: Recueil périodique et critique de jurisprudence, de législation et de doctrine*. Part 4. "Lois, décrets et arrêtés, avec dapports et discussions législatives." Paris: Bureau de la jurisprudence générale.

Dazet, Georges, and Georges Dupuy. 1900. *Revision de la loi sur la naturalisation en Algérie et du décret Crémieux*. Algiers: Imprimerie typographique et lithographique S. Léon.

de Bussy, P. Genty. 1833. *De l'établissement des Français dans la régence d'Alger et des moyens d'en assurer la prospérité*. Algiers: Imprimerie du gouvernement.

Demontès, Victor. 1906. *Le peuple algérien: Essai de démographie algérienne*. Algiers: Imprimerie Algérienne.

Dunant, J. Henry. 1858. *Notice sur la Régence de Tunis*. Geneva: Jules Gme. Fick.

Faucon, Narcisse. 1893. *La Tunisie avant et depuis l'occupation française*. Vol. 2, *Colonisation*. Paris: Augustin Challamel.

Lacoste, L. 1931. *La colonisation maritime en Algérie*. Paris: Librairie Larose.

Leroy-Beaulieu, Paul. 1887. *L'Algérie et la Tunisie*. Paris: Librairie Guillaumin.

Morell, John Reynell. 1854. *Algeria: The Topography and History, Political, Social, and Natural, of French Africa*. London: Nathaniel Cooke.

Peyerimhoff, M. de. 1906. *Enquête sur les résultats de la colonisation officielle de 1871 à 1895*. Rapport à Monsieur Jonnart, gouverneur général de l'Algérie. Gouvernement Général de l'Algérie. Direction de l'agriculture, du commerce, et de l'industrie. Algiers: Imprimerie J. Torrent.

Ricoux, René. 1880. *La démographie figurée de l'Algérie: Etude statistique des populations européennes qui habitent l'Algérie*. Paris: G. Masson.

Wilkin, Anthony. 1900. *Among the Berbers of Algeria*. London: T. Fisher Unwin.

SECONDARY SOURCES

Ageron, Charles-Robert. 1960. "La France a-t-elle un politique kabyle?" *Revue historique* 223:311–52.

———. 1968. *Les Algériens musulmans et la France (1871–1919)*. 2 vols. Paris: Presses Universitaires de France.

———. 1979. *Histoire de l'Algérie contemporaine*. Vol. 2, *1870–1954*. Paris: Presses Universitaires de France.

———. 1991. *Modern Algeria: A History from 1830 to the Present*. Trans. Michael Brett. London: Hurst.

———. 1994. *La décolonisation française*. Paris: Armand Collin.

Alba, Richard, and Roxane Silberman. 2002. "Decolonization Immigrations and the Social Origins of the Second Generation: The Case of North Africans in France." *International Migration Review* 36 (4): 1169–93.

Alexander, Martin, Martin Evans, and J. F. V. Keiger, eds. 2002. *The Algerian War and the French Army, 1954–62: Experiences, Images, Testimonies*. New York: Palgrave Macmillan.

Alonso, Ana María. 1988. "The Effects of Truth: Re-presentations of the Past and the Imagining of Community." *Journal of Historical Sociology* 1 (1): 33–57.

———. 1995. *Thread of Blood: Colonialism, Revolution, and Gender on Mexico's Northern Frontier*. Tucson: University of Arizona Press.

Anderson, Benedict. 1991. *Imagined Communities: Reflections on the Origin and Spread of Nationalism*. London: Verso.

Arnaud, Louis. 1960. *Bône: Son histoire, ses histoires*. Constantine: Damrémont.

Asad, Talal. 1973. Introduction to *Anthropology and the Colonial Encounter*, ed. Talal Asad, 9–19. New York: Humanities.

Aussaresses, Général. 2001. *Services spéciaux: Algérie, 1955–1957*. Paris: Perrin.

Bahloul, Joëlle. 1996. *The Architecture of Memory: A Jewish-Muslim Household in Colonial Algeria, 1937–1962*. Cambridge: Cambridge University Press.

Baillet, Pierre. 1975. "L'intégration des rapatriés d'Algérie en France." *Population* 30 (2): 303–13.

Bakhtin, Mikhail M. 1981. *The Dialogic Imagination: Four Essays*. Trans. Caryl Emerson and Michael Holquist, ed. Michael Holquist. Austin: University of Texas Press.

———. 1986. *Speech Genres and Other Late Essays*. Trans. Vern McGee, ed. Caryl Emerson and Michael Holquist. Austin: University of Texas Press.

Balandier, Georges. 1951. "La situation coloniale." *Cahiers Internationaux de Sociologie* 11:44–79. Paris: Aux Éditions du Seuil.

Balibar, Etienne. 1984. "Sujets ou citoyens." *Les temps modernes* 452 (3–4): 1726–53.

Balibar, Etienne, and Immanuel Wallerstein. 1991. *Race, Nation, Class: Ambiguous Identities*. New York: Verso.

Baroli, Marc. 1967. *La vie quotidienne des Français en Algérie, 1830–1914*. Paris: Hachette.

Barth, Fredrik, ed. 1969. *Ethnic Groups and Boundaries: The Social Organization of Culture Difference*. Bergen-Oslo: Universitetsforlaget.

Basu, Joseph. 2001. "Hunting Down Home: Reflections on Homeland and the Search for Identity in the Scottish Diaspora." In *Contested Landscapes: Movement, Exile, and Place*, ed. Barbara Bender and Margot Winer, 333–48. Oxford: Berg.

Battaglia, Debbora. 1992. "The Body in the Gift: Memory and Forgetting in Sabarl Mortuary Exchange." *American Ethnologist* 19 (1): 3–18.

Baussant, Michèle. 2002. *Pieds-noirs: Mémoires d'exils*. Paris: Stock.

Beidelman, Thomas O. 1981. *Colonial Evangelism: A Socio-historical Study of an East African Mission at the Grassroots*. Bloomington: Indiana University Press.

Bénichou, Marcel. 1992. "Sémantique et histoire: 'Les Rapatriés' . . . ?" In *Les rapatriés d'Algérie en Languedoc-Roussillon, 1962–1992*, ed. Mohand Khellil and Jules Maurin, 199–207. Montpellier: Université Paul Valéry–Montpellier III.

Bennoune, Mahfoud. 1988. *The Making of Contemporary Algeria, 1830–1987: Colonial Upheavals and Post-independence Development.* Cambridge: Cambridge University Press.

Berger, Peter, Brigitte Berger, and Hansfried Kellner. 1973. *The Homeless Mind: Modernization and Consciousness.* New York: Random House.

Beriss, David. 1990. "Scarves, Schools, and Segregation: The Foulard Affair." *French Politics and Society* 8 (1): 1–13.

———. 2004. *Black Skins, French Voices: Caribbean Ethnicity and Activism in Urban France.* Boulder: Westview.

Bertrand, Louis. 1920 [1899]. *Le sang des races.* Paris: Ollendorf.

———. 1920 [1904]. *Pépète le bien-aimé.* Paris: Ollendorf.

Bhabha, Homi K., ed 1990. *Nation and Narration.* London: Routledge.

Bicharat, George. 1997. "Exile to Compatriot: Transformations in the Social Identity of Palestinian Refugees in the West Bank." In *Culture, Power, Place: Explorations in Critical Anthropology,* ed. Akhil Gupta and James Ferguson, 203–33. Durham, N.C.: Duke University Press.

Blondy, Alain. 1994. "L'ordre de Saint-Jean et l'essor économique de Malte, 1530–1798." *Revue du monde musulman et de la Méditerranée* 71 (1): 75–90.

Blum, Alain. 2002. "Resistance to Identity Categorization in France." In *Census and Identity: The Politics of Race, Ethnicity, and Language in National Censuses,* ed. David Kertzer and Dominique Arel, 121–47. Cambridge: Cambridge University Press.

Bonacich, Edna. 1972. "A Theory of Ethnic Antagonism: The Split Labor Market." *American Sociological Review* 37 (5): 547–59.

Boserup, Esther. 1965. *The Conditions of Agricultural Growth.* Chicago: Aldine.

Bourdieu, Pierre. 1962 [1958]. *The Algerians.* Originally published as *Sociologie de l'Algérie.* Trans. Alan Ross. Boston: Beacon.

Boussevain, Jeremy. 1965. *Saints and Fireworks: Religion and Politics in Rural Malta.* London: Athlone.

Boyarin, Jonathan. 1991. *Polish Jews in Paris: The Ethnography of Memory.* Bloomington: Indiana University Press.

Brincat, Joseph. 1991. "Language and Demography in Malta: The Social Foundations of the Symbiosis between Semitic and Romance in Standard Maltese." In *Malta: A Case Study in International Cross-Currents,* ed. Stanley Fiorini and Victor Mallia-Milanes, 91–110. Malta: Salesian Press.

Brodkin, Karen. 1998. *How Jews Became White Folks and What That Says about Race in America.* New Brunswick, N.J.: Rutgers University Press.

Brubaker, William Rogers. 1992. *Citizenship and Nationhood in France and Germany.* Cambridge, Mass.: Harvard University Press.

———, ed. 1989. *Immigration and the Politics of Citizenship in Europe and North America.* Lanham, Md.: University Press of America.

Burton, Antoinette, ed. 2003. *After the Imperial Turn: Thinking with and through the Nation.* Durham, N.C.: Duke University Press.

Calmein, Maurice. 1994. *Les associations pieds-noirs, 1962–1994.* Carcassone: SOS Outre-Mer.

Camilleri, Carmel. 1985. "Une communauté maltaise en Tunisie entre les groupes Arabo-Berbère et Français." *Les temps modernes* 470:486–513.

Casey, Edward. 1993. *Getting Back into Place: Toward a Renewed Understanding of the Place-World.* Bloomington: Indiana University Press.

———. 1996. "How to Get from Space to Place in a Fairly Short Stretch of Time: Phenomenological Prolegomena." In *Senses of Place,* ed. Steven Feld and Keith Basso, 13–52. Santa Fe, N.M.: School of American Research Press.

Cassar, Carmel. 2000. *Society, Culture, and Identity in Early Modern Malta.* Msida, Malta: Mireva.

———. 2001. "Malta: Language, Literacy, and Identity in a Mediterranean Island Society." *National Identities* 3 (3): 257–75.

Castles, Stephen, Heather Booth, and Tina Wallace. 1984. *Here for Good: Western Europe's New Ethnic Minorities.* London: Pluto.

Césaire, Aimé. 1955. *Discours sur le colonialisme.* Paris: Éditions Presence Africaine.

Chouraqui, André. 1968. *Between East and West: A History of the Jews in North Africa.* Trans. Michael Bernet. Philadelphia: Jewish Publication Society of America.

Ciappara, Frans. 2001. *Society and the Inquisition in Early Modern Malta.* San Gwann, Malta: Publishers Enterprises Group.

Clancy-Smith, Julia. 1994. *Rebel and Saint: Muslim Notables, Populist Protest, Colonial Encounters (Algeria and Tunisia, 1800–1904).* Berkeley: University of California Press.

Clayton, Anthony. 1988. *France, Soldiers, and Africa.* London: Brassey's Defence Publishers.

———. 1994. *The Wars of French Decolonization.* London: Longman.

Clifford, James. 1992. "Traveling Cultures." In *Cultural Studies,* ed. Lawrence Grossberg, Cary Nelson, and Paula Treichler, 96–116. New York: Routledge.

———. 1994. "Diasporas." *Cultural Anthropology* 9 (3): 302–38.

Cohen, Robin. 1997. *Global Diasporas: An Introduction.* Seattle: University of Washington Press.

Cohn, Bernard. 1996. *Colonialism and Its Forms of Knowledge: The British in India.* Princeton, N.J.: Princeton University Press.

Cole, Jeffrey. 1997. *The New Racism in Europe: A Sicilian Ethnography.* Cambridge: Cambridge University Press.

Cole, Jennifer. 2001. *Forget Colonialism? Sacrifice and the Art of Memory in Madagascar.* Berkeley: University of California Press.

Colonna, Fanny. 1975. *Instituteurs algériens, 1833–1939.* Paris: Presses de la Fondation nationale des sciences politiques.

Comaroff, John. 1987. "Of Totemism and Ethnicity: Consciousness, Practice, and the Signs of Inequality." *Ethnos* 52 (3–4): 301–23.

Connerton, Paul. 1989. *How Societies Remember.* Cambridge: Cambridge University Press.

Cooke, Miriam, and Angela Woollacott, eds. 1993. *Gendering War Talk.* Princeton, N.J.: Princeton University Press.

Cooper, Frederick, and Ann L. Stoler. 1989. "Introduction: Tensions of Empire; Colonial Control and Visions of Rule." *American Ethnologist* 16 (4): 609–21.

Corrigan, Philip, and Derek Sayer. 1985. *The Great Arch: English State Formation as Cultural Revolution.* Oxford: Basil Blackwell.

Crespo, Gérard. 1994. *Les Italiens en Algérie, 1830–1960: Histoire et sociologie d'une migration.* Calvisson: Éditions Jacques Gandini.

Crespo, Gérard, and Jean-Jacques Jordi. 1991. *Les Espagnols dans l'Algérois, de 1830 à 1914: Histoire d'une migration.* Versailles: Éditions de l'Atlanthrope.

Debbasch, Charles, and Jacques Bourdon. 1995. *Les associations.* 5th ed. Paris: Presses Universitaires de France.

Defrasne, Jean. 1995. *La vie associative en France.* Paris: Presses Universitaires de France.

Dembour, Marie-Benedicte. 2000. *Recalling the Belgian Congo: Conversations and Introspection.* New York: Bergahn.

Dine, Philip. 1998. "French Culture and the Algerian War: Mobilizing Icons." *Journal of European Studies* 28:51–68.

Diner, Hasia. 2001. *Hungering for America: Italian, Irish, and Jewish Foodways in the Age of Migration.* Cambridge, Mass.: Harvard University Press.

Dinh, Trong Hieu. 1997. "Notre quotidien exotique: Les repères culturels dans l'alimentation de l'Asie en France." *Ethnologie française* 27 (1): 27–38.

Dirks, Nicholas B., ed. 1992. *Colonialism and Culture.* Ann Arbor: University of Michigan Press.

Donato, Marc. 1985. *L'émigration des Maltais en Algérie au XIXème siècle.* Montpellier: Collection Africa Nostra.

Douglas, Mary. 1966. *Purity and Danger: An Analysis of the Concepts of Pollution and Taboo.* New York: Frederick Praeger.

Drakulić, Slavenka. 1993. *Balkan Express.* Trans. Maja Soljan. London: Hutchinson. Quoted in Jansen 1998.

Dubois, Colette. 1994. "La nation et les Français d'outre-mer: Rapatriés ou sinistrés de la décolonisation?" In *L'Europe retrouvée: Les migrations de la décolonisation,* ed. Jean-Louis Miège and Colette Dubois, 75–134. Paris: L'Harmattan.

Duranti, Alessandro. 1997. *Linguistic Anthropology.* Cambridge: Cambridge University Press.

Elgey, G. 2001. "Crimes de la guerre d'Algérie: Divulger pour ne pas répéter." *Le monde,* May 5, pp. 1, 16.

Eriksen, Thomas Hylland. 2002. *Ethnicity and Nationalism.* 2nd ed. London: Pluto.

Espitallier, Jean-Michel. 1987. "Un habitant de Descartes se souvient." In "Algérie: Histoire et nostalgie, 1830–1987," special issue, *Historia* 486:116–19.

Evans, Martin. 1997. *The Memory of Resistance: French Opposition to the Algerian War (1954–1962).* Oxford: Berg.

———. 2002. "The Harkis: The Experience and Memory of France's Muslim Auxiliaries." In *The Algerian War and the French Army: Experiences, Images, Testimonies,* ed. Martin S. Alexander, Martin Evans, and J. F. V. Keiger, 117–33. New York: Palgrave Macmillan.

Ezra, Elizabeth. 2000. *The Colonial Unconscious: Race and Culture in Interwar France.* Ithaca, N.Y.: Cornell University Press.

Fabian, Johannes. 1983. *Time and the Other: How Anthropology Makes Its Object.* New York: Columbia University Press.

Fanon, Frantz. 1961. *Les damnés de la terre.* Paris: Maspero.

Feld, Steven. 1990. *Sound and Sentiment: Birds, Weeping, Poetics, and Song in Kaluli Expression.* Philadelphia: University of Pennsylvania Press.

———. 1996. "Waterfalls of Song: An Acoustemology of Place Resounding in Bosavi, Papua New Guinea." In *Senses of Place,* ed. Steven Feld and Keith Basso, 91–135. Santa Fe, N.M.: School of American Research Press.

Feld, Steven, and Keith H. Basso, eds. 1996. *Senses of Place.* Santa Fe, N.M.: School of American Research Press.

Fenech, Eugène, and Richard Spiteri. 2001. *Mémoires d'un officier de santé maltais dans l'armée française, 1786–1839.* Récit de la vie de Charles-Eugène Fenech. Paris: La Vouivre.

Fernandez, James. 1988. "Andalusia on Our Minds: Two Contrasting Places in Spain as Seen in a Vernacular Poetic Duel of the Late 19th Century." *Cultural Anthropology* 3 (1): 21–35.

Font, Christine. 1996. "De Nemours à Largentière, une solidarité: Le réseau des officiers de la DBFM." In *Marseille et le choc des décolonisations,* ed. Jean-Jacques Jordi and Emile Temime, 92–102. Aix-en-Provence: Edisud.

Frémeaux, Jacques. 1996. "Le reflux des Français d'Afrique du Nord (1956–1962)." In *Marseille et le choc des décolonisations,* ed. Jean-Jacques Jordi and Emile Temime, 13–28. Aix-en-Provence: Edisud.

Frendo, Henry. 1988. "Maltese Colonial Identity: Latin Mediterranean or British Empire?" In *The British Colonial Experience, 1800–1964: The Impact on Maltese Society,* ed. Victor Mallia-Milanes, 185–214. Amsterdam: Mireva.

Freud, Sigmund. 1965 [1901]. *The Psychopathology of Everyday Life: Forgetting, Slips of the Tongue, Bungled Actions, Superstitions, and Errors.* Trans. Alan Tyson, ed. James Strachey. New York: W. W. Norton.

Friedman, Elizabeth. 1988. *Colonialism and After: An Algerian Jewish Community.* South Hadley, Mass.: Bergin and Garvey.

Gallisot, René. 1975. "Precolonial Algeria." *Economy and Society* 4 (4): 418–45.

Gerson, Stéphane. 2003. *The Pride of Place: Local Memories and Political Culture in Nineteenth-Century France.* Ithaca, N.Y.: Cornell University Press.

Gignoux, C. J., and Bernard Simiot, ed. 1961. "Les pieds noirs: La question du jour." *Les documents de la revue des deux mondes* 18:1–57.

Gilmore, David. 1982. "Anthropology of the Mediterranean Area." *Annual Review of Anthropology* 11:175–205.

Gittins, Diana. 1998. "Silences: The Case of a Psychiatric Hospital." In *Narrative and Genre,* ed. Mary Chamberlain and Joseph Thompson, 46–62. London: Routledge.

Glazer, Nathan, and Daniel Patrick Moynihan. 1963. *Beyond the Melting Pot: The Negroes, Puerto Ricans, Jews, Italians, and Irish of New York City.* Cambridge, Mass.: MIT Press.

Goebel, Stephan. 2001. "Intersecting Memories: War and Remembrance in Twentieth-Century Europe." *Historical Journal* 44 (3): 853–58.

Goodwin, Charles, and Alessandro Duranti. 1992. "Rethinking Context: An Introduction." In *Rethinking Context: Language as an Interactive Phenomenon,* ed. Alessandro Duranti and Charles Goodwin, 1–42. Cambridge: Cambridge University Press.

Gordon, Milton. 1964. *Assimilation in American Life: The Role of Race, Religion, and National Origins.* New York: Oxford University Press.

Gosnell, Jonathan. 2002. *The Politics of Frenchness in Colonial Algeria, 1930–1954.* Rochester, N.Y.: University of Rochester Press.

Gough, Kathleen. 1968. "New Proposals for Anthropologists." *Current Anthropology* 9 (5): 403–407.

Gramsci, Antonio. 1971. *Selections from the Prison Notebooks of Antonio Gramsci.* Trans. and ed. Quintin Hoare and Geoffrey Nowell Smith. New York: International Publishers.

Green, Nancy. 1991. "L'immigration en France et aux États-Unis: Historiographie comparée." *Vingtième siècle* 29:67–82.

Greene, Naomi. 1999. *Landscapes of Loss: The National Past in Postwar French Cinema.* Princeton, N.J.: Princeton University Press.

Grillo, R. D. 1985. *Ideologies and Institutions in Urban France: The Representation of Immigrants.* Cambridge: Cambridge University Press.

Gross, Joan, David McMurray, and Ted Swedenburg. 1996. "Arab Noise and Ramadan Nights: Rai, Rap, and Franco-Maghrebi Identities." In *Displacement, Diaspora, and Geographies of Identity,* ed. Smadar Lavie and Ted Swedenburg, 119–55. Durham, N.C.: Duke University Press.

Gumperz, John. 1982. *Discourse Strategies.* Cambridge: Cambridge University Press.

Gupta, Akhil, and James Ferguson. 1997a. "Beyond 'Culture': Space, Identity, and the Politics of Difference." In *Culture, Power, Place: Explorations in Critical Anthropology,* ed. Akhil Gupta and James Ferguson, 33–51. Durham, N.C.: Duke University Press.

———. 1997b. "Culture, Power, Place: Ethnography at the End of an Era." In *Culture, Power, Place: Explorations in Critical Anthropology,* ed. Akhil Gupta and James Ferguson, 1–29. Durham, N.C.: Duke University Press.

Halbwachs, Maurice. 1941. *La topographie légendaire des évangiles en terre sainte: Étude de mémoire collective.* Paris: Presses Universitaires de France.

———. 1980 [1950]. *The Collective Memory.* New York: Harper & Row.

———. 1992. *On Collective Memory.* Trans. and ed. Lewis Coser. Chicago: University of Chicago Press.

Hamoumou, Mohand. 2004. "L'histoire des harkis et Français musulmans: La fin d'un tabou?" In *La Guerre d'Algérie, 1954–2004: La fin de l'amnésie,* ed. Mohammed Harbi and Benjamin Stora, 317–44. Paris: Robert Laffont.

Handler, Richard. 1988. *Nationalism and the Politics of Culture in Quebec.* Madison: University of Wisconsin Press.

Harbi, Mohammed, and Benjamin Stora, eds. 2004. *La Guerre d'Algérie, 1954–2004: La fin de l'amnésie.* Paris: Robert Laffont.

Hargreaves, Alec G. 1995. *Immigration, "Race," and Ethnicity in Contemporary France.* London: Routledge.

Hargreaves, Alec G., and Mark McKinney, eds. 1997. *Post-colonial Cultures in France.* London: Routledge.

Heggoy, Alf Andrew, and John Haar. 1984. *The Military in Imperial History: The French Connection.* New York: Garland.

Henry, Jean-Robert. 1996. "Rapatriés, réfugiés, repliés: Le poids des mots." In *Marseille et le choc des décolonisations,* ed. Jean-Jacques Jordi and Emile Temime, 150–57. Aix-en-Provence: Edisud.

Herzfeld, Michael. 1987. *Anthropology through the Looking-Glass: Critical Ethnography in the Margins of Europe.* Cambridge: Cambridge University Press.

———. 1991. *A Place in History: Social and Monumental Time in a Cretan Town.* Princeton, N.J.: Princeton University Press.

Hill, Jane. 1985. "The Grammar of Consciousness and the Consciousness of Grammar." *American Ethnologist* 12:725–37.

Hirschberg, H. Z. 1981. *A History of the Jews in North Africa.* 2nd rev. ed. Ed. Eliezer Bashan and Robert Attal. Leiden: E. J. Brill.

Hirschon, Renée. 1989. *Heirs of the Greek Catastrophe: The Social Life of Asia Minor Refugees in Piraeus.* Oxford: Clarendon.

Holmes, Douglas. 2000. *Integral Europe: Fast-Capitalism, Multiculturalism, Neofascism.* Princeton, N.J.: Princeton University Press.

Horne, Alistair. 1977. *A Savage War of Peace: Algeria, 1954–1962.* London: Macmillan.

House, Deborah. 2002. *Language Shift among the Navajos: Identity Politics and Cultural Continuity.* Tucson: University of Arizona Press.

Houtsma, M. T., T. W. Arnold, R. Basset, and R. Hartmann, eds. 1987. *E. J. Brill's First Encyclopaedia of Islam, 1913–1936.* Leiden: E. J. Brill.

Hunt, Jennifer. 1992. "The Impact of the 1962 Repatriates from Algeria on the French Labor Market." *Industrial and Labor Relations Review* 45 (3): 556–72.

Hureau, Joëlle. 1987. *La mémoire des pieds-noirs.* France: Olivier Orban.

Irvine, Judith, and Susan Gal. 2000. "Language Ideology and Linguistic Differentiation." In *Regimes of Language: Ideologies, Polities, and Identities,* ed. Paul V. Kroskrity, 35–83. Santa Fe, N.M.: School of American Research Press.

Irwin-Zarecka, Iwona. 1994. *Frames of Remembrances: The Dynamics of Collective Memory.* New Brunswick, N.J.: Transaction.

Jaffe, Alexandra. 1999. *Ideologies in Action: Language Policies on Corsica.* New York: Mouton de Gruyter.

Jansen, Stef. 1998. "Homeless at Home: Narrations of Post-Yugoslav Identities." In *Migrants of Identity: Perceptions of Home in a World of Movement,* ed. Nigel Rapport and Andrew Dawson, 85–109. Oxford: Berg.

Jordi, Jean-Jacques. 1986. *Les Espagnols en Oranie, 1830–1914: Histoire d'une migration.* Montpellier: Collection Africa Nostra.

———. 1993. *De l'exode à l'exil: Rapatriés et pieds-noirs en France; L'exemple marseillais, 1954–1992.* Paris: L'Harmattan.

———. 1995. *1962: L'arrivée des pieds-noirs.* Paris: Autrement.

———. 1996. "L'été '62 à Marseille: Tensions et incompréhensions." In *Marseille et le choc des décolonisations*, ed. Jean-Jacques Jordi and Emile Temime, 66–74. Aix-en-Provence: Edisud.

———. 2003. "The Creation of the Pieds-Noirs: Arrival and Settlement in Marseilles, 1962." In *Europe's Invisible Migrants*, ed. Andrea L. Smith, 61–74. Amsterdam: Amsterdam University Press.

Joutard, Philippe. 1983. *Ces voix qui nous viennent du passé*. Paris: Hachette.

Julien, Charles-André. 1964. *Histoire de l'Algérie contemporaine*. Vol. 1, *1827–1871*. Paris: Presses Universitaires de France.

Kennedy, Dane. 1996. "Imperial History and Post-colonial Theory." *Journal of Imperial and Colonial History* 24 (3): 345–63.

Kondo, Dorinne. 1996. "The Narrative Production of 'Home,' Community, and Political Identity in Asian American Theater." In *Displacement, Diaspora, and Geographies of Identity*, ed. Smadar Lavie and Ted Swedenburg, 97–117. Durham, N.C.: Duke University Press.

Kosansky, Oren. 2002. "Tourism, Charity, and Profit: The Movement of Money in Moroccan Jewish Pilgrimage." *Cultural Anthropology* 17 (3): 359–400.

Kramer, Jane. 1980. *Unsettling Europe*. New York: Random House.

Krautwurst, Udo. 2003. "What Is Settler Colonialism? An Anthropological Meditation on Frantz Fanon's 'Concerning Violence.'" *History and Anthropology* 14 (1): 55–72.

Kugelmass, Jack, and Jonathan Boyarin, eds. 1998. *From a Ruined Garden: The Memorial Books of Polish Jewry*. 2nd ed. Bloomington: Indiana University Press.

Kumar, Krishan. 2003. *The Making of English National Identity*. Cambridge: Cambridge University Press.

Laffly, Georges. 1987. "Culture: La France commence à se souvenir de ce qui fut la 'France d'en face.'" In "L'irrésistible ascension des Pieds Noirs," special issue, *Le Figaro* (June 27), no. 13319, pp. 7–11.

Laloum, Jean, and Jean-Luc Allouche, eds. 1987. *Les Juifs d'Algerie: Images et textes*. Paris: Éditions du Scribe.

Lanly, A. 1970. *Le Français d'Afrique du Nord: Etude linguistique*. Paris: Bordas.

Lavie, Smadar. 1996. "Blowups in the Borderzones: Third World Israeli Authors' Gropings for Home." In *Displacement, Diaspora, and Geographies of Identity*, ed. Smadar Lavie and Ted Swedenburg, 55–96. Durham, N.C.: Duke University Press.

Lavie, Smadar, and Ted Swedenburg. 1996. "Introduction: Displacement, Diaspora, and Geographies of Identity." In *Displacement, Diaspora, and Geographies of Identity*, ed. Smadar Lavie and Ted Swedenburg, 1–25. Durham, N.C.: Duke University Press.

Leach, Edmund. 1964. "Anthropological Aspects of Language: Animal Categories and Verbal Abuse." In *New Directions in the Study of Language*. Cambridge, Mass.: MIT Press.

Lebovics, Herman. 2004. *Bringing the Empire Back Home: France in the Global Age*. Durham, N.C.: Duke University Press.

Lees, Christiane. 1996. "L'établissement des pieds-noirs dans le Midi méditerranéen français." In *Marseille et le choc des décolonisations*, ed. Jean-Jacques Jordi and Emile Temime, 105–16. Aix-en-Provence: Edisud.

Lefeuvre, Daniel. 2004. "Les pieds-noirs." In *La Guerre d'Algérie, 1954–2004: La fin de l'amnésie*, ed. Mohammed Harbi and Benjamin Stora, 267–86. Paris: Robert Laffont.

Lorcin, Patricia M. E. 1995. *Imperial Identities: Stereotyping, Prejudice, and Race in Colonial Algeria*. London: I. B. Tauris.

Lowenthal, David. 1985. *The Past Is a Foreign Country*. Cambridge: Cambridge University Press.

Luttrell, Anthony. 1977. "Girolamo Manduca and Gian Francesco Abela: Tradition and Invention in Maltese Historiography." *Melita Historica* 7 (2): 105–32.

———. 1994. "L'effritement de l'Islam (1091–1282)." *Revue du monde musulman et de la Méditerranée* 71 (1): 49–61.

Luttrell, Anthony, ed. 1975. *Medieval Malta: Studies on Malta before the Knights.* London: British School at Rome.

Malefakis, Edward. 1970. *Agrarian Reform and Peasant Revolution in Spain: Origins of the Civil War.* New Haven, Conn.: Yale University Press.

Malkki, Liisa. 1997. "National Geographic: The Rooting of Peoples and the Territorialization of National Identity among Scholars and Refugees." In *Culture, Power, Place: Explorations in Critical Anthropology,* ed. Akhil Gupta and James Ferguson, 52–74. Durham, N.C.: Duke University Press.

Mallia-Milanes, Victor. 1992a. "Corsairs Parading Crosses: The Hospitallers and Venice, 1530–1798." In *The Military Orders: Fighting for the Faith and Caring for the Sick,* ed. Malcolm Barber, 103–12. Aldershot, U.K.: Variorum.

———. 1992b. *Venice and Hospitaller Malta, 1530–1798: Aspects of a Relationship.* Marsa, Malta : Publishers Enterprises Group.

Marcus, George, and Michael Fischer. 1986. *Anthropology as Cultural Critique: An Experimental Moment in the Human Sciences.* Chicago: University of Chicago Press.

McDonald, Maryon. 1989. *"We Are Not French!" Language, Culture, and Identity in Brittany.* London: Routledge.

Memmi, Albert. 1962. *Portrait d'un Juif.* Paris: Gallimard.

———. 1966. *La statue de sel.* Paris: Gallimard.

———. 1967. *The Colonizer and the Colonized.* Trans. Howard Greenfeld. Boston: Beacon.

Mendras, Henri. 1988. *La seconde révolution française, 1965–1984.* Paris: Gallimard.

Meynier, Gilbert. 1981. *L'Algérie révélée.* Geneva: Librairie Droz.

Michaud, Yves, and Raphaëlle Branche, eds. 2004. *La guerre d'Algérie: 1954–1962.* Paris: Odile Jacob.

Michel, Marc. 1984. "Les troupes coloniales arrivent." *Histoire* 69:116–21.

Mitchell, Jon. 2002. *Ambivalent Europeans: Ritual, Memory, and the Public Sphere in Malta.* London: Routledge.

Myers, Fred. 1986. *Pintupi Country, Pintupi Self: Sentiment, Place, and Politics among Western Desert Aborigines.* Berkeley: University of California Press.

Naficy, Hamid. 1991. "The Poetics and Practice of Iranian Nostalgia in Exile." *Diaspora* 1 (3): 285–302.

Naylor, Phillip, and Alf A. Heggoy, eds. 1994. *Historical Dictionary of Algeria.* 2nd ed. Metuchen, N.J.: Scarecrow.

Netting, Robert McC. 1977. *Cultural Ecology.* Menlo Park, Calif.: Cummings.

Noiriel, Gérard. 1996 [1988]. *The French Melting Pot: Immigration, Citizenship, and National Identity.* Originally published as *Le creuset français: Histoire de l'immigration, XIXe–XXe siècles.* Trans. Geoffroy de Laforcade. Minneapolis: University of Minnesota Press.

Nora, Pierre. 1984. *Les lieux de mémoire.* Vol. 1, *La République.* Paris: Gallimard.

———. 1989. "Between Memory and History: *Les lieux de mémoire.*" Trans. Marc Roudebush. *Representations* 26: 7–25.

———. 1996 [1984]. *Realms of Memory: Rethinking the French Past.* Vol. 1: *Conflicts and Divisions.* Trans. Arthur Goldhammer, ed. Lawrence Kritzman. New York: Columbia University Press.

———. 1998 [1992]. *Realms of Memory: The Construction of the French Past.* Vol. 3, *Symbols.* English-language edition ed. Lawrence Kritzman. Trans. Arthur Goldhammer. New York: Columbia University Press.

Nosco, Peter. 1990. *Remembering Paradise: Nativism and Nostalgia in Eighteenth-Century Japan.* Cambridge, Mass.: Harvard University Press.

Nouschi, André. 1961. *Enquête sur le niveau de vie des populations rurales constantinoises de la conquête jusqu'en 1919.* Paris: Presses Universitaires de France.

Olick, Jeffrey. 1999. "Genre Memories and Memory Genres: A Dialogical Analysis of May 8, 1945, Commemorations in the Federal Republic of Germany." *American Sociological Review* 64:381–402.

Olick, Jeffrey, and Joyce Robbins. 1998. "Social Memory Studies: From 'Collective Memory' to the Historical Sociology of Mnemonic Practices." *Annual Review of Sociology* 24:105–40.

Olwig, Karen Fog, and Kirsten Hastrup. 1997. *Siting Culture: The Shifting Anthropological Object.* London: Routledge.

Pascaud, Dominique. 1986. "Les appelés d'Algérie: Témoignages et silences." *Cahiers d'histoire* 31 (3–4): 317–45.

Peer, Shanny. 1998. *France on Display: Peasants, Provincials, and Folklore in the 1937 World's Fair.* Albany: State University of New York Press.

Pels, Peter. 1997. "The Anthropology of Colonialism: Culture, History, and the Emergence of Western Governmentality." *Annual Review of Anthropology* 26:163–83.

Perkins, Kenneth J. 1997. *Historical Dictionary of Tunisia.* Lanham, Md.: Scarecrow.

Pervillé, Guy. 2004. "La Guerre d'Algérie: Combien de morts?" In *La Guerre d'Algérie, 1954–2004: La fin de l'amnésie,* ed. Mohammed Harbi and Benjamin Stora, 477–93. Paris: Pierre Laffont.

Popular Memory Group. 1982. "Popular Memory: Theory, Politics, Method." In *Making Histories: Studies in History Writing and Politics,* ed. Richard Johnson et al., 205–52. Minneapolis: University of Minnesota Press.

Portelli, Alessandro. 1997. *The Battle of Valle Giulia: Oral History and the Art of Dialogue.* Madison: University of Wisconsin Press.

Pouillon, Francois. 1993. "Simplification ethnique en Afrique du Nord: Maures, Arabes, Berbères (XVIIIe–XXe siècles)." *Cahiers d'études africaines* 33 (1): 37–49.

Price, Charles Archibald. 1954. *Malta and the Maltese: A Study in Nineteenth Century Migration.* Melbourne: Georgian House.

Prochaska, David. 1990. *Making Algeria French: Colonialism in Bône, 1870–1920.* Cambridge: Cambridge University Press.

———. 1996. "History as Literature, Literature as History: Cagayous of Algiers." *American Historical Review* 101 (3): 671–711.

Proschan, Frank. 1997. "'We are all Kmhmu, just the same': Ethnonyms, Ethnic Identities, and Ethnic Groups." *American Ethnologist* 24 (1): 91–113.

Pullicino, Joseph Cassar. 1979. "The Mediterranean Islands as Places of Synthesis between Arab Culture and European Cultures." *Journal of Maltese Studies* 13:17–42.

Randau, Robert. 1911. *Les algérianistes.* Paris: Sansot.

Rapport, Nigel, and Andrew Dawson. 1998. *Migrants of Identity: Perceptions of Home in a World of Movement.* Oxford: Berg.

Reed-Danahay, Deborah. 1996. *Education and Identity in Rural France: The Politics of Schooling.* Cambridge: Cambridge University Press.

Roche, Anne, and Marie-Claude Taranger. 1995. *Celles qui n'ont pas écrit: Récits de femmes dans la region marseillaise, 1914–1945.* Aix-en-Provence: Edisud.

Rogers, Susan Carol. 1991. *Shaping Modern Times in Rural France: The Transformation and Reproduction of an Aveyronnais Community.* Princeton, N.J.: Princeton University Press.

Rosaldo, Renato. 1989. *Culture and Truth: The Remaking of Social Analysis.* Boston: Beacon.

Rotman, Patrick, and Bertrand Tavernier. 1992. *La guerre sans nom: Les appelés d'Algérie, 1954–1962.* Paris: Éditions du Seuil.

Ruedy, John. 1967. *Land Policy in Colonial Algeria: The Origins of the Rural Public Domain.* Near Eastern Studies, vol. 10. Berkeley: University of California Press.

———. 1992. *Modern Algeria: The Origins and Development of a Nation.* Bloomington: Indiana University Press.

Safran, William. 1991. "Diasporas in Modern Societies: Myths of Homeland and Return." *Diaspora* 1 (1): 83–99.

Said, Edward. 1978. *Orientalism.* New York: Random House.

———. 1989. "Representing the Colonized: Anthropology's Interlocutors." *Critical Inquiry* 15:205–25.

———. 1993. *Culture and Imperialism.* New York: Knopf.

Salloum, Habeeb. 1997. "Malta's Arab heritage." *Aljadid* 21 (3): 34–45.

Schnapper, Dominique. 1992. *L'Europe des immigrés.* Paris: Jeanne Bourin.

———. 1998. *Community of Citizens: On the Modern Idea of Nationality.* New Brunswick, N.J.: Transaction.

Schneider, Jane, and Peter Schneider. 1976. *Culture and Political Economy in Western Sicily.* New York: Academic.

Schwartzfuchs, Simon. 1980. "Colonialisme français et colonialisme juif en Algérie, 1830–1845." In *Judaisme d'Afrique du Nord aux XIXe–XXe siècles,* ed. Michel Abitbol, 37–48. Jerusalem: Institut Ben Zvi.

Scott, James. 1990. *Domination and the Arts of Resistance: Hidden Transcripts.* New Haven, Conn.: Yale University Press.

Selwood, Dominic. 1999. *Knights of the Cloister: Templars and Hospitallers in Central-Southern Occitania, c. 1100–1300.* Woodbridge: Boydell.

Sherzer, Joel. 1987. "A Discourse-Centered Approach to Language and Culture." *American Anthropologist* 89:295–309.

Silverblatt, Irene. 1987. *Moon, Sun, and Witches: Gender Ideologies and Class in Inca and Colonial Peru.* Princeton, N.J.: Princeton University Press.

Silverman, Maxim. 1992. *Deconstructing the Nation: Immigration, Racism and Citizenship in Modern France.* London: Routledge.

Sivan, E. 1980. "Stéréotypes antijuifs dans la mentalité pied-noir." In *Les relations entre Juifs et Musulmans en Afrique du Nord, XIXe–XXe siècles,* 160–69. Paris: Éditions du Centre National de la Recherche Scientifique.

Slyomovics, Susan. 1995. "Algeria Elsewhere: The Pilgrimage of the Virgin of Santa Cruz in Oran, Algeria, and in Nîmes, France." In *Folklore Interpreted: Essays in Honor of Alan Dundes,* ed. Regina Bendix and Rosemary Zumwalt, 337–53. New York: Garland.

———. 1998. *The Object of Memory: Arab and Jew Narrate the Palestinian Village.* Philadelphia: University of Pennsylvania Press.

Smith, Andrea L. 2003. "Introduction: Europe's Invisible Migrants." In *Europe's Invisible Migrants,* ed. Andrea L. Smith, 9–32. Amsterdam: Amsterdam University Press.

Solal, Edouard. n.d. *Philippeville et sa région, 1837–1870.* Alger: La Maison des Livres.

Stasiulis, Daiva, and Nira Yuval-Davis. 1995. *Unsettling Settler Societies: Articulations of Gender, Race, Ethnicity, and Class.* London: Sage.

Steinberg, Stephen. 1989. *The Ethnic Myth: Race, Ethnicity, and Class in America.* Boston: Beacon.

Stillman, Norman. 1976. *The Jews of Arab Lands: A History and Source Book.* Philadelphia, Penn.: Jewish Publication Society of America.

Stocking, George W., ed. 1991. *Colonial Situations: Essays on the Contextualization of Ethnographic Knowledge.* History of Anthropology, vol. 7. Madison: University of Wisconsin Press.

Stoler, Ann Laura. 1989. "Rethinking Colonial Categories: European Communities and the Boundaries of Rule." *Comparative Studies of Society and History* 31:134–59.

————. 1992. "Sexual Affronts and Racial Frontiers: European Identities and the Cultural Politics of Exclusion in Colonial Southeast Asia." *Comparative Studies in Society and History* 34 (3): 514–51.

Stoler, Ann Laura, and Frederick Cooper. 1997. "Between Metropole and Colony: Rethinking a Research Agenda." In *Tensions of Empire: Colonial Cultures in a Bourgeois World*, ed. Frederick Cooper and Ann Laura Stoler, 1–56. Berkeley: University of California Press.

Stoller, Paul. 1995. *Embodying Colonial Memories: Spirit Possession, Power, and the Hauka in West Africa*. New York: Routledge.

Stora, Benjamin. 1991. *Histoire de l'Algérie coloniale, 1830–1954*. Paris: Éditions La Découverte.

————. 1992. *La gangrène et l'oubli: La mémoire de la guerre d'Algérie*. Paris: Éditions La Découverte.

————. 1993. *Histoire de la guerre d'Algérie (1954–1962)*. Paris: Éditions La Découverte.

————. 1999. *Le transfert d'une mémoire: De l'"Algérie française" au racisme anti-arabe*. Paris: Éditions La Découverte.

Sueur, James. 2001. *Uncivil War: Intellectuals and Identity Politics during the Decolonization of Algeria*. Philadelphia: University of Pennsylvania Press.

Sznycer, Maurice. 1973. "Les Phéniciens à Malte d'après les témoignages épigraphiques." In *Proceedings of the First Congress on Mediterranean Studies of Arabo-Berber Influence*, ed. Micheline Galley in collaboration with David R. Marshall, 147–51. Algiers: Société Nationale d'Édition et de Diffusion.

Talbott, John. 1980. *The War without a Name: France in Algeria, 1954–1962*. New York: Knopf.

Thernstrom, Stephan. 2004. "Rediscovering the Melting Pot—Still Going Strong." In *Reinventing the Melting Pot: The New Immigrants and What It Means to be American*, ed. Tamar Jacoby, 47–59. New York: Basic.

Thomas, Nicholas. 1994. *Colonialism's Culture: Anthropology, Travel, and Government*. Princeton, N.J.: Princeton University Press.

Thomson, Ann. 1993. "La classification raciale de l'Afrique du Nord au début du XIXe siècle." *Cahiers d'études africaines* 33 (1): 19–36.

Tilly, Charles. 1996. Foreward to *The French Melting Pot: Immigration, Citizenship, and National Identity*, by Gérard Noiriel, vii–ix. Minneapolis: University of Minnesota Press.

Tonkin, Elizabeth. 1992. *Narrating Our Pasts: The Social Construction of Oral History*. Cambridge: Cambridge University Press.

Trouillot, Michel-Rolph. 1995. *Silencing the Past: Power and the Production of History*. Boston: Beacon.

Turner, Victor. 1969. *The Ritual Process: Structure and Anti-structure*. Chicago: Aldine.

Vadala, Ramiro. 1911. *Les Maltais hors de Malte: Étude sur l'émigration maltaise*. Paris: Arthur Rousseau.

Valensi, Lucette. 1967. "Esclaves chrétiens et esclaves noirs à Tunis au XVIIIe siècle." *Annales: Economies, sociétés, civilizations* 22 (4–6): 1267–88.

————. 1977. *On the Eve of Colonialism: North Africa before the French Conquest*. New York: Africana.

————. 1986. "La tour de Babel: Groupes et relations ethniques au Moyen-Orient et en Afrique du Nord." *Annales: Economies, sociétés, civilizations* 41 (4): 817–38.

————. 1990. "From Sacred History to Historical Memory and Back: The Jewish Past." In *Between Memory and History*, ed. Marie-Noëlle Bourguet, Lucette Valensi, and Nathan Wachtel, 77–99. Chur, Switzerland: Harwood Academic.

————. 1995. "Histoire nationale, historie monumentale: Les lieux de mémoire (note critique)." *Annales HSS* 6:1271–77.

Vanhove, Martine. 1994. "La langue maltaise: Un carrefour linguistique." *Revue du monde musulman et de la Méditerranée* 71 (1): 167–83.

Vidal-Naquet, Pierre. 1983 [1972]. *La torture dans la République*. Paris: La Découverte.

Wachtel, Nathan. 1990. "Remember and Never Forget." In *Between Memory and History*, ed. Marie-Noëlle Bourguet, Lucette Valensi, and Nathan Wachtel, 101–29. Chur, Switzerland: Harwood Academic.

Weaver, John C. 2003. *The Great Land Rush and the Making of the Modern World, 1650–1900*. Montreal: McGill–Queen's University Press.

Weber, Eugen. 1976. *Peasants into Frenchmen: The Modernization of Rural France, 1870–1914*. Stanford, Calif.: Stanford University Press.

Weil, Patrick. 1991. *La France et ses étrangers*. Paris: Calmann-Lévy.

Weill, N. 2001. "La torture en Algérie entre tabou, occultation et mémoire." *Le monde*, May 8, p. 5.

Wettinger, Godrey. 1972. "Arabo-Berber Influences in Malta: Onomastic Evidence." In *Proceedings of the First Congress on Mediterranean Studies of Arabo-Berber Influence*, ed. Micheline Galley in collaboration with David R. Marshall, 484–95. Algiers: Société Nationale d'Édition et de Diffusion.

———. 1986. "The Arabs in Malta." In *Malta: Studies of Its Heritage and History*, 87–104. Malta: Mid-Med Bank.

———. 2000. *Place-Names of the Maltese Islands, ca. 1300–1800*. San Gwann, Malta: Publishers Enterprise Group.

Wieviorka, Michel. 1992. *La France raciste*. Paris: Éditions du Seuil.

Wihtol de Wenden, Catherine. 1987. *Citoyenneté, nationalité et immigration*. Paris: Arcantère.

Williams, Brackette. 1991. *Stains on My Name, War in My Veins: Guyana and the Politics of Cultural Struggle*. Durham, N.C.: Duke University Press.

Williams, Raymond. 1977. *Marxism and Literature*. Oxford: Oxford University Press.

Wilson, Kathleen. 2003. *The Island Race: Englishness, Empire, and Gender in the Eighteenth Century*. London: Routledge.

Wolfe, Patrick. 1999. *Settler Colonialism and the Transformation of Anthropology: The Politics and Poetics of an Ethnographic Event*. London: Cassell.

Wood, Nancy. 1999. *Vectors of Memory: Legacies of Trauma in Postwar Europe*. Oxford: Berg.

Wylie, Laurence. 1957. *Village in the Vaucluse*. Cambridge, Mass.: Harvard University Press.

Zangwill, Israel. 1926. *The Melting Pot*. New York: Macmillan.

Zytnicki, Colette. 1998. "L'administration face à l'arrivée des rapatriés d'Algérie: L'exemple de la région Midi-Pyrénées (1962–1964)." *Annales du Midi* 110:501–21.

INDEX

References to illustrations appear in italics.

accueil: definition of, 175; and nostalgia, 173. *See also* hospitality

African Americans: and *pieds-noirs,* 31–32

Ageron, Charles-Robert, 100, 101, 108, 233n7, 234n17

Aix-en-Provence: and associations, 38, 207; fieldwork in, 6, 13–16, 33, 35–36, 171, 176; *pied-noir* settlement in, 35–36, 51, 167

Algeria: nostalgia for, 31–32; recreated in France, 189, *189*–193; as Wild West, 28

Algerian colonial history, alternative reading of, 151

Algerian independence, 145

Algerian melting pot. *See creuset algérien*

Algerian War (1954–1962): 3, 5, 110; *attentats* (bombings), 144; disruption in France, 5; exodus and exile, 161–162; fatalities in, 5; and fieldwork, 6–8; history, 141–145; in the imagination, 7; literature, 241n1; military service, 5; narratives of, 153–157; official recognition as war in 1999, 158, 242n10; referred to as "the events," 145; referred to by different names, 233n9; silenced, 145–150; torture, 5, 143, 158, 233n6

Algerianistes, 114–115, 136

Algerians in French army, 107, 241n4, *See also* military service

Algiers

—city of: capital, 81; *Mahonnais* in, 68; migration to, 19; neighborhoods of, 117; in settler discourse, 112, 129; settlers in, 54–65, *58,* 61–63, 70, 95, 100

—province of (*département*): 77

—Regency of. *See* Ottoman Algeria

All Saints' Day, 171

alienation, 16, 203; of Algerians from French, 66; of Algerians from land, 65;

Amicales, 41; in Europe, 16; of Franco-Maltese, 195–197. *See also* displacement; expropriation; liminality

alterity, 117

ALN, 141

Amicale France-Malte, 2, 6, 11, 18, 33, 35–37, 39, 40, 54–55, 63, 140, 154, 188, 206, 208, 210; alienation, 41; association, 37; club names, 206; France's failure, 40

amicales: defined, 37; *pied-noir,* 190–193. *See also Amicale France-Malte;* Franco-Maltese clubs

Annaba (Bône), 51, 166, 190, ethnic neighborhoods, 116; origins of interviewees, 51, 166, 192; *pied-noir* clubs, 121, 193

anthropology: and colonialism, 25, 28–29; and colonists, 29; of Europe, 28

Anti-Arab sentiment in France, 186

Antilleans in France, 184

anti-Maltese sentiment: in Algeria, 62, 89–90, 92–95; in France, 197

anti-*pied-noir* sentiment, 175, 179–188, 209

anti-Semitism: and colonial categories, 91, 105; and Crémieux decree, 105; and *péril étranger,* 109; *pied-noir,* 193–194; popular culture, 114–115

Arab culture in *pied-noir* culture, 220

Arabic: in Algeria, 111; in France, 220; in Malta, 1–2, 222–223; and Maltese language, 22, 221; *pied-noir* knowledge of, 53, 128, 220–221

archival research, 17

Arles, 7, 39, 172

Armée de libération nationale. See ALN

Arnaud, Louis, 95

arsch, 65

Ascension Day, 7, 39

New Anthropologies of Europe

Daphne Berdahl, Matti Bunzl, and Michael Herzfeld, editors

ANDREA L. SMITH is Assistant Professor of Anthropology at Lafayette College. She is editor of *Europe's Invisible Migrants*.